The Sea Against Hunger

AN INTERNATIONAL OCEANOGRAPHIC
FOUNDATION SELECTION

The Sea
Against Hunger

C. P. IDYLL

THOMAS Y. CROWELL
COMPANY
New York   Established 1834

To my father
Albert Charles Idyll

Contents

Introduction

At a time when the United States was still an infant republic, an English economist named Thomas Robert Malthus aroused a storm of criticism with his prediction that mankind was doomed to famine and poverty.

In his *Essay on the Principle of Population,* first published in 1798, Malthus asserted that man will never be able to produce food fast enough to keep up with population growth. Population, he said, increases geometrically; food production goes up only at an arithmetical rate. Thus, he concluded, mankind must inevitably starve to death.

Few people believed Malthus, and much abuse was heaped on his head. And for a time history seemed to prove him wrong. The New World offered thousands of square miles of rich farmland. Emigration helped reduce Europe's problems of overcrowding. And science and technology kept improving food production with new farm machines and better crops.

Meanwhile, however, population kept growing, especially because of a sharp drop in the death rate. At the time of Malthus' death, in the early 1830's, only a billion people lived on earth. In a century another billion had been added, and in just thirty years still another billion. Today the curve is shooting up so fast that economists freely predict a staggering population of 7.5 billion by the year 2000!

Was Malthus right after all? Will the famines that have become common in India soon become the problem of much of the rest of the world?

The answer is far from easy, as Dr. C. P. Idyll shows in this admirable survey of the problem. At least a third of the world's people are already suffering from malnutrition or outright starvation—and the fraction could easily be a half or more. Basic requirements call for doubling the total world food supply by 1980 and tripling it by 2000.

At the same time, most of the world's land suitable for farming has already gone under cultivation. "The blunt truth is," says Dr. Idyll, "we do not have enough food now, and no matter what miracles the agricultural sciences perform we will not have enough food in the future if we wait for the farms to produce it."

At present the ocean produces only 2 or 3 per cent of the total calories consumed by human beings, but its potential prospects will, I think, astonish most readers.

While Dr. Idyll does not draw pictures of vast stretches of submerged fields waving in the currents, he does make an exciting assessment of how we might increase our efficiency in making use of the sea.

I have read this book with more than ordinary interest because of the author's connection with the University of Miami's Institute of Marine and Atmospheric Sciences, where he is chairman of the Division of Fishery Sciences. Over the last two decades I have watched this Institute grow from a small, struggling laboratory to one of the nation's large and prestigious marine science organizations—and Dr. Idyll has played an important role in that growth.

On my frequent visits to the institute I have always found special pleasure in talking to Dr. Idyll. He has infused his new book with the same clarity and breadth of knowledge that I find in his conversation, as well as in the several articles he has written for the *National Geographic Magazine.* He is very much at home when he writes about the lore and science of the sea.

And if hunger cannot be banished by the fruits of the sea alone, at least Dr. Idyll has given valuable prescriptions for one of the major ailments of "this small, shrinking, and misused planet."

MELVILLE BELL GROSVENOR
BOARD CHAIRMAN, NATIONAL GEOGRAPHIC SOCIETY

Preface

The first chapter tells in detail my purpose in preparing this book; briefly, it is to make a critical examination of mankind's chance of avoiding widespread hunger by increasing the use of food from the sea. A belief has been created by highly colored newspaper and magazine articles—and even encouraged by some scientists—that man needs only to turn his attention seriously to the oceans and the world food problems will be solved. Phrases like "the harvest of plankton" and "farming the sea" have misled the public and some lawmakers, and the perpetuation of such misconceptions can be dangerous, if only because they distract from the proper kinds of scientific and technological efforts that are so badly needed if man is to make the best use of his total resources.

The book looks critically at several major aspects of the problem, drawing first on the current status of science and technology to evaluate man's realistic prospects. In addition to the limits imposed by natural law, the harvest of the sea is restricted by human institutions and behavior—economics, politics, taste, prejudice—and part of the analysis examines how these operate in this field of human effort.

Among the many people to whom I am indebted for help in the preparation of this book I owe special gratitude to my wife, both for her patient forbearance and for her exceptional skill as an editor. In a very real sense this book is also hers.

I have been fortunate also to have the generous help and advice of many expert friends. Colleagues who have read one or more chapters include Dr. F. G. Walton Smith, dean of the School of Marine and Atmospheric Sciences at the University of Miami; Dr. Edwin S. Iversen, Dr. E. Ferguson Wood, and Professor Dennis O'Connor, members of the faculty of the University of Miami; Dr. Harold Humm, University of South Florida, Tampa; Dr. Milner B. Schaefer, University of California, La Jolla; Dr. Hiroshi Kasahara, United Nations Development Programme, New York; Dr. Harold Webber, Groton Associates, Groton, Massachusetts; Monroe Bush, formerly of the Population Reference Bureau, Washington, D.C., now head of Monroe Bush Associates in that city; Dr. Ferris Neave, Fisheries Research Board of Canada, Nanaimo, British Columbia; Dr. Donald Snyder and Harvey Bullis, both of the Bureau of Commercial Fisheries of the U.S. Fish and Wildlife Service; George Parman, U.S. Agency for International Development (AID); and Roy Jackson, Fisheries Department, Food and Agriculture Organization of the United Nations, Rome, Italy.

C. P. IDYLL

The Sea Against Hunger

1 *Hunger*

Man has nothing to fear but man. Lord of living things, he has a high degree of control over the rest of the earth's creatures. He manipulates, molds, and changes the plant populations, bidding them to grow here and not there, in this manner and form and not in that. With somewhat less skill but with equal enthusiasm, he changes the shape of animals, shifts them from place to place over the globe, and suppresses those that irritate or harm him. Man has no predators in the sense that a rabbit has, in the form of foxes and stoats, and he has learned to control pestilence, which in an earlier era devastated his ranks. After a few hundred thousand years—a single breath in the life of the earth—he is able to stand erect in the jungle, breathing hard perhaps, but able to look about and see the rest of the creatures enslaved or retreating, never again seriously to threaten his life or his works.

But man has not learned to control himself. He has devised no treatment of the rest of the animals as savage as that to which he subjects his fellow man, no enslavement as cruel. Having filled all the empty places of the planet he is destroying its bounty and tossing the garbage over his shoulder. Having crushed the bodies and souls of millions in war, he feverishly wages more war. He quakes in his collective shoes over the possibility that some hand, trembling with fear or drunk with power, will press the button that will unleash nuclear warfare.

But a prospect even more horrifying than the hydrogen bomb faces the world today—the prospect that man may continue to reproduce at such a high rate that he will scrape the last crumb of food from the surface of the earth. In the headlong crush preceding this, such a desperate struggle might take place among the swarming people that

[1]

atomic war would be only one aspect of the calamity that would annihilate mankind.

Many believe that this calamity can be prevented by greater use of the sea as a source of food, with the expectation that the oceans can produce as much food as the land, or even more.

The theoretical basis for the hope that the sea can save man from hunger is that over 70 per cent of the solar energy reaching the earth (the ultimate source of all food on earth) falls on the surface of the sea. In addition, sea water is a dilute broth, holding in solution all the chemical nutrients necessary for the growth of plants. The supposition that the sea is rich seems to be confirmed by the immense swarms of fish and other life that can sometimes be seen in the ocean—great schools of herring in the North Atlantic, seemingly endless numbers of tunas rolling in the central Pacific, hordes of salmon surging up the spawning streams of Alaska.

And yet, in the face of the theory and of these observations, the sea produces only 2 to 3 per cent of the calories consumed by mankind. The purpose of this book is to find out why this percentage is so low, and to analyze the prospect for wresting a greater quantity of food from the sea.

The rate of population rise is dismaying. Its causes and its impact on man and all his works and hopes are matters everyone should know and ponder.

The date 1650 is a benchmark in the history of mankind. The human population was about 500 million and had been nearly stable for a very long time. But about then it began its upward curve. At first the rise was insignificant, and even the most perceptive did not notice the change. Within another century the rate had gained momentum, but the rise was still so slow and so smooth that few paid any attention. But some did. In 1798, when the number of people had reached perhaps three quarters of a billion, the Reverend Thomas Malthus of England expressed alarm that the population was in danger of outrunning its food. He was ridiculed.

The population reached a billion about 1830, having doubled in less than 200 years. Now the line curved upward more sharply still, and in a mere 100 years another doubling took place. By 1930 mankind was in the midst of a worldwide economic crisis and hunger was common. It began to occur to a few more people that the world's bounty would go further if the sharing could be done among fewer consumers, but no general understanding existed even then of the alarming import of human increase. Meanwhile, the next billion people appeared in only thirty years, with 1960 showing a total of about 3 billion.

[2]

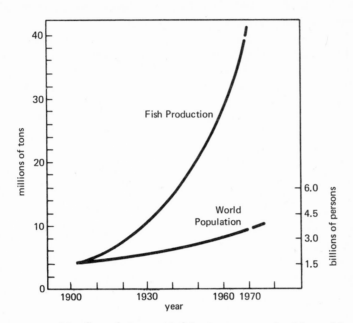

FIGURE 1.1. *Growth in world fisheries compared with world population increase.*

Fisheries of North America

And the pace continues to quicken. Sixty million more people are added to the total every year—more than enough to populate a new France, another Italy. There could be a second United Kingdom every ten months, another New York City or Tokyo every two. If the United States were suddenly emptied of all its people it could be re-populated in three years with the world's new inhabitants.

Human population growth rates are increasing by leaps of larger and larger magnitude. This is because the increments occur not arithmetically, by adding fixed amounts to the present total, but geometrically, by multiplying the current numbers by the rate of increase, and then multiplying the new, larger number again—and then again.

At present the multiplier—the yearly rate of population increase—is more than 3 per cent in many countries. The present worldwide rate is about 2.1 per cent. A rate of 2 per cent per year means that the number of people *doubles every thirty-five years.* If the present trend continues until the year 2000 there will be 7.5 billion people—twice as many as now; by 2035 there will be 12 billion. At the rate of 3 per cent exhibited by some countries, their populations will double in 24 years.

[3]

Between 1960 and 2000, the "underdeveloped" world—meaning the part with the least capacity to care for more people—will have increased from 2 billion to 4.7 billion. Meanwhile the "developed" world of the West will grow less rapidly, from 1.0 billion to 1.4 billion.

Many demographers assume that the rate of increase will not, in fact, continue to be as high as it is now, and some have guessed that the year 2050 will see a population of "only" 10 billion; the year 2100, 20 billion. But even the "conservative" estimates are staggering.

This rapid rise in population has occurred because man, an animal, has broken a fundamental law of nature, the law controlling animal numbers. The numbers of individuals in normal animal populations are controlled and prevented from overrunning their living space by the checks and balances of predators, disease, and starvation. Beginning about 300 years ago mankind first learned to loosen the grip of these factors, and his skill in this has increased rapidly, especially during the present century.

"Mature" populations of wild animals come into equilibrium with their environment, meaning that their numbers are nicely balanced with living space, predators, and available food, and births are balanced by deaths. Thus the number of animals remains constant, on the average, from year to year. Man would not be in his present perilous situation if he had not discovered how to beat the odds and to bypass the causes of death.

The surge in human population is not the result of a general increase in birth rate, but a very significant drop in death rate. Over most of the world the birth rate has either fallen or remained stable, but death rates are lower. In 1560 in the Western world the annual death rate was about 40 per 1,000 population; in Europe today it is about 10 per 1,000. This dramatic reduction can be attributed to increased knowledge of nutrition and sanitation, and to the discoveries of methods for controlling disease.

Advances in public health—the development of methods of keeping food and water clean, and the education of mankind to make use of these new skills—have been dramatic. In the United States deaths from typhoid fever, a killer carried by unclean water and food, were reduced from 36 per 1,000 population in 1900 to virtually zero (a total of 14 cases) in 1964. Equally rapid advances have been made in the control of the major infectious diseases—the great killers of the past such as yellow fever, smallpox, malaria, yaws, and the plague. Man has not faced a worldwide pestilence since 1918–19, when about 15 million people died of influenza.

In addition, he enjoys a greatly lengthened average life span. Thus, the world is not only filling up far faster than in the past, but people are staying around far longer to occupy their allotted niches and consume their share of the globe's bounty.

A fundamental truth that has not been stated often enough is that regardless of the miracles of science and technology, everything required by man for his comfort and existence must come from the earth. A great many of the necessities exist in fixed amounts, and once consumed are gone forever; other resources are renewable, and, if skillfully managed may produce considerable quantities of material as long as the energy of the sun is supplied.

The most urgent problem arising from the increase in human population is the inadequate supply of consumables—food, fresh water, minerals, energy. Food is the most critical of these. Man has a serious food problem now and it is getting worse.

If it is really true that man is in danger of outrunning food supplies by increases in numbers of people, how long will it be before there are serious shortages of food? The answer is, man has long since passed this point, and he is falling farther behind every day.

It is hard for people in well-fed countries like the United States to accept the fact that mankind is failing to make progress in the war

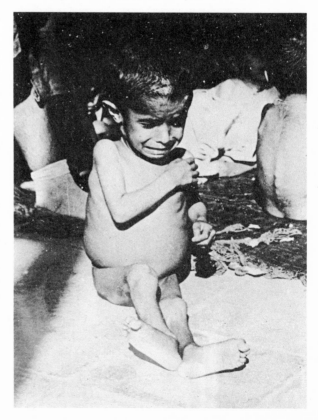

FIGURE 1.2. *Sekeneh, a small girl from Teheran, Iran, suffering from kwashiorkor, an extreme level of malnutrition. Countless people over the world are starving, and far more are the victims of various levels of malnutrition.*

Food and Agriculture Organization

against hunger. It is hard because it flies in the face of their experience at home, where most people are overfed rather than in want; it is hard because it is contrary to the comfortable thesis that mankind is progressing along all fronts. The trouble with the theory that technology will take care of all the new inhabitants of the earth is that it never has been true throughout the world, and it is less true today than ever before. A highly creditable increase of 8 per cent took place in the world's food supply in the period 1947–53, but in the same interval world population increased 11 per cent. From 1961 to 1966 the food production of Latin America declined 6 per cent and in Asia 4 per cent, while the population zoomed in both areas. The Malthusian Theory is operating with a vengeance.

Hunger has two aspects, a shortage of food and a shortage of the right kind of food. And the latter is more prevalent and more damaging than the first; there are far more people without enough protein in their diet than without enough calories. A man may have enough food to fill his stomach, but if this food is largely bulky starches such as manioc, yams, or maize flour he may still be "hungry." Without a high proportion of proteins and certain vitamins and minerals the body suffers varying degrees of illness.

FIGURE 1.3. *The geography of hunger.*

Food and Agriculture Organization

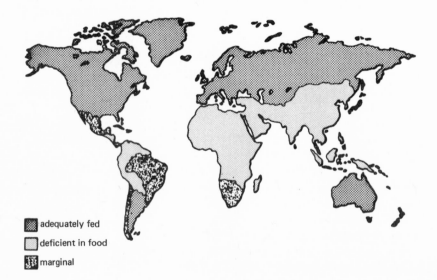

adequately fed
deficient in food
marginal

Many of the plants constituting the bulk of the food of some under-developed countries have a tenth or less of the protein per calorie that fish contains.

When proteins are lacking in the human diet, especially during infancy and childhood, reduced body efficiency and mental apathy result; when proteins are seriously lacking, disease is prevalent. One of the commonest of protein deficiency diseases is kwashiorkor, the crippler of children.

No one can say for sure how many people are hungry, but it is not far off the mark to conclude that at least a third of the world's people are suffering from malnutrition or outright starvation, and the fraction could easily be a half or more. The Population Reference Bureau says that of the 3.3 billion people on the globe in 1966 *two-thirds* suffered from hunger!

A doubling of the total world food supplies is required by 1980 and a tripling by 2000. In the really hungry parts of the world four times the present available amount of food will be needed by 2000, and six times the present supplies of animal products.

Thus the problem is clear: the number of people on the earth is already so large that between 1.5 and 2 billion of them are hungry, and the numbers are increasing at such fast rates that mankind is faced with a truly disastrous situation, with starvation, misery, and wars as probable consequences.

The ultimate answer can only be a marked reduction in the rate of increase in population. No one would seriously advocate stemming the downward trend in death rates, so the remaining alternative is a reduction in birth rates. This is inevitable if mankind is to survive, despite social and religious resistance.

But even with wholehearted and widespread agreement and active implementation of effective birth-control measures over the world—an impossibility for a very long time—it would be decades or generations before any large impact would be made on the population curve.

So in the meantime, men must turn their efforts energetically to the problem of producing more food for the swarming numbers of additional people who will inhabit our planet in the next few years.

At the present time more than 96 per cent of human food comes from the land, and it is certain that a high proportion will continue to come from this source in the foreseeable future.

The land can grow a great deal more food. In fact, with major advances in the development of high-yield varieties of the major grains —developments of such importance they have been dubbed "The Green Revolution"—possibilities exist for doubling or tripling production if

[7]

adequate supplies of water, fertilizer, pesticides, and modern equipment are made available. But whether land farming *will* produce enough to take care of man's needs is still very much in doubt because of the multitude of economic, political, and social barriers he has erected. It is pointless to argue that the people of the world could be fed if these barriers did not exist. The blunt truth is that man does behave irrationally; he does not have enough food now, and no matter what miracles the agricultural sciences perform he will probably not have enough food in the future if he relies solely on farms to produce it.

Perhaps instead man can turn science loose, bypass the farms, and develop entirely new ways of producing food. It is theoretically possible to produce food from organic or inorganic substances. Some kinds of unicellular algae, and some yeasts and fungi, can convert sugar to proteins in the presence of inorganic nitrogen. Thousands of tons of food yeast were produced and consumed in Germany in World War II. A product called "torula," a yeast protein, is sold on a small scale today. But these processes start with sugar, and this must be grown on farms.

A French scientist, Alfred Champagnat, has harnessed a species of fungus to the job of converting petroleum into protein. If this can be converted into foods that are palatable, an enormous advance will have been made. But there is no indication how far this development will go in solving the problem, nor is there any other method of producing synthetic food that holds real promise at the moment.

It is this situation, in which mankind is faced with starvation, that has turned the attention of experts and the lay public alike to the possibility that the sea may hold the key to human survival.

2   *Present Contribution of the Sea*

A complex mystique has grown up about the sea, partly because of its immense size, its strange inhabitants, its menace, and its complexity, and partly because of the common belief that no matter how men may overrun the earth or change the face of the land, when life gets really hard the sea will provide. In order to assess the validity of this feeling about the ultimate ability of the sea to fill the gap between men's needs and their satisfaction, it is pertinent first to determine the present contribution of the sea to the world food supply.

Expressed in terms of gross weight of total food, or in calories consumed, the contribution of the sea to human feeding is statistically insignificant.

In 1968 the world catch of marine products was 57.4 million metric tons (a metric ton is 2,204 pounds). A little over 36 per cent of this total consisted of fish used for purposes other than human food, being made into products such as fish meal and oil, bait or fertilizer. Other large quantities were inedible seaweeds, clam and lobster shells, and other wastes. Perhaps 35 per cent of the gross weight was in the form of edible fish flesh, producing a total of about 21.1 million metric tons, or 46.5 billion pounds. Assuming a world population of 3.5 billion, the average consumption of fish over the world was approximately 13.5 pounds per person. This is a little over 1 per cent of the total weight of food or calories consumed.

But this method of expressing the role of fish in human feeding does not assess its importance accurately. The nutrition problem of the human race is to an important degree a shortage of animal protein, and the proportionate contribution of the sea to supplies of this kind of food is much more impressive.

[9]

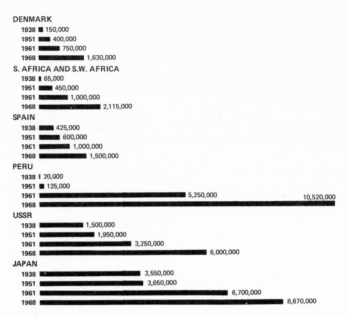

FIGURE 2.1. *Increased production of fish from the sea by certain nations.*

Food and Agriculture Organization

The considerable nutritional advantage of animal flesh over plant material in terms of two of the essential amino acids that make up various proteins is illustrated by the fact that one pound of fish flesh supplies as much tryptophan as three one-pound loaves of wheat flour bread and as much lysine as eight such loaves. As a rough generality, plant protein is about half as valuable nutritionally as animal protein.

Fish is approximately 70–75 per cent water, 19 per cent protein, 5 per cent fat, 3 per cent nitrogen, and 1 per cent phosphorus. It provides about 500 calories per pound. The protein content of many kinds of lean fish is higher than that of beef (about 17–24 per cent), which is sometimes held up as the standard of prime food. And the nutritional value of fish protein is equal to that of protein from beef, veal, lamb, and pork, the relative amounts of the essential amino acids being almost identical.

In 1960 the world total of animal protein available for human consumption was 24,500,000 metric tons. Of this, fish supplied 3,200,000 tons, or 13.1 per cent; this was about as much protein as provided by pork and about three quarters as much as from beef; it was more than twice the amount supplied by eggs and more than three times as much as from poultry.

[10]

For some countries of the world, fish is the major source of animal protein. Worldwide it provides protein for a great many more people than milk or meat, since consumption of these foods is concentrated in a few fortunate countries: more than two thirds of the milk and meat are consumed by fewer than 60 million people—2 per cent of the world population. More than half the human population depends on fish for the greatest part of their animal protein.

Portugal is an example of a country where fish is of great importance in the diet: 36 per cent of the animal protein consumed by its people comes from the sea. In other countries—Japan, Norway, Chile, and India, for example—fish proteins are also of major significance. By contrast, fish plays a minor role in Argentina, Brazil, Turkey, Australia, and other lands.

The cost of producing animal protein from the sea is significantly lower than the cost on land. On a worldwide basis it costs half as much to produce a ton of protein from fish as from beef, a third as much as from pork. In labor expended, fish requires a third as many man-hours to process as pork. In the United States fish sells for about a third the price of competitive meat protein.

According to some experts there is actually an excess of calories produced in the world. But there is no such surplus of animal proteins: here a serious world shortage exists.

It has been estimated that total food supplies have been increasing

FIGURE 2.2. *A large catch of ocean perch, or redfish. Beyond the deck flooded with fish the lower end of the trawl contains another huge load.*

Gerhard Binanzer, Stuttgart

much more slowly than the human population: about 0.5 per cent per year compared to 2 per cent. In contrast, landings of fish are increasing at a rate between two and three times as fast as the population. This is a relatively new trend—or rather, the renewal of an earlier trend. Before the middle of the nineteenth century world fisheries had a period of rapid expansion as maritime nations awakened to the availability of fish in their waters. Then new methods of farming and new agricultural machines turned attention to the land and the fisheries declined in relative importance. This trend was especially marked in North America. It is only in recent times that fishing has picked up momentum again over the world, as the arable lands are occupied.

Records are imperfect, but it may be that world fish production (including freshwater fish) was about 1.5 to 2.25 million metric tons in 1850. In the next half century this doubled. Between 1900 and 1962 production jumped eightfold from 4 million metric tons to more than 40 million. The biggest increases have come since World War II. In the early 1950's landings rose between 4 and 4.5 per cent per year, over twice the rate of human increase. In the late fifties and early sixties rates surged to between 6 and 8 per cent per year, three to four times the rate of increase of the world population.

Thus, while the sea provides a very small proportion of the total food consumed by humans, it has shown a rapid growth in the production of vital and scarce animal protein. A continuation of this trend would be a boon to mankind.

TABLE 1

WORLD CATCH OF MARINE FISH AND OTHER PRODUCTS [a]

Year	Catch in Millions of Metric Tons [b]	Year	Catch in Millions of Metric Tons
1850	1.50-2.25	1959	30.56
1900	4.00	1960	33.39
1930	10.00	1961	36.44
1938	17.50	1962	40.22
1948	17.02	1963	41.26
1955	21.21	1964	45.46
1956	22.61	1965	45.75
1957	26.44	1966	49.17
1958	27.64	1967	52.28
		1968	57.40

[a] Source: Food and Agriculture Organization *Yearbooks of Fishery Statistics*
[b] One metric ton = 2204 pounds

TABLE 2

WORLD CATCH BY GROUPS OF SPECIES, 1967 [a]

Species	Catch in Metric Tons [b]
Herring, sardines, anchovies, etc.	19,680,000
Cod, hake, haddock, etc.	8,150,000
Redfish, bass, etc.	3,140,000
Mackerel, billfish, etc.	2,680,000
Jack, mullet, etc.	2,030,000
Tuna, bonita, etc.	1,330,000
Flounders, halibut, sole, etc.	1,200,000
Salmon, trout	1,070,000
Sharks, rays, etc.	440,000
Crustaceans	1,350,000
Mollusks	3,080,000
Unsorted and unidentified	8,290,000

[a] Source: Food and Agriculture Organization *Yearbook of Fishery Statistics,* Vol. 24.

[b] One metric ton = 2204 pounds

3 *Food Production in the Sea*

Despite the differences between the land and ocean environments, food production follows the same basic principles in the sea as on land. All food is derived from living material, plant or animal, and all living matter originates as plant substance. Animals are sustained by eating plants directly or by eating other animals that have eaten plants.

The chemical factories of plants operate by combining carbon dioxide, water, and inorganic chemicals into more complex living substances. The energy required for this transformation is supplied by the sun, with the green substance chlorophyll (or some other photosynthetic pigment) acting as a catalyst, or chemical helper.

The sun supplies the earth with 240 trillion horsepower of energy per day, about one horsepower per square yard of surface in twenty-four hours. Since the area of the sea is approximately 71 per cent of the surface of the earth, about this proportion of the sun's energy falling on the earth becomes the sea's share. Only a small amount of the total light energy is used by the plants for photosynthesis. In some special cases the proportion is high, since a thick forest canopy traps as much as 99 per cent, but in desert areas the amount may be zero. Ponds with heavy concentrations of algae use up to 14 per cent of the light, but in the open ocean the proportion is less than 1 per cent.

Besides carbon dioxide and water, certain other materials must be present for plants to manufacture the complex carbohydrates, proteins, and fats from the original carbohydrate molecules. These may include mineral salts such as phosphates and nitrates and such "trace elements" as iron, copper, and magnesium. In the whole bulk of the ocean there are enormous amounts of all the essential nutrients. For example, it has been estimated that the ocean contains 250,000 million tons of nitrate nitrogen, 75,000 million tons of phosphate phosphorus, and similarly large quantities of potassium salts. The ocean has by far the greatest part of the earth's carbon dioxide—fifteen to thirty times as much as the atmosphere—and of the soluble carbonates. All the trace elements, some of which are essential to the production of protoplasm, are present in the sea in substantial quantities.

Like so many of the land's riches, the plant nutrients of the sea are very unevenly distributed. Consequently the productivity of the ocean varies enormously from place to place, probably with at least as wide a range as on land. Coastal areas generally are about as productive as some forests, moist grasslands, and lands under ordinary cultivation, but some parts of the ocean support no more plants and animals than deserts on land. Shallow regions at the edge of the ocean are often six to nine times richer than the poorer parts of the open sea, and coral reefs forty times as productive. Some estuaries are similar in productivity to evergreen forests and lands under intensive cultivation: they are fifty times as productive as some barren regions of the open sea.

These striking contrasts in the capacity of various parts of the ocean to produce and sustain living creatures are caused largely by variations in the amounts of chemical nutrients in solution. In the relatively barren areas it is ordinarily the phosphates, nitrates, and nitrites that are in short supply. This is exactly like the situation on land, where some soils must be fertilized by adding these minerals.

Whatever the momentary supply of the nutrient minerals in any part of the ocean, there is a gradual loss as the chemicals are carried downward with the sinking bodies of dead animals and plants. The cells decompose, releasing the minerals below the level at which light is strong enough for photosynthesis. The depth at which plant growth stops varies with latitude, angle of the sun, water clarity, and other factors, but it is always relatively shallow. Light is extinguished with surprising rapidity in water: half of it is blocked out in as little as six feet in some inshore waters, and 90 per cent is gone at twenty-five feet. Offshore water is usually clearer, and light may penetrate five times deeper than it does near the land. Light strong enough for photosynthesis penetrates to a maximum depth of only about 100–130 feet in inshore areas, and to about 325 feet in clear, offshore, tropical waters. The growth of plants, of course, may prevent light from reaching such depths. The heavy production of the microscopic single cells of marine plants sometimes creates a living "sediment" in the water, causing shade like that produced by a forest canopy—and plant production is slowed down exactly as it is on a bare forest floor.

After minerals have sunk into the lower, lightless depths of the sea they are lost to the plants unless they are swept upward to the surface layers again. The rich parts of the sea are those where the nutrients are returned quickly and in large amounts. Hence, in some manner the sea must be "plowed" in order to sustain plant growth.

One of the important oceanic plowing mechanisms is convection. When the upper layer of the sea cools and sinks, the water beneath is forced to the top, carrying with it fresh supplies of minerals. This happens in the temperate zones and arctic regions, where surface waters become cold in winter and winds help to mix the layers. Shallow areas are richer partly because the nutrients are trapped on the bottom within, or close to, the lighted zone. Thus a rich store of phosphates, nitrates, and other minerals may accumulate in the sediments, to be swept upward by seasonal overturns and storm winds.

The overturning of the oceans from top to bottom is the principal key to the enormously abundant fish populations of such regions as the Grand Banks and the North Sea. The cold far-southern seas also bloom with great vigor in the spring and summer, supporting teeming new life and making the antarctic waters among the richest of the ocean. But there is little or no convection in tropical and subtropical oceans. In these regions the nutrients are permanently trapped in unlighted depths unless some other kind of plowing takes place.

This occurs in some favored areas, both tropical and temperate, where the prevailing winds blow offshore, carrying large masses of water away from the land. The surface water, perhaps spent of its nutrients, is replaced by mineral-laden water from the depths. This happens on the western coasts of continents—in South America off Peru and Chile for example—sustaining their enormously large anchovy populations, and off the west coast of Africa, where some of the richest fishing grounds in the world are beginning to be exploited.

In still other areas of the ocean another kind of enrichment takes place when two ocean currents meet head-on, forcing deeper water to the surface by the resulting turbulence. This mechanism is less important than the convection and wind processes, but it may be locally significant. It operates, for example, in the northwestern Atlantic, where the Gulf Stream and the Labrador Current meet, and it is partly responsible for the productivity of this rich region.

To make an estimate of how much human food the oceans can yield, the first step is a calculation of the total amount produced there. This sets the upper limit, since no more food can be extracted from the seas than is manufactured.

Experts disagree in their estimates of the capacity of the sea to

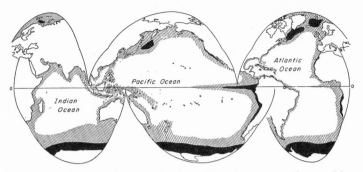

FIGURE 3.1. *Distribution of mineral nutrients over the world ocean. The black areas are the richest, the white the poorest.*

produce living material. The lack of agreement results from the scarcity of accurate information about the amounts of essential chemicals available and the rates of the basic chemical processes.

Since all living protoplasm is formed by combining (or "fixing") carbon with other chemical elements into complex organic substances through the process of photosynthesis, one way to measure the total amount of living material produced in the sea is to determine the total weight of carbon fixed. This is done by lowering marine plants in bottles or other containers to various depths and measuring the amounts of carbon transformed into plant material.

An estimate by Dr. Gordon A. Riley of Yale University in the 1940's set the total productivity of the ocean at 126 billion tons of carbon per year. More recent estimates have tended to be smaller than this. One by the Danish scientists E. Steeman-Nielsen and Aabie Jensen places the value at 12 to 15 billion tons. In 1962 Moses Pike and Athelstan Spilhaus reported for the National Academy of Sciences "on very inadequate data" that about 19 billion tons of carbon are annually synthesized into living organic matter. Using observations from over a large area of the Pacific Ocean the Soviet scientist O. I. Koblenz-Mishke calculated in 1965 that 13 billion tons of carbon are fixed each year (with a possible range of error of plus or minus 50 per cent). Estimates of recent years are on the same order of magnitude. It is of interest to note that these amounts are about the same as the total carbon fixed on land in a year.

Both on land and in the sea, plants are eaten by herbivorous (plant-eating) animals, these in turn by carnivores, and the first group of carnivores by another level of flesh eaters, through several steps, or

[17]

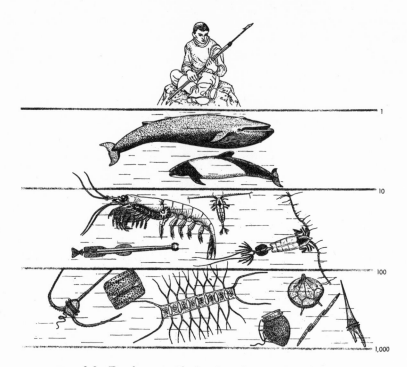

FIGURE 3.2. *Food pyramid showing the energy relations between whales and the principal elements in their food chain. The numbers to the right of the pyramid indicate the ratio of phytoplankton net production to production of zooplankton and whales.*

From "Whales, Plankton and Man," by W. E. Pequegnat,
© January 1958, *Scientific American*

links in a chain. Each link involves a great loss of energy and material, since an animal can retain in its body only a small fraction of the substance of its prey. The rest is spun off as energy or waste material. Thus there is a far greater amount of substance and energy spread among plants than among plant eaters, a correspondingly greater amount among herbivores than among primary carnivores, far more among the latter than among secondary carnivores, and so on for a step or two more. Because of this progressive reduction in the quantities of material and energy, their transfer from plants through the animals is often depicted as a "food pyramid," with the plants as its base. Each block of the pyramid is called a "trophic" (nutritional) level.

To determine the amount of useful food obtainable from the sea (with our present methods of harvest, mostly fishes at the second, third, and higher levels of the food pyramid), calculations must be made of the fraction passed from each trophic level to the next. There is considerable uncertainty about the values of these figures because scientists have not yet learned enough about the complicated processes of life in the sea to be able to assign trustworthy rates to them. The concepts of chains and pyramids, helpful as they are in clarifying complex systems, are oversimplifications. The flow of material and energy is not a simple progression from one link of the food chain or one level of the food pyramid to the next. Instead of being consumed directly, plants or animals may die and be decomposed by bacteria, and the bacteria may be consumed by animals. Furthermore, predators and prey are bound together in "food webs," in which the material and energy are shunted back and forth, and some of it becomes "dead-ended" as far as man is concerned by being tied up in such creatures as jelly-fishes, corals, or barnacles. A simplified account of part of the intricate relationship among herring and its predators and prey will help to show the intricacy of energy-flow patterns.

The herring do not occupy one isolated link in the food chain by eating plankton and accumulating the material thus derived. Instead, a bewildering number of animals enter the herring's food web, as predators or prey. Young and adult herring are the food of a great many species of carnivorous fishes, including salmon, rockfish, cod, haddock, pollock, hake, albacore, and dogfish; squids, whales, seals, and porpoises eat them too. The eggs and the young of herring also constitute a source of food for many animals, including such occupants of the plankton as arrowworns, jellyfishes, and comb jellies. The herring, along with mackerel, salmon, and other fishes, then consume arrowworms that have eaten the young of the fish.

These food webs become more complicated to the extent that the predator is adaptable in its food choice, and that food requirements change with different stages of life. Both types of variation are common. In some instances, as noted in the case of the herring and arrowworms, prey and predator change roles.

The food-chain concept, while an oversimplification, is still helpful for illustrating certain points. One of these is the greater number of energy transformations—and consequent energy losses—required before food becomes available to man from the sea compared to number required for food from land. On land most human food derived from animal flesh comes from the shortest possible (two-link) chains (e.g., grass to sheep and cattle). But two-link chains are not common in the sea, some of the few examples being plant plankton to menhaden, or to anchovies. There are no three-, four-, or five-link chains on land that are important in the food economy of humans, but these long chains are normal in the sea. Three-link chains (e.g., diatoms to copepods (small crustaceans) to fish or mammal) include those leading to shad, basking sharks, whalebone whales, and numerous plankton-eating fishes. Four-link chains (diatoms to copepods to zooplankton-eating fishes to predatory fishes) include those leading to salmon, haddock, cod, and halibut. Sharks are at the end of five-link chains.

It may be that the transfer of energy from plants to animals, or from one animal to its predator, is more efficient in the sea than on land. In calculations of energy flow between trophic levels it is usual to assume that only 10 per cent is passed from one level to the next. This may be a fair average among land animals, but not necessarily among those in the sea. Furthermore, even on land there are some notable exceptions: with the help of carefully selected and controlled diets 20 per cent of a chicken's food may be transformed into body substance. Thus if the 10 per cent rate is used without discrimination, gross errors result.

Dr. Milner B. Schaefer of the University of California points out that instead of all the "decomposition" being returned to the food-chain system only after reduction to inorganics, a considerable amount of the food material is short-circuited back into the system at various higher trophic levels in three ways: it is eaten by detritus feeders (clams and oysters, and a host of animals with similar feeding habits); absorbed by bacteria and other creatures, which are then eaten by higher animals; and eaten directly after death by scavengers. Instead of the flat 10 per cent efficiency these processes in the sea may result in higher ecological transfers: "Fifteen per cent would not seem an unreasonable guess, and 20 per cent should be possible," according to Schaefer.

Taking these same factors into consideration, Dr. William Ricker of the Fisheries Research Board of Canada estimated in 1968 that the "transfer efficiency" between plants and herbivores in the sea may be 10 per cent, but that this may rise to 15 per cent between each animal trophic level.

Having estimated annual plant production in the sea and fixed on a range of reasonable rates of transfer between trophic levels, one more factor must be analyzed before the quantities of food available to humans can be determined. This factor is the relative use that can be made by humans of the protoplasm in its various forms: as plant material, as the bodies of herbivores, or as first-, second-, or higher-level carnivores.

Men can make very little use of the plants constituting the first trophic level. Most of the plant material in the sea is in the form

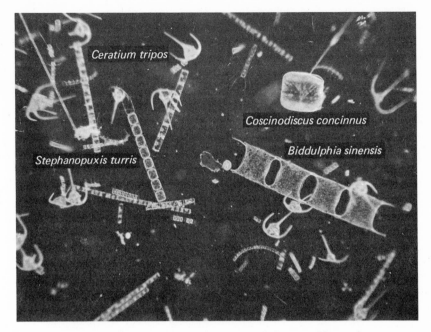

Ceratium tripos

Coscinodiscus concinnus

Biddulphia sinensis

Stephanopuxis turris

FIGURE 3.3. *The "grass" and "trees" of the sea. Shown here photographed alive are the two principal groups of the plant plankton: diatoms* (Biddulphia, Stephanopuxis, Coscinodiscus) *and dinoflagellates* (*anchor-shaped* Ceratium tripos).

Douglas P. Wilson

of plankton—microscopic diatoms and flagellates—which are not edible by humans. Neither are the herbivorous plankton animals (those at the second trophic level) usually used as human food, since the chief marine herbivores are copepods and euphausids, small relatives of the shrimp, which are difficult to capture and to process into edible form.

Men do make considerable use of such abundant fishes as the anchovies, sardines, menhaden, and other herringlike species. These feed on both plankton plants and herbivorous planktonic animals, and thus occupy an intermediate position between trophic level two (the plant eaters) and trophic level three (the primary carnivores). About 40 per cent of the commercial catch today is of fishes at this intermediate level. Traditionally, however, the bulk of the food that man has obtained from the sea has consisted of such secondary carnivores (trophic level four) as salmon, cod, mackerel, and tuna.

Starting with the kinds of data summarized above, various

[21]

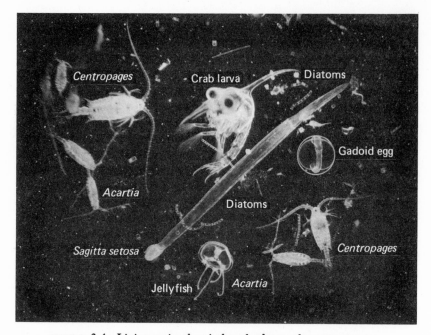

FIGURE 3.4. *Living animals of the plankton: the transparent arrowworm* Sagitta setosa, *the zoea (early larva) of a crab, a round gadoid egg with a developing fish inside, and a small jellyfish. The larger copepods are* Centropages *and the smaller ones* Acartia. *Diatoms can be seen as small chains and squares of cells.*

Douglas P. Wilson

estimates have been made of the total amount of material from the sea available to man in forms suitable for food.

In 1962 Herbert Graham and Robert Edwards of the U.S. Bureau of Commerical Fisheries calculated that the annual production of bony fishes (i.e., species like salmon and cod, but not including sharks) was 230 million tons. Assuming that all the harvest was at level four in the food pyramid and that half the available amount could be taken each year without depleting the stocks, they supposed that the potential to man is 115 million tons.

In 1965 Dr. Milner B. Schaefer started with the National Academy of Sciences figure of total plant carbon production of 19 billion metric tons. Unlike Graham and Edwards who assumed that all the catch is of stage-four fishes, Schaefer took account of the high proportion of sardinelike "stage-two and a half" fishes harvested. Schaefer calculated the total of these potential harvests to be 1.08 billion tons at a 10 per cent efficiency and 2.42 billion tons at a 15 per cent rate. Taking into account the various reasons why not all of this material can be harvested, Schaefer's "minimum, conservative" estimate is an actual catch of 200 million tons a year.

In 1968 Dr. William Ricker used Koblenz-Mishke's primary production figure of 130 billion tons of plants. He assumed that the average edible product harvested is between trophic levels three and four, but he put the average closer to level four. Using transfer rates of 10 per cent between the plants and the herbivores and 15 per cent thereafter, Ricker calculated that there are 300 million tons of material available for harvest. The value is 2 billion tons if the harvest is made at level three, so if Schaefer's view is correct, that more of the harvest is toward this level, the potential available would be correspondingly higher by Ricker's method of calculation.

Some scientists have put the potential much higher than the figures set forth here. In 1965 Dr. Wilbert M. Chapman of the Ralston-Purina Company, using the same base figure and rates of transfer as Schaefer but assuming that humans can use a larger share of animals at the lower trophic level (smaller fishes and zooplankton), said that "the ocean is producing at least 2 billion tons per year of organisms of size and form that are capable of practical harvest by man with known technology."

The higher estimates may eventually prove to be closer to the

FIGURE 3.5. *The herring,* Clupea harengus. *This abundant species represents trophic level three, the eaters of animal plankon. But herring and other similar fishes also consume some plant plankton, and thus occupy a level somewhere between two (the plant eaters) and three.*

truth for two reasons. First, most of the larger estimates were made with traditional scientific conservatism, using the lowest available quantities or rates. If average values were used instead, some of these estimates would be considerably higher. Great uncertainties exist about the accuracy of the basic figures, but while estimates of the total quantity of carbon fixed per year have been smaller in the last few decades, the calculated values of the other pertinent variables (efficiency between successive trophic levels, levels of harvest) have increased. To the extent that incorrectly low estimates of these rates have been used, the potentials as stated are lower than reality.

The second reason for optimism concerning the size of the potential harvest of food from the sea is that techniques and markets are being developed for harvesting and using kinds of animals that previously seemed out of reach—small fishes, squids, antarctic krill, Pacific red crabs, and perhaps many more. As the harvest moves closer to the herbivore level (by continuing the trend to use more and more sardine-like fishes) it approaches a potential figure of 7.2 billion tons at the 20 per cent conversion level. If man learns to use herbivores, this figure would be 38 billion tons.

I would venture to guess that at least 400 million metric tons of food material can be caught and used annually from the sea—and I will not be astonished if this proves to be considerably short of the truth.

Thus, it turns out that the sea produces every year such enormous quantities of living material that not only the present population of the world but the enormously increased crowds of future years could theoretically be sustained by the sea alone, with no dependence on land farms. By far the greatest part of the material produced in the sea is unavailable or is in forms unusable or unacceptable by man, but even after a conservative discounting of these two categories, it is obvious that the sea is producing edible protoplasm ("packaged" in the form of fishes and other animals so that it is perfectly acceptable and useful to man) in quantities far greater than are now being used.

If Dr. Chapman was right in fixing on 2 billion metric tons as the potential (and he believed even his estimate to be conservative), only about 2.5 per cent of the potential is being used.

Since as much plant material is created annually in the sea by photosynthesis as on land, it would seem possible to harvest as much food from the ocean as from land farms. But this plant material in the sea is not available to be harvested all at one time. Instead of growing by one generation a year and ripening for harvest at one time of the year, the little plants of the sea appear in a whole series of short genera-

FIGURE 3.6. *The cod end, or bag, of a trawl dumping its load on the deck of a North Atlantic vessel. Many of these fishes represent trophic level four —the carnivorous fishes such as cod and haddock.*

F. Krügler

FIGURE 3.7. *A big catch of dogfish sharks. These fishes represent trophic level five, fish that eat fish that eat fish.*

Bureau of
Commercial Fisheries

tions, each producing a fraction of the bulk of the whole. Thus, while the standing crop of many plants on land is about equal to the annual production, in the sea it is usually 1 per cent or less of annual production. Furthermore, individual atoms of carbon and other elements are used many times in a year, passing from one plant to another as photosynthesis and breakdown follow in succession. If plants were harvested, these atoms would be removed and thus be unavailable to form part of the substance of the next generation of plants; this would reduce the annual production.

This is very different from the pattern of plant production on land, a pattern that makes possible the large harvests of farms. Because of the longer lives of most land plants, the amount of living material existing at any one time is either about the same as annual production (in the case of the grasses and grain crops) or actually larger than annual production (trees and shrubs). The pattern of plant production in the sea accounts to an important degree for that fact pointed out in Chapter 2 that only 1 to 2 per cent of human food comes from the world oceans.

The fundamental differences between the land and the sea environment, which make the harvest of sea animals much harder than that of land animals, are also partly responsible for the great disparity in production. The most important of these differences is the great bulk of the ocean, which allows the material to be spread so thinly that collection is difficult. On land most of the harvestable material is concentrated in a very limited region, mostly a few feet thick on the land surface. In the sea the addition of the third dimension, hundreds and sometimes thousands of feet in extent, complicates the gathering process enormously.

Despite these problems, there is no doubt that the sea can be persuaded to yield far greater bounty, and several ways for enlarging the harvest have been suggested. The methods most often proposed for increasing the contribution of the sea to the fight against hunger include the following:

First, humans might take direct advantage of the immense bulk of plant and animal plankton—the small floating creatures that form the base of the food pyramid. Virtually no use is now made of the plants and the plant-eating animals of the sea, the equivalent of the materials constituting the overwhelming bulk of our food from the land, and the suggestion is often made that plankton is the chief hope of a hungry world.

Second, the bigger plants, the seaweeds, might yield far greater amounts of food than they do at present. The Japanese eat thousands of tons of seaweed yearly—why can't the rest of the world?

Third, most people believe that fishing is a primitive way to gather food, equivalent to the hunting economy of many centuries ago. The greatest hope of many is that mankind will learn to farm the sea, turning vast tracts of sea bottom into marine equivalents of Iowa cornfields, and herding fishes and whales with submarine-mounted cowboys.

Fourth, we might transplant useful marine animals from one part of the ocean to another, filling gaps that nature has left with food fishes, mammals, and plants for ready harvest.

The last way of increasing food from the sea is to make more use of the kinds of fishes, mammals, and other animals already caught in at least small quantities. Clearly some of these creatures are unexploited or underexploited, and more effort with more efficient tools should give greater yields.

In the remainder of this book each of these possible methods of increasing the contribution of the sea to the fight against hunger will be examined.

[27]

4   *The Harvest of Plankton*

Suppose that the food supplies of mankind were suddenly reduced by the loss of the edible land plants. Then men could no longer eat any grains (wheat, rice, corn, and countless others), any tubers (potatoes, yams, carrots), any fruits or vegetables, any nuts, any sugar—indeed any of the enormously varied and abundant plant materials that are the basis of the human diet. The result would be disaster, swift and overwhelming. In 1965 this would have resulted in a loss of over 1,518 million metric tons of food—something like 3,345,900,000,000 pounds. For the peoples of the Far East, the Near East, Africa, and most of Latin America—70 per cent of the world's population—it would represent a loss of 85 per cent of their food; for the rest of the world—the relatively well-fed 30 per cent—an average loss of 70 per cent.

But if with the same swift stroke the world were deprived of all the sea plants men now eat the event would hardly be noticed. Humans eat virtually no marine plants; furthermore, they consume only minor quantities of marine herbivorous animals. Yet the plants and the herbivores are by far the most abundant of living creatures, and their total quantity in the sea is enormous, probably far greater than on land. Why do men fail to use these food resources? To answer this question one must examine the nature of the food now used from the sea, and of the neglected oceanic plants and herbivores.

Most of the human food derived from the sea consists of carnivorous fishes—tuna, cod, salmon, and others with similar feeding habits. These fishes have eaten other animals; these in turn may also have eaten animals, and there may be several links down the food chain to the plants. Every time a link is added there is a loss of substance and

[28]

energy of perhaps 80 to 90 per cent. Thus a mackerel, which eats fishes that eat smaller fishes that eat small shrimplike animals that finally eat small floating plants, is the product of a whole series of energy transformations, each undergoing a loss of as much as 90 per cent of the former stage. On land the animals in the same wasteful position in the food chain are such creatures as the weasels, the foxes, the cats, and the wolverines. Even if fried fox or broiled wolverine were delicious, the dishes would not often be served since these animals would be too expensive to raise as food. The cows, pigs, and sheep consumed by humans are plant eaters, making immediate use of grasses and grains; by undergoing only a single transformation of tissue they suffer only one loss of energy and substance. Thus, far greater efficiency is attained in the use of land-derived foods. The plants most used as food possess roots that may swell into edible tubers, or flowers that may develop into grains, fruits, or nuts. But the plants from the sea eaten by humans consist entirely of leafy vegetables—the equivalent of cabbage, lettuce, and dandelion leaves. Grains, roots, fruits, and nuts are not harvested from the sea because for practical purposes there are none there.

At present the overwhelming proportion of human food from the sea consists of animals, only a trivial 0.005 per cent being plant material; on land from 40 to 85 per cent comes from plants in various countries.

A casual observer might think that the sea has very few plants of any kind. Along the shore and in shallow bays are glistening growths of seaweeds that move languidly back and forth with the currents when the tide is in, or lie spinelessly in the sand at low tide; and in a few shallow areas there are rooted plants.

Neither the sparse "fields" of rooted plants nor the somewhat greater areas of seaweeds exist in anything like the vast expanses of the grassy prairies or the forests of the land. Only in a narrow strip around some edges of the sea, in the shallowest of waters, is vegetation of this sort found.

Yet the sea must have plants in great abundance because its immense populations of animals cannot exist without them. Animals cannot manufacture their food; they derive it directly by grazing on plants or indirectly by eating other animals that have eaten plants, one or more steps down the food pyramid. The very base of all food chains, the broad and indispensable foundation on which all life rests, is composed of the plants.

Ocean pastures do exist, and they are enormous. But instead of being grasses, shrubs, and trees, the marine plants are mostly one-celled creatures floating passively in the water as part of the plankton.

[29]

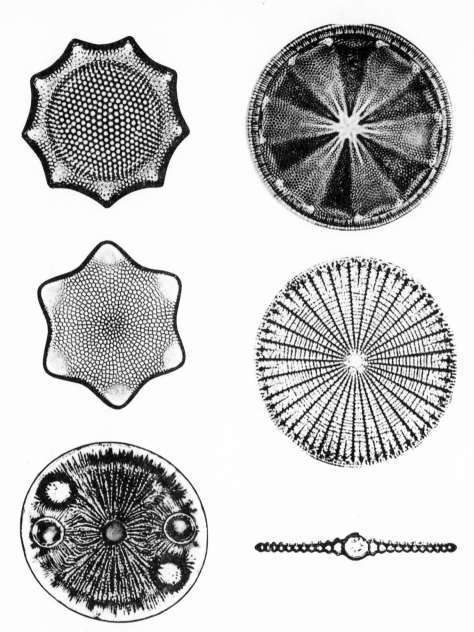

FIGURE 4.1. *Diatoms, one of the principal groups of microscopic planktonic plants of the sea. The little plants are encased in boxes of silica, whose shapes and patterns are as beautiful as they are varied. Diatoms form the food of countless billions of herbivorous animals, and they are a major part of the broad base of the food pyramid in the sea.*

Dr. Albert Mann

They usually are so small that it requires a microscope to see the individuals, giving the illusion that the sea lacks its proper complement of plants.

The plants of the sea are of little use as human food directly. The rooted plants can be dismissed both because of their scarcity and because they have no edible tubers, grains, or fruits. The more abundant algae, or seaweeds, constitute the bulk of large-sized marine plant material. Like the algae from the land, which are ignored as food since they are distasteful, sometimes poisonous, and usually unnutritious, most of the seaweeds are likewise not edible, or are barely so to most tastes. The planktonic plants are so diffused over the ocean's bulk that it is very much more difficult to harvest them than it is to send a reaper into a field of wheat. And even if harvest were easy, other characteristics of the oceanic plants make them unsatisfactory as food.

The most numerous of the small plants of the sea are the flagellates, so called because they possess one or two whiplike appendages called flagella. Many species in this group are naked, but an immense number have external skeletons of cellulose. This is the same kind of material that composes the supporting parts of land plants; it is tough, chemically complex, and indigestible. Human beings put up with it in land plants, passing it through their systems for the sake of the digestible parts of the plants enclosed by the cellulose. But the cellulose proportions of many flagellates are high compared to the whole plants, reducing their value as food.

Another great group of the flagellates is the coccolithophores. These are among the smallest of the small plants of the sea. They have tiny

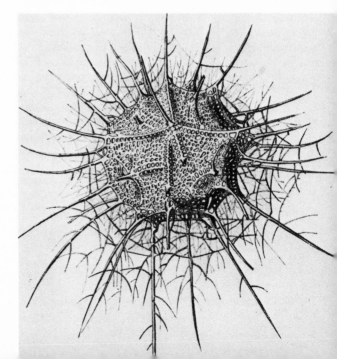

FIGURE 4.2. *A radiolarian,* Oroscena, *showing the complex radiating spikes of silica that would render it an uncomfortable kind of food.*

Valdivia Expedition

skeletons of calcareous plates, fitting neatly together to form multitudes of fanciful shapes. Here, too, the proportion of skeleton to digestible substance is high.

And worse is yet to come. The other group of oceanic plants is the diatoms, tiny specks of protoplasm encased in shells of silica. Silica is the main ingredient of glass—definitely not a food substance.

At certain times great flowerings of the plankton plants take place so that they make a soup of the sea, coloring it red, brown, or green as billions of billions of organisms explode into being. The "red tides" of the coastal waters of Florida, California, and Peru are typical of such blooms. In these enormous outbursts 60 million dinoflagellates have been counted in a liter (a little more than a quart) of seawater, and in other places blooms of diatoms have resulted in the production of 7 to 8 billion individuals under a square meter (something over a square yard) of sea surface. At such times of heavy plant growth, plankton hauls are exclusively of one kind of organism, and nets quickly become clogged and inoperative. And when dinoflagellate "red tide" blooms occur, the tremendous chemical activity (including the production of poisonous metabolic wastes of the little plants) kills fish and other creatures and causes respiratory discomfort to humans.

But these great blooms of oceanic plants are abnormal occurrences. Under ordinary circumstances the amount of material available at a given time is very small, even in highly productive parts of the ocean. Over a year the total production is high, but this is made possible by a very short generation time for the little plants—in many cases only two or three days or less.

Nearly everyone who talks about plankton as food means the animals in the plankton, whether he says so or not. Furthermore, implicitly or explicitly, in almost all cases the plankton animals under discussion are crustaceans. The most familiar of the crustaceans are the shrimps, crabs, and lobsters, but their less well known cousins, the copepods and euphausids, are immensely more important in the economy of the sea. The average-sized copepod is no bigger than the head of a pin. The importance of the copepods is not in proportion to their size, but to their numbers and to their intermediate position in the food chain. It has been estimated that the number of individual copepods is larger than that of all the other multicelled animals of the world combined. Hardly a plankton haul made in any part of the ocean comes up without some copepods, and they often make up 75 to 95 per cent of all individuals caught.

The copepods are the chief grazers of the sea, devouring little plants and converting their substance into animal tissue. The copepods,

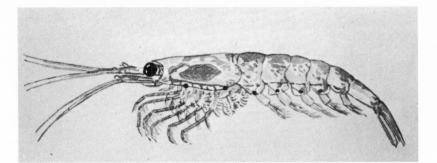

FIGURE 4.3. *The krill,* Euphausia superba, *which may some day support a major fishery in the Antarctic. If it does, it will help enormously in the problem of harvesting more food from the sea, since krill are very abundant and, more importantly, represent a layer in the marine food pyramid that is being poorly used at present.*

Sir Alister Hardy, *Great Waters,* Harper & Row

in turn, are eaten by an immense variety of other sea creatures, including fishes and mammals.

The other very important crustacean hebivores are the euphausids. They are usually bigger than the copepods—up to two inches long. Some are immensely numerous in the Antarctic, where the whalers know them as "krill." During the far southern summer they swarm in fantastic numbers at the edge of the ice pack, feeding on the blooms of diatoms and forming fodder for the great whales.

Thus the available supplies of animal plankton in the sea are exceedingly large. The next question to examine is whether they are nutritious and palatable.

Animal plankton appears to be rich in the nutrient materials essential for the human diet. Some types are especially high in protein, and this is significant since hunger involves not only shortages of calories but critical shortages of protein, and especially animal protein.

In addition, some other nutrients occur in important concentrations in planktonic crustaceans. Vitamins A and D, for which cod-liver oil is famous, are derived from crustaceans. In the krill, vitamin A is found in large quantities, especially in the eyes; as much as 12,000 international units has been assayed per gram of dry weight of euphausids, compared to 70 international units per gram in mammals.

It is not enough, however, that a substance contain the materials that constitute animal food, however richly. This is merely the potential, and it must be shown in addition that an animal eating the food is capable of extracting the energy from the substance. There is some evidence that only a small portion of the nutritive value of the plankton can be realized by the digestive systems of land mammals. This evidence comes from limited experiments with rats, which did poorly on a diet of plankton. Although the tests are by no means conclusive, the results suggest that one should go slowly in claiming zooplankton as the solution to the world's food problem. At the same time it is obvious that some animals thrive on natural diets that include crustacean plankton creatures. The largest mammals in the world, the largest fishes and the most numerous fishes all eat plankton; in fact, it is almost their sole food.

The sperm whale is the only one of the very large whales to eat sizeable prey—mostly squids. The other big whales, the baleen or whalebone whales, strain enormous quantities of zooplankton from the water.

One of the baleen species, the blue whale, is not only the largest animal in the world today but the largest animal that has ever lived, greatly exceeding the size of any of the ancient dinosaurs. It reaches a length of 100 feet and a weight of 100 tons. This animal supports its immense body largely from a diet of a planktonic crustacean, the antarctic krill *Euphausia superba*.

The blue whale catches euphausids by swimming through the water, often at the surface, with its mouth open. Accordion pleats in the throat allow the already gigantic mouth to expand greatly. After a mouthful of water and plankton is taken in, the pleats are contracted, the mouth is closed, and the tongue forces the water out sideways through curtains of whalebone, gigantic sieves that hang "like a vast internal mustache" (to use Sir Alister Hardy's phrase) from inside the upper jaw. The krill are strained from the water, wiped off the mustache by the tongue, and swallowed. The stomach of one blue whale taken in the Antarctic was found to contain 1,200 quarts of krill. A single whale may consume up to three tons of krill a day.

The biggest of all fishes is the whale shark, *Rhineodon typus,* which reaches a length of at least fifty feet. In *Kon Tiki* Thor Heyerdahl tells of a visit by one of these enormous creatures to his drifting raft. It provided an awesome sight, with its head appearing under the bow and its tail under the stern simultaneously. The whale shark subsists on plankton.

So does another immense fish, the basking shark, *Cetorhinus maximus,* which grows to a length of forty feet and a weight of several tons. These animals are seen commonly off the coasts of Ireland and Scotland in the summer, especially when their principal food, the copepod *Calanus,* is swarming. The shark cruises slowly just below the surface, filtering approximately 2,000 tons of water in a day. One basking shark caught off Scotland had 1,000 quarts of the *Calanus* copepods in its stomach.

The most numerous of the fishes of the ocean also depend exclusively or very heavily on planktonic organisms. These are the herring, the sardines, the anchovies, and similar species, which swarm the seas in astonishing numbers. Off Peru a single species of anchovettas, *Engraulis ringens,* is so numerous that it supports a fishery whose landings exceed the weight of the *combined* landings of *all* species of fish of any other country in the world. A total of 10 million metric tons of anchovettas were landed in Peru in 1967, and this may represent only half the numbers of these fish in the ocean off her shores. California landed 550,000 tons of sardines, *Sardinops caerulea,* when that fishery was in its heyday in the 1930's; again perhaps as many more were left swimming free. In good years, fishermen have landed 2 billion pounds of menhaden, *Brevoortia,* off the east and Gulf coasts of the United States. And all these thousands of billions of fish exist chiefly through the consumption of planktonic animals. Many species of tuna, salmon, and mackerel do likewise.

Of course, it cannot be assumed that crustacean plankton will turn out to be manna for man merely because it is the bread and butter of the blue whale and the Peruvian anchovetta. But on the basis of the high content of basic food materials, and from long experience in successful consumption by humans of shrimp, lobsters, crabs, and many other seafoods closely related in body characteristics to the planktonic crustaceans, it seems likely that the latter would prove to be satisfactory food.

The experiments with rats suggested that one reason these animals failed to flourish on plankton was that they simply did not like it. Humans are also notoriously fussy about what they eat, and some starve in the presence of perfectly edible foods for the unreasonable reason that they don't like them.

However, people have learned to eat—and like—crustacean plankton. Among the earliest accounts of its consumption by humans is Sir William Herdman's. He relates that in Norway in 1891 a yachting party ate it without strong objections.

In 1952 Dr. Alain Bombard, a physician, subjected himself to grueling hardships in order to prove that a man could survive a considerable period of time on a raft or small boat, living exclusively on what he could get from the sea. Ten days was usually regarded as about the maximum survival time under such circumstances, but Dr. Bombard

[35]

came out alive after sixty-five days, drifting from the Canary Islands to the West Indies. This was made possible partly through the consumption of plankton. He had no rain for twenty-five days, and the plankton supplied some of his water requirements as well as his food. He described it as tasting "like lobster, at times like shrimp and at times some vegetable."

Experiments were carried out in 1948 by George Clarke and David Bishop of Harvard to determine whether plankton could be used as emergency food for persons cast adrift at sea. Members of the scientific group reported, "the plankton has a mildly pleasant taste, being somewhat reminiscent of shrimp or oysters." However, the most that could be eaten before it became unacceptable and distasteful was something less than a quarter of a pound. Even a third of this amount "gave the impression of remaining undigested in the stomach after several hours."

Thor Heyerdahl and his companions caught and sampled plankton from their famous raft, *Kon Tiki,* during its drifting voyage from Peru to islands of the Polynesian archipelago in the Pacific. They ate it "not for the sake of the smell, for that was bad. Not because the sight was appetizing, for it looked a horrible mess." But "bad as it smelled it tasted correspondingly good if one just plucked up courage and put a spoonful into one's mouth."

Sir Alister Hardy, the eminent British marine scientist, says that some copepods are delicious. "Boiled in sea water for a moment, strained and then fried in butter and served on toast, *Euchaeta* is a delicacy which one day might support a small fishery to supply a luxury market. Its deep blue clusters of eggs turn a brilliant orange when cooked. *Calanus,* served in the same way, make a pleasant shrimp paste." Prince Albert of Monaco, the royal amateur whose energetic interest advanced marine biology so effectively around the turn of the last century, regarded plankton as a palatable food when cooked in oil.

These are either casual or incidental essays into the nearly unknown area of plankton consumption, or instances of trials of its use on an emergency basis. But there are some areas of the world where plankton is an established food. Peter Freuchen, the Norwegian explorer, reported that plankton is eaten in the high Arctic: "I have seen it boiled; it turns bright red like lobsters and forms a sort of porridge which can be eaten with a spoon." In the Mediterranean the euphausid *Meganyctiphanes* supports a small fishery.

The Japanese conduct an important fishery for several kinds of planktonic crustaceans that are cooked in soya sauce to make a dish called tsudadani, and for at least a century the peoples of Southeast Asia and some other areas have prepared fermented fish pastes from a wide variety of sea animals, including several planktonic crustaceans. These pastes, variously called mam, belachan, terassi, and other names in different regions, serve the important function of condiments, brightening an otherwise somewhat drab diet consisting largely of rice, vegetables, salt fish, and various soups. Residents of the north coast of China make a shrimp paste that is eaten by the poor all over China, especially in the winter. Sea-derived pastes are also manufactured and consumed in Japan, India, the Philippines, and Indochina.

Fish and shrimp pastes are indispensable parts of the diet in Thailand. "Kapi," or shrimp paste, is used as a relish throughout the year by nearly everyone. To make "dry" kapi, having the consistency of cottage cheese, the plankton is drained, mixed with fine salt, dried in the sun for six to eight hours, crushed finely, and drained and dried again. Then it is packed tightly in wooden tubs, covered with layers of banana

FIGURE 4.4. *Other euphausids besides the krill might form the material for plankton fisheries if efficient methods of capture could be devised, and markets could be found for the catch.*

N. B. Marshall, *Aspects of Deep Sea Biology*

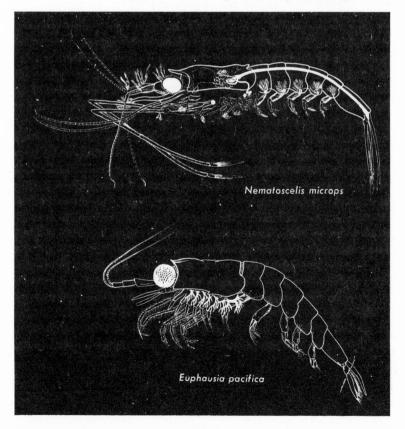

Nematoscelis microps

Euphausia pacifica

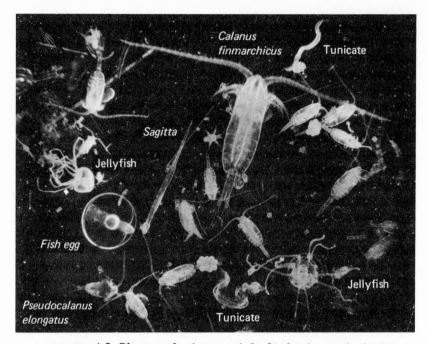

FIGURE 4.5. *Photograph of some of the kinds of animals that would form the human diet if plankton were harvested as food. The biggest animal in the picture is the copepod* Calanus finmarchicus, *which is only an eighth of an inch long.* Pseudocalanus elongatus *is another copepod;* Sagitta *is an arrowworm; tunicates are primitive chordates; the fish egg is that of the cod family.*

Douglas P. Wilson

leaves and straw matting weighted with stones and put in a well-shaded place to ferment. Two weeks is the minimum time for fermentation, and six months is ideal for the best ripening.

"The flavor of these condiments is highly appreciated by the natives but seems to be unpalatable to Europeans," according to a report by Dr. J. Westenberg, of the Service of Sea Fisheries of Indonesia. But while fermented shrimp paste may never appear as a delicacy on the menus of the Western world, it is obvious that plankton is already firmly established as food among a large part of the earth's population, and there is no reason to doubt that other kinds of food products made from planktonic crustaceans could be developed that would be fully acceptable to other palates.

The final question, of course, is whether plankton can be harvested economically. The outlook is not promising.

Vast misconceptions surround this matter. Learning that the sea produces an estimated 19 billion tons of living matter a year, some people conceive that it is soup that waits only to be strained. Unfortunately, it is an extremely thin soup. There are approximately 331 million cubic miles of water in the sea—301,471,060,000,000,000,-000 gallons. This is a very great amount of water, and the little plants and animals that inhabit it are so widely spaced that the vast majority of them are perfectly safe from capture by man. Of course, the plankton are not evenly scattered over the whole breadth and depth of the ocean, but are concentrated near the lighted upper regions, and are collected into schools and patches of various concentrations at different times of the year. Otherwise it would be a completely hopeless task to try to collect them in quantity. As it is, the task is extremely difficult.

Outside of a few places like Thailand and Japan, most plankton captured now is collected for research purposes by marine scientists, who usually gather it by means of nets made of a metal ring supporting a conical bag of fine-meshed material. The standard net is one meter (a little over a yard) in diameter at the mouth, about ten feet long, and has a bottle at the small end in which the plankton is collected. The nets are towed slowly through the water or are held in place while the tide streams through them. They are regarded as being about 20 per cent efficient, capturing only this proportion of the plankton organisms because the meshes become clogged with the early part of the catch, and because water and some of the plankton it contains spill around the opening without passing through the meshes.

The present outlook for commercial fishing of plankton is so poor that most expert observers have dismissed the idea as hopeless. For example, Dr. Gordon A. Riley of the Bingham Oceanographic Laboratories of Yale University has said that "to harvest any considerable fraction of the plankton of the world seems as fantastic as the old dream of extracting gold from seawater. By and large we must leave the plankton to the fishes." Dr. Daniel Merriman, also at Yale, has been equally forthright:

. . . the harvesting of a plankton crop would require the continuous filtering of stupendous quantities of water and would demand such an enormous output of energy that any large-scale process of this sort is completely impractical—at least until atomic energy is turned to constructive rather than destructive ends, and even then the problems would be complex. Such harvesting still belongs in the realm of fantasy.

The evidence supporting these statements is solid. Dr. George

Clarke of Harvard calculated that if diatoms were sought in times of maximum abundance, about a quart could be caught in six hours by three men using a forty-foot power boat. This is in the relatively rich areas of the Atlantic between Cape Cod and Chesapeake Bay. Copepods and other comparatively large animal plankton are somewhat easier to catch in quantity. Coarser nets and faster towing speeds are possible, and a two-meter net fishing at two knots would catch about a pound and a half (dry weight) in three and a quarter hours in periods of summer abundance. By using two such nets and fishing them alternately in a continuous operation, it would be possible to collect twelve pounds of animal plankton (dry weight) in a day. At this rate of capture, in order to satisfy the daily food requirements of the average human, the zooplankton from an area approximately the size of a football field and four and a half feet deep would be required. Under the conditions assumed, this would take two and a half hours to accomplish. Dr. Clarke was "forced to conclude, therefore, that if the marketing of plankton on a commercial scale is to become a practical reality, either areas of greatly increased richness must be located or some method must be found for making the above rate of producing plankton economically feasible."

Philip Jackson of the Scottish Institute of Seaweed Research also came to a pessimistic conclusion. He estimated that it would cost from $5,040 to $8,000 a dry ton to produce the plankton by various methods.

Dr. Chancey Juday, an American freshwater biologist, and Dr. James Fraser, an eminent planktologist from Aberdeen, have discussed the use of large centrifuges as an alternative to catching plankton by nets. These devices whirl heavier particles or components of a mixture to the outer rim, where they can be separated out. Fraser has not been very sanguine about this method, since he has pointed out that it would require large amounts of power to filter the very large quantities of water. Where power is free or cheap, as in some tidal estuaries with powerfull currents, the supply of plankton is unreliable. Conversely, in the Antarctic and other places where plankton is abundant, power is scarce and expensive, and markets are far away.

R. F. Shropshire of the Dow Chemical Company designed a plankton harvester he believed would be practical. His device consisted of a large rotary cylinder, covered with bolting cloth. When water passed through the open end, the plankton was collected against the cloth. It was flushed off the cloth by a series of nozzles whose jets of water washed the catch into a trough, and the nearly gelatinous material was led to a filter press and formed into a cake. But in most plankton-rich areas this machine is estimated to be capable of collecting only about 35.2 pounds per day.

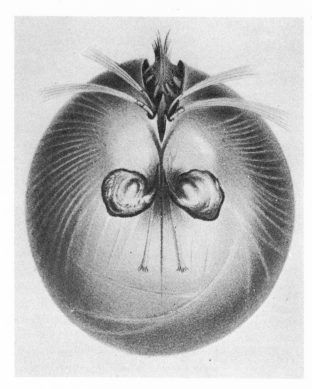

FIGURE 4.6. *An ostracod,* Gigantocypris agassizii, *one of the many kinds of crustaceans in the plankton. This species occurs in the deep sea, its size of about half an inch makes it much larger than most others of the group.*

Valdivia Expedition

If the nets of scientists cannot catch enough plankton to pay for their operation, and neither can the centrifuge of the dairyman nor the specially devised revolving cylinder of the engineer, what about trying the technique of the whale? An "artificial whale" might be a vessel with a gaping opening in its bow, backed by some kind of filtering device. The ship would plow as rapidly as possible through the water and sweep up the plankton. Dr. James Fraser designed a ship with a fifteen-foot-wide oval opening below the surface, to avoid picking up floating debris. The water and plankton would be passed over revolving fine-meshed drums of monel metal. Pumps would remove the plankton in concentrated form, and other pumps would pour the water back overboard. The catch would be dried and packed in airtight containers for shipment to market. But Fraser's calculation of the financial return from such a ship is not encouraging. On a twenty-one-day trip the vessel might catch 2,500 pounds on the passage out, 44,000 pounds at the main fishing grounds, and another 2,500 pounds en route home, for a total of 22 metric tons of wet plankton, or 2.75 tons dry weight. But a trawler on a similar trip could catch 30 to 120 tons of fish at less than half the cost and worth more per ton on the market.

Sir Alister Hardy was at one time optimistic about commercial plankton fishing. But after serious attempts he was obliged to concede that it was not feasible in British waters under existing conditions:

The plankton is so very uneven in its distribution and such an enormous quantity of water has to be filtered to give sufficient yield in even a very rich area. Plankton may help to save the marooned sailor or airman on a raft from starvation but it is unlikely to support a fishery in our own waters, except perhaps as a luxury food. . . . It is possible that some harvesting of plankton in the extremely rich areas of krill . . . in polar seas might prove a success.

The crack in the door, left open by Hardy and other observers, is the possibility of harvesting the antarctic krill, *Euphausia superba*. The way to break open any difficult problem is to attack it at its easiest point; then experience may help provide answers to its other initially unsolvable facets. In the Antarctic, the quantities and concentrations of krill are large enough to offer hope of successful harvest. In recent years the Soviets have carried out experiments testing special gear for gathering these planktonic animals. They have approached the problem with the attitude that plankton harvesting must be regarded as a specialized type of fishery and that the fisherman must have knowledge of the occurrence, seasonal abundance, and behavior of his planktonic prey. No fisherman can make a living by dragging his gear haphazardly through the water, as has been implied in some schemes for harvesting plankton. For success in such a venture special plankton fisheries must be developed, with experienced crews searching for concentrations of commercially valuable species and catching them with particular kinds of efficient gear.

Although it has been commonly assumed in the past that plankton would be used directly as human food, the Soviets started their investigations specifically for fish meal to be used as a feed supplement for poultry and swine. One estimate in October 1961 put their supplies of fish meal at only 19 per cent of needs. Thus, the research vessel *Muksun*, a fishing trawler attached to the Atlantic Scientific Institute for Fisheries and Oceanography, sailed for the Scotia Sea, an especially rich krill area in the Antarctic. Her mission was to discover whether the swarming krill of those waters could be caught economically, and whether satisfactory meal could be made from them.

Euphausia superba is one of the biggest of the multitudinous forms of plankton crustaceans, ranging in size from about an inch and a half to two inches. In the summer and fall these swarm in enormous shoals at and near the surface of the sea, staining the water various reddish, yellowish, and brownish shades. These are apparently feeding con-

FIGURE 4.7. *Intestines and stomach of the blue whale cut open to show its recent meal of krill.*

N. A. Macintosh

centrations, the little "shrimp" eating the still more numerous diatom plants that bloom in the antarctic seas.

The numbers of krill boggle the imagination. In one three-day reconaissance in January 1962 the Soviets founds "feeding fields" over twenty miles in width that covered an area of at least 3,600 square miles. Other masses were also found, some denser (if smaller) than this one.

It is very difficult to make estimates of the total amounts of krill in the sea, and calculations vary considerably. But even the smallest estimates indicate that the quantities are immense. The most conservative estimate of the size of krill stocks is about 40 million tons, but 100 million may be closer to the truth, and the actual amount may easily be far higher. Probably a minimum of 50 million tons is available for harvest annually—about the total catch of the world fisheries in the late 1960's. Hence it is an immense resource that the Soviets set out to investigate.

Their vessel *Muksun* took three kinds of fishing gear to the Antarctic to try on the krill—a mid-water trawl designed for herring and sardines, a conical trawl used to catch fingerlings near the surface, and a combination of the fingerling trawl and a fish pump. With the latter gear, as the trawl caught the krill a pump pushed the catch aboard the vessel. Despite the small quantities caught with this device, its possibilities appeared promising. Most of the catches were made near the surface, to about sixteen feet, but good concentrations were found down to eighty feet or more.

The results of the expedition were encouraging enough that the *Muksun* was sent back to Antarctica in October 1963 to conduct further trials. A "side trawl" proved effective. This was a refinement of the combination fingerling trawl and pump. The entire length of the trawl was made of fine mesh to prevent the escape of the euphausids, and the device was dragged from a rigid frame on a boom held perpendicular to the side of the vessel.

The 1963 expedition caught about seventy tons of krill. From part of this, eleven tons of meal were made on board the vessel. The meal was orange in color, as a result of the high content of carotene, a reddish chemical which can be transformed into vitamin A.

The food value of krill compares favorably with that of other crustaceans such as shrimp, crabs, and lobsters. The protein and fat contents are high, and one pound supplies 460 calories. Krill spoils quickly, even in the cold antarctic temperatures. The first *Muksun* expedition salted down two barrels, but these spoiled before they could be delivered to Kaliningrad. Even so brief an exposure as three hours on deck at 32°F. resulted in a 16 per cent weight loss. After eight to twelve hours the krill turned soft and yellowish gray; longer exposure produced black spots followed by rapid disintegration. Hence there can be no thought of returning the catch to a distant port for processing: the meal must be made on the spot, and within a few hours of capture.

Scientists at the Kaliningrad Regional Experimental Agriculture Station found that one ton of krill meal fed to weanling piglets produced as much meat on the pigs as seven to eight tons of grain. The pigs grew to usable size more quickly, and thus more cheaply and efficiently. This was regarded as "an enormous economic benefit."

Consideration was also given to the possibility of using krill directly as human food, instead of feeding it to livestock. It tastes fine— "as good as shrimp"—according to the Soviet experimenters. But its small size is a severe handicap. The body of an average-sized animal weighs only about one gram (a little over three one-hundredths of an ounce). The edible portion of the body is about a quarter to a third of this, and the problems of cleaning such a tiny shrimp are formidable. If it is eaten without being shelled a high proportion of indigestible chitinous exoskeleton (more than 25 per cent) is ingested.

Some trials were carried out despite these problems. Four recipes were tried, involving the manufacture of canned "meat pies." Two of these proved worthless; the other two were acceptable. But the use of krill as human food is less promising at the moment than that of making meal for farm animals.

If the Soviets are able to establish the first krill fishery, the next one may be organized by the Norwegians. Many species of euphausids exist in their waters in large quantities, and show up on the echo sounders of fishermen seeking sprat and other prey. In the Hardanger Fjord strong lights have been strung along the water from the quays, and dense shoals have been attracted. Between 176 and 440 pounds in a night can be caught with bag nets supported on the end of a pole. More efficient gears are being tried, including mid-water trawls, lights, pumps, and other devices.

If the Soviets and Norwegians succeed in catching and using krill economically, there are scores of other species of euphausids (about eighty-five), thousands of other planktonic crustaceans, and hundreds of thousands of additional animals that men might learn to harvest. After the krill the next creature to support a plankton fishery may be the "red crab," a galatheid crustacean, *Pleuroncodes planipes*. During its adult life it lives on the bottom, where it might support a trawl fishery, as a related "crab," *Munida,* already does in Chile. Young red crabs swarm in the plankton in exceedingly large numbers, especially at the southern end of the California Current off Baja California. One oceanographer observed that "a ship sometimes appears to crunch through almost a solid mass of crabs for miles on end."

The red crab occurs both over the continental shelf and beyond it. It has been caught at least 1,000 miles to the southwest of Baja California, in the extension of the California Current. The bottom-living adults occur in deep water on the continental slope. Both the planktonic young and the adults might be fished. Concentrations of plankton are heavy enough to support catches of 550 pounds per hour with a small mid-water trawl. This may be exceeded by ten times under favorable conditions. The Russians are reported to have fished red crabs off California on a test basis.

The pessimism expressed by most observers about the possibility of developing plankton fisheries is well-founded, in view of the current level of man's skills and technology, but the picture is not entirely bleak. It would be foolish to think the problem is nearly solved merely because there seems to be a chance of harvesting antarctic krill on an economic basis. But one step at a time. Perhaps Antarctica first, then Norway or the California Current. Then enormous riches of food might be harvestable.

5   *The Harvest of Seaweed*

Besides the plankton plants, which are of little use as human food because of their glassy or calcareous shells, the ocean has another kind of algae, the seaweeds. Because they are relatively unpalatable and unnutritious, little use is made of them as food except in Asia, especially Japan. Somewhat more use is made of them to extract certain substances, and some are fed to livestock.

Seaweeds differ biologically from most land plants in that they are usually attached by "holdfasts," or anchoring devices, but they do not have true roots. Roots absorb mineral nutrients from the soil, but seaweeds absorb the nutrients through their "leaves." They have no flowers, fruits, or edible tubers.

The seaweeds of greatest economic importance are the brown algae and the red algae; a few green algae are also harvested. Although rarely used as food, the brown algae (including sugar wrack, *Laminaria,* and the giant kelps, *Macrocystis* and *Nereocystis*) are important in the production of extractives called algins. The red algae, including Irish moss and dulse, are those most often eaten, but their chief use is to make extractives, the agars and carrageenins. A red alga, laver, is the object of an extensive Japanese farming operation. Of the green algae, *Ulva* (called sea lettuce because of its resemblance to the land vegetable) and one or two other genera are used to a slight degree.

The use of seaweeds is increasing somewhat over the world, but not so much for food as for the production of chemicals and other useful substances. For 1967, the Food and Agriculture Organization of the United Nations reported a world production of 800,000 metric tons of seaweeds—about the quantity of prunes produced in the United States,

[47]

FIGURE 5.1. *A seaweed garden. This shallow area in Hammond Bay, near Nanaimo, British Columbia, has an unusually varied aggregation of marine plants. At the top are eelgrass (the only flowering plant in the picture) and Laminaria, a brown seaweed. Other brown seaweeds include Costaria, at the lower left, and a small example of the giant kelp Nereocystis in the center (its fronds here are only about three feet long, compared to a possible length of 150 feet or more). Gracilaria (a red seaweed) is attached to a rock at the left; broad fronds of the sea lettuce Ulva (a green alga) are at the bottom of the photograph.*

Fisheries Research Board of Canada, Biological Station, Nanaimo and approximately one tenth of this country's production of tomatoes.

Most European countries use seaweeds sparingly. In Great Britain, in the middle of the nineteenth century, sugar wrack and other species were sold in the streets of Edinburgh by vendors crying, "Buy dulse and tangle!", but in Britain the general consumption of marine algae stopped 50 to 100 years ago. Only in poorer areas, where food is scarce or where long tradition exists, do seaweeds form any part of the diet. South Wales is the center of seaweed consumption, but even there the amount of laver, the main species eaten, is a trivial 200 tons a year compared to 78,000 tons consumed in Japan, the world's principal user of seaweeds.

Laver is the Devon and Welsh name for the red seaweed *Porphyra.* In places where there are moderately dense growths, such as the Pembroke coast of South Wales, it is collected at low tide and sent fresh to Swansea by passenger train. Some is consumed raw as a salad but most goes into "laverbread." In the preparation of laverbread the plant is first washed very thoroughly. With typical British understatement, a report on this process says: "The more tenacious sand is removed from twisted sections and knots by hand. This cleaning is extremely important, as the presence of any sand in the finished product is highly detrimental." The laver is cooked in salted water in copper boilers for twelve hours, and then is spread on stone slabs to cool. It is minced, and coloring matter is added.

The final product is a unique kind of bread—a shiny, gelatinous mass with a pleasant flavor of the sea. It is either warmed in fat or is made into small cakes coated with oatmeal, which are fried and eaten with bacon and eggs. In the Swansea market there are several stalls where only laverbread is sold, and cockle women of Penclawdd sell it through the Welsh valleys.

In South Wales and Scotland a small amount of Irish moss is eaten. It is boiled in milk to produce a sort of blancmange. Some dulse is chewed like tobacco, and small quantities of the young tender stalks of *Laminaria* are eaten. In former times *Ulva,* the sea lettuce, was used raw in salads and cooked in soups.

In Iceland, dulse has been eaten since at least the eighth century, usually with dried fish, butter, and potatoes. In times of famine bread also was made from dulse.

On the coast of Armorica (present-day Brittany) "pain des algues" was once manufactured from *Laminaria* and *Chondrus.* This is a laverbread in that it is more of a jelly than a true bread. During periods of serious food shortages in World War II, German occupiers of Norway set up two bakeries to manufacture a more familiar kind of bread from dried, ground, and desalted algae.

[49]

In modern times the Soviets, in line with their vigorous exploitation of the sea, have tried seaweeds as ingredients of certain dishes. One recipe gives instructions for preparing a sauce from "sea cabbage" (*Laminaria*) and vegetables. Fresh sea cabbage is cleaned, rinsed, and dried. Then it is soaked in fresh water for three or four hours, rinsed again, and chopped into small pieces. The chopped seaweed is fried in vegetable oil for five or six minutes and quickly cooled. After tomato sauce is added to a "stuffing" of sea cabbage, carrots, and beets, the mixture is canned.

An even more intriguing Soviet recipe consists of "sea cabbage stuffed with mussels and rice." Cleaned and rinsed sea cabbage is cooked in boiling water or steam for about sixty to eighty minutes, then fried in vegetable oil for one to one and a half minutes. It is used as wrapping or "pie covering" for a mussel-and-rice mixture, flavored with fried onions, pepper, and oil. Again the pies are canned with tomato sauce.

In North America seaweed production is concentrated in California and the New England-Maritime Provinces coastal areas. The habit of using marine algae spread to the latter region from the British Isles and France. Irish moss, *Chondrus crispus,* and dulse, *Rhodymenia palmata,* are the important species—the former for the manufacture of gels and the latter for food.

Irish moss, one of the red seaweeds, supports the oldest seaweed industry of the United States. It is not eaten directly, but for generations its extractives have found their way into food in the production of blancmange and as thickeners for soups and similar dishes.

In the Maritime Provinces dulse, a red alga, is eaten in its dried form. It can be bought in stores as crackly, dark bits of material, smelling and tasting faintly of the sea (and a bit reminiscent of leather).

In North America in general, outside of the small pockets on the eastern seaboard where dulse is eaten, seaweed is consumed only by health faddists in special proprietary foods. A little is added to some breakfast foods as roughage, and some goes into low-calorie bakery goods.

In the Caribbean a small amount of seaweed is eaten. On the island of Grenada I saw *Gracilaria* (one of the red seaweeds) spread in the sun to dry. It had been washed with detergent, and several days of exposure to the sun had bleached it almost white. It is prepared as a kind of porridge. Some dried *Gracilaria* is sold as a gelling agent in various Caribbean islands.

The Eastern world values seaweed as food more than the Western. The Polynesians, a true people of the sea, are said to maintain aquatic gardens where they raise edible seaweeds. In Hawaii more than forty kinds are used as food. People in China, the Philippines, and Indonesia all eat a certain amount of marine algae.

But of all the countries of the world Japan is the only one making full use of these resources. Not only do the Japanese harvest as much wild seaweed as possible, but for centuries they have grown algae in aquatic farms. Over a third of the total production of the country (over half a million tons in 1962) comes from culture. The most popular variety in Japan is "nori" (laver), but several other kinds are also used.

Japanese laver culture constitutes the only really substantial seaweed food industry in the world. More than 61,000 Japanese raise marine-plant crops, and more than 300,000 people are supported by the industry. In 1960, 57 per cent of all the area under culture in Japan for any kind of marine product—animal or vegetable—was given over to laver, and 81.5 per cent of sea-farm workers were engaged in this activity.

Artificial culture of laver is successful because of the peculiar life history of this red alga. The first attempts were made more than 300 years ago, and there are accounts of laver farms in Tokyo Bay from 1670. In the intervening years this activity has grown enormously. Vast areas of shallow water are given over to laver culture, mostly in the Inland Sea and on the Pacific shores of the three southern islands. The best areas are in great demand and are leased under strict terms by the government. Because the most suitable areas near the mouths of rivers (where the concentrations of nutrient salts are high) have already been put into cultivation, the industry can expand only with great difficulty.

The principal species cultivated in Japan is "asakusa-nori" (purple laver), *Porphyra tenera.* An inferior product is also made from "awonori" (green laver), *Enteromorpha,* and from "wakame," *Undaria.*

Like the land farmer, the seaweed culturist adjusts the rhythm of his life to the seasonal pattern of his crop. For the laver this pattern is unlike that of most land crops, the best growth occurring in winter. While the seeds of land plants burst into life under the influence of rising temperature in the spring, the monospores of laver swarm in the water with the declining temperature of autumn. If they settle on a firm, rough surface in the intertidal zone, they develop into "leafy" plants, which grow so rapidly they can be harvested after a few weeks. In March this luxuriant growth ceases and the plants disappear. Until about half a century ago the life cycle of the laver plant was a mystery, and no one knew what happened to the alga or in what form it existed from the time the leafy plants disappeared to the reappearance of the spores six months later.

[51]

But laver farmers knew that the size of their crop depended on the number of spores settling on intertidal rocks, or on the artificial spore collectors ("hibi") that they set out. In the first laver farms the hibi were sticks of bamboo or oak stripped of their leaves and thrust into the mud of shallow bays. The spore collectors were moved at the end of October or into mid-November to intertidal areas, often near river or sewer outfalls to take advantage of the lower salinity and the increased fertility of these regions. The wooden hibi were commonly grouped into rafts or "farms" 120 feet long and 7 feet wide. Over the decades suitable bays became crowded with these curious structures, and the industry gained steadily in importance.

Then a British botanist, Dr. Kathleen Drew, solved the mystery of the missing half of the life of the laver plant, enabling the Japanese industry to increase its production rapidly. Her contribution was so important that the Japanese have erected a granite monument in her memory at Uzuchi, near Tokyo. Dr. Drew's research uncovered the curious fact that in the spring the dying laver plant releases carpospores (minute spores freed during the sexual phase of red algae) that attach themselves to oyster or clam shells and bore into the matrix of the shell material. The carpospores then grow small filaments on the surface of the shells. These little algae had been previously observed but had been described as a separate plant, under the name of *Conchocelis rosea*. This is a masquerade, and the little filaments are actually one phase of the life cycle of *Porphyra*. They release the monospores that the seaweed farmers had collected on their hibi over the years.

With this new understanding of the life history and ecological requirements of laver, farmers quickly made improvements in their techniques. Clean oyster shells are now put into the water in the spring to collect the carpospores. As the spores push their filaments through the shells, the shells turn black. At the proper time in the fall the shells, now bearing the filmentous conchocelis phase, are placed in the water beneath the hibi in vinyl bags or wedged into pieces of split bamboo. Enormous swarms of the monospores attach themselves to the collectors —in far greater numbers than under natural conditions.

Harvesting of the laver is done by hand, usually when the fronds are three to eight inches long. The strap-shaped fronds are washed, chopped, ground, and dried in the sun on mats of fine bamboo splints.

The resulting product, resembling rough paper, is a thin, dark sheet, purple to nearly black, about seven inches square and weighing one tenth of an ounce. It is mottled in appearance, since some of the fragments of algae are thicker than others. It has a faint "sea" odor and very little taste. Bundles of ten sheets are packed into tin cans or paper boxes. Laver is expensive, up to $8 a pound, and one sheet costs the housewife about as much as a hen's egg. Over 78,000 tons of laver (about 4 billion sheets) were consumed annually in the early 1960's, and even more in recent years.

Laver is used in many ways. Sometimes it is toasted over a charcoal fire, turning green under the heat. Then it is broken into bits and added to soups and sauces. A very common dish, sushi, consists of laver wrapped around vinegared rice, meat, prawns, eggs, or fish. It may be dipped into soy sauce and eaten by itself, or eaten wrapped around boiled rice.

Japan's use of laver to the contrary, there are excellent reasons why little use is made of seaweeds for food worldwide. One of these is that their nutritional value is small: they are poor sources of energy, their protein content is only fair, and their fat content is low. The small value they have as food resides chiefly in the presence of trace elements and secondarily in a high vitamin content.

The proteins of algae are less assimilable by the human digestive system than those of other plants, which in turn are poorer than animal protein in this respect. Many of the seaweeds compare favorably with rice in terms of calories, but these figures are misleading since a high proportion of the energy is unavailable as indigestible, complex carbohydrates.

The usual inefficiency of the human digestive system when confronted with these carbohydrates may be partly a consequence of lack

FIGURE 5.1A. *Algae of shallow-water areas. These plants are attached to the bottom by holdfasts, but not roots; they have no fruits or flowers.*

International Oceanographic Foundation

of experience in dealing with them. Japanese and other Orientals who habitually eat algae may have developed a specialized bacterial flora more capable of digesting the polysaccharides than the flora of people with different food habits. Hence, if consumption of seaweeds were to become common, the ability to digest them might increase too. It has also been suggested that the contribution of seaweeds to human nutrition could be increased by predigestion of the carbohydrates by suitable enzymes or bacterial cultures, as is done in Japan to some extent.

But if seaweeds are low in energy and protein, they are excellent sources of trace elements. For example, some species have 300 times more iodine and 50 times more iron than whole wheat. They are also high in potassium and in a number of trace minerals, but relatively low in nitrogen and phosphorus.

The mineral and vitamin content of seaweeds makes them valuable in the prevention and treatment of deficiency diseases. The crews of whaling ships in the nineteenth century are said to have used them to avoid the effects of scurvy. In modern times the trace elements of giant kelp have been successfully used to treat such ailments as anemia, digestive problems, and the disabilities of geriatric patients.

An interesting atomic-age use of sodium alginate has been discovered by McGill University biologists. This is to protect people from the effects of eating radioactive strontium, one of the most feared components of nuclear fallout. Strontium 90 can be ingested with milk, and can cause leukemia and bone cancer. Sodium alginate eaten as seaweed can absorb and harmlessly eliminate from the digestive tract up to 93 per cent of the strontium 90. Even after it has reached the bone tissue, up to 25 per cent can be removed, leaving untouched the essential but chemically related calcium.

People tasting seaweeds for the first time normally do not like them. Characteristically they have very little flavor, although in large amounts or in the dried form they may have a distinctive taste. Dr. V. J. Chapman, an American botanist, quotes a French algologist on his opinion of a salad of sea lettuce (*Ulva lactuca*): "It was leathery and waxy in taste, and in spite of good digestion I thought I would be ill." However, a different reaction was expressed by another intrepid pioneer, who made a salad of the green algae *Enteromorpha* and *Monostroma* (both related to sea lettuce). Having flavored it heavily with salad dressing, vinegar, lemon, pepper, onions, and oil, he described it as "wonderfully nice; slightly piquant, and not inferior to the best garden salad." Which proves again that tastes differ, or that the condiments overwhelmed the flavor of the seaweeds, or both.

Dr. Josephine Tilden, a well-known American algologist, said that seaweed chopped and mixed with softened butter "makes a delicious sandwich." She described some seaweeds as "tasting like peanuts." But Dr. Tilden's liking for seaweed is not shared by most people. An old (1862) summation of the reaction of the people of Britain probably describes the general attitude in Western nations: "John Bull, though so truly a man of the sea, does not take kindly to an alginic diet."

Except in Japan, then, and to a lesser extent in China, very little use is made of seaweeds directly as food, either raw or processed. But a considerable and important use is made of *extracts* of seaweeds for what might be called "supporting" food uses. Because seaweeds contain substances called phycocolloids, with properties that make them excellent gels, they have widespread and expanding uses in a large variety of food products.

There are three main classes of these organic extractives: agars, carrageenins, and algins. The first two of these are from red algae, the last from brown.

Agar-agar derives its name from the Malayan word for the alga *Eucheuma,* from which the gel was originally extracted. The name, usually shortened to agar, now refers to the extracts of several kinds of red seaweeds, including *Gelidium* and *Gracilaria.* Over many centuries a sweetened form has been used as a relish in the Orient.

Agar was the first seaweed product to become an important item of commerce. Its chief characteristic is that it produces a firm, jellylike substance. Its best-known use has been in bacteriology, as a gelling agent for culture media. Tradition has it that this use originated in Germany in 1881 when Frau Fanni Eilshemius Hesse suggested the idea to her husband, Walther Hesse, who worked with the eminent bacteriologist Robert Koch. Frau Hesse used agar in her kitchen, having obtained the recipe from a Dutch family who had lived in Java, where Japanese agar from the seaweed *Gelidium* was used domestically. Agar is especially useful as a bacterial medium since it forms a jelly at ordinary temperatures and is not attacked by the organisms growing on it.

The agar industry in Japan has a long history, beginning in about 1769. By World War II the Japanese had a virtual world monopoly, but with loss of Japanese supplies at the outbreak of war other countries began to increase their own production. In the United States it sells for $4 to $6 a pound, and about 80 per cent of it is purchased by manufacturers of microbiological culture media.

Agar is also used in food where firm gels are required—in ice creams as a thickener, in chiffon pies and meringues, and in icings to prevent them from sticking to their packaging.

The principal product of brown algae is algin, or alginic acid. It is

[55]

FIGURE 5.1B. *Fronds of the giant kelp,* Macrocystis pyrifera, *one of the brown algae.*

Jack W. Schott, California Department of Fish and Game

not especially useful in itself, but its derivatives, the soluble metallic alginates, have an impressive list of uses in the food, pharmaceutical, rubber, dairy, and textile industries. Alginic acid occurs in the cell walls of the plant. It has large molecules, and its salts have the capacity to produce tough, clear, flexible, films, and to serve well as thickeners, coagulants, and flocculating agents in many foods.

By far the most important use of the alginates is in the manufacture of ice cream. They prevent the formation of ice or sugar crystals and the separation of fat globules. Sodium alginate is also used as a thickener and stabilizer for soups, mayonnaise, and sauces. Sausage casings are made from it. It is formed into a thin film over herring and other fish before they are frozen in order to prevent "freezer-burn"—oxidation and drying. It is put into wrapped cakes to keep them moist. In all of these uses only small quantities are required, but the total amount of alginates used is substantial.

Alginic acid can be made into a fiber and spun into cloth. The fiber can be dissolved out in the "disappearing fiber" technique of weaving, to produce unusual patterns and textures. Algin can also be made into nonflammable fibers. During World War II this property was useful in the manufacture of camouflage netting for gun sites.

The principal source of algin in the United States is the giant kelp *Macrocystis pyrifera,* exploited in California. This brown alga is perhaps the largest of all marine plants, and the fastest growing of all plants on land or water. Giant, shiny stems grow from holdfasts in the bottom of the sea, looping 165 feet or more to the surface and bearing 3-foot leaves that stream out with the tide. Big, bulbous floats buoy up the leaves. Kelp harvesting started in California in 1910, spurred by fears that supplies of potash were about to be cut off from Germany as restrictions were imposed on exports from the Strassburg deposits. When total loss of these supplies followed declaration of war, activity quickened to a feverish boom, with as much as 400,000 tons of kelp being harvested annually to produce potash for explosives. This phase of the industry ended in 1919, and a second, more stable period began in the mid-1920's. This time the principal products have been algin and kelp meal for stock feed, and production has been only a fraction of that during the older period.

Kelp is harvested by mechanized barges designed to cut the surface canopy of the beds like hay reapers. Adjustable moving sickles cut the weed down to a legal four feet below the surface, and the fronds are taken aboard an open barge by conveyor. A given area is harvested three or four times a year. From 10 to 60 per cent of the plant is removed when it is harvested, but it can grow two feet in one day and double its size in fourteen days.

The third of the important derived products from seaweeds are the carrageenins. These are extracted from red algae, principally Irish

FIGURE 5.2. *Irish moss,* Chondrus crispus, *one of the red algae.*

Department of Fisheries and Forestry of Canada

FIGURE 5.3. *Drying Irish moss near the village of Sturgeon, Prince Edward Island. Bleaching it in the sun on the wooden "flakes" improves the quality of the seaweed as a stabilizing agent in such foods as mayonnaise.*

Department of Fisheries and Forestry of Canada

moss, *Chondrus*, and to a lesser extent from false Irish moss, *Gigartina*. Like algin, the carrageenins were first used extensively in Europe, especially in Scotland. There, and in coastal France and some other areas, they have been used for generations as a gelling agent for desserts such as blancmange. The American colonists brought this use to the New England states, but for many years they thought it necessary to import their carrageenin from Ireland at a considerable price. Then, in 1835, a former mayor of Boston, Dr. J. V. C. Smith, recognized that Irish moss was abundant on the rocky shores of Massachusetts, and he stimulated a local industry. Now it is harvested in many New England states and in the Maritime Provinces of Canada.

When prepared gelatins came onto the market the carrageenins were pushed somewhat into the background, but now the superior quality of seaweed derivatives has revived interest in them. Carrageenin is used in soft ice cream as a stabilizer; in chocolate milk to keep the particles of flavoring in suspension; in salad dressings, flavorings, emulsions, and fruit syrups as a thickener; in the coatings of jellied poultry, fish, and aspics as the thickening agent.

Other food uses for carrageenin include the "fining" or clarifying of beer. During the brewing process small amounts of carrageenin are added twice, first to the hot beer wort and later when the brew is at 60°F.—the "cold break."

Thus, in a single meal a person may eat derivatives of the seaweeds in a substantial number of forms. They are so disguised, however, that one could be forgiven for going through life without realizing that he was in the habit of eating seaweed.

Humans also consume seaweed indirectly in the form of animal flesh, but the amount is so small as to be almost of no consequence. Its relatively low nutritive value and contradictory reports of the effect of seaweed on the health of farm animals are chiefly responsible for this lack of popularity. Palatability and digestibility are poor as well.

In Norway and Scotland some seaweeds are boiled and fed to stock. Factories in Norway, France, Ireland, Scotland, Denmark, the Netherlands, and a few other countries produce small amounts of seaweed meal. It is made also in South Africa, the United States, and Canada, but on an even smaller scale. The total European production in a recent year was less than 50,000 tons—no more than the monthly output of one moderate-sized fish meal plant.

Domestic animals do not ordinarily like seaweed, at least in the beginning. Sheep, pigs, and horses seem to be less choosy than cows, which usually take longest to become accustomed to this diet.

The nutritional value of seaweeds for farm animals is similar to that for humans: their main value is in the trace elements and some of the vitamins. Digestibility by farm animals is lower than that of many land plants and this reduces the food value of seaweeds, but domestic animals have less trouble than humans digesting the complex polysaccharides. With proper choice of material and judicious balance of proportions—perhaps not above 15 per cent for cattle and 10 per cent for poultry—seaweeds are valuable sources of fodder, and thus indirectly of food for man.

Seaweeds serve as land fertilizers in the production of food for humans. Once used only in coastal areas, where farmers carried the seaweed from the beach to their land, algae fertilizer is available almost everywhere now that it is packaged in easily transported meal and liquid forms.

The use of seaweeds by coastal farmers goes back to prehistoric times. Later there are records of this use from Asia, Europe, North America, and Oceania, and it probably has been a practice in every other part of the world to some degree. In Great Britain, France, Canada, and the New England states some farmers living within about ten miles of the coast still carry loads of fresh seaweed to the fields. In

FIGURE 5.4. *A field of nori nets in the Seto Inland Sea of Japan.*

John Ryther

the Madras Presidency of India seaweeds are used to fertilize coconut palms; they are chopped up and put in pits around the trees, three to four feet away from the trunks, and covered with earth.

Fresh seaweeds are slippery, bulky, and hard to handle. They are usually not satisfactory as a dressing for the surface of the soil, and in some cases are not useful even when they have been chopped and buried. Nearly all the potash they contain is water-soluble, so this material is released quickly, but the nitrogen and the phosphoric acid become available only when the algae rot.

Seaweeds are most effective in light, sandy soil. Their nutritive value as plant fertilizers is about the same as that of barnyard manure when the various constituents are averaged. The nitrogen content of the algae is at least two thirds that of manure; the phosphoric acid content is half or less. Their chief virtue is their potash content, which is usually about twice that of manure. The high content of trace elements and vitamins also increases their value, as does the freedom from weed seeds and the spores of crop diseases.

Seaweed meal is especially good for root crops such as potatoes and beets, since they require large quantities of potash, but some types of meal gave poor results with tomatoes, beets, and radish crops. These results are associated with manganese toxicity and phosphorus deficiency.

Besides adding nutrients, seaweed fertilizers change the characteristics of the soil. Sometimes these changes are undesirable, but properly used, seaweed fertilizers can be valuable soil conditioners, increasing water-holding power, the stability of soil crumbs, and the availability of oxygen to the plants and microorganisms.

Perhaps the most significant advance in this field has been the development in Scotland of liquid seaweed fertilizers. This goes back only to 1950, but in ten years ending in 1965 their use increased twelve times, and they are replacing meals. Their virtue is in the efficient use of the nutrients. This advance promises to increase their use materially.

The total quantities of seaweeds available for harvest over the world are unknown, since few area surveys have been made. Except for a few species, principally *Sargassum*, they live attached to the bottom, so only shallow, near-shore areas will produce them. And because they are plants, they depend upon light energy for their life processes. Thus they can flourish only in water shallow enough for light to penetrate—perhaps 160 feet or less in most areas, and to 500 or 600 feet in the clearest water.

Data on potential resources are better for Scotland than for any other part of the world. The Institute of Seaweed Research estimates that there are about 180,000 tons of brown seaweeds (principally *Ascophyllum nodosum* and *Fucus vesiculosus*) available in densities sufficient to support economic exploitation. The high-density areas are mostly in the Outer Hebrides and the Orkney Islands, where annual yields have ranged from 7.8 to 18.1 tons per acre, suggesting that greater exploitation is possible here, as well as expansion to other areas not cropped at present. Standing crops of *Laminaria* in Scotland have been estimated to total 3,868,000 tons. Red seaweeds (*Gigartina* and to a lesser extent *Chondrus*) occur in much smaller amounts: 360.2 tons of marketable standing crop in Scotland and 11.5 tons in England.

Very considerable increases can take place in the exploitation of the California kelp beds described earlier. But in recent years the beds have been seriously damaged by sea urchins, which set the plants adrift by nibbling through their holdfasts. Progress is being made in controlling

FIGURE 5.5. *A kelp harvester in southern California shears and gathers the seaweed, cutting only four feet below the surface. This regulation is to help ensure maximum harvest; the sun penetrates to the plants and encourages growth, which may be as much as eighteen inches a day. The kelp can be harvested once a month.*

George A. Stokes, California Institute of Technology

the urchins with quicklime, and in some areas the beds are recovering. Production in the 1960's is about 100,000 tons annually, only about a quarter of the landings of fifty years ago, when the market was better. It appears that only about 5 per cent of the sustainable yield is being cropped at the present time, and one expert has estimated that these beds could sustain an annual harvest of 3 million tons.

It may appear at first glance that seaweeds are greatly under-exploited in many parts of the world because yields are low in comparison to supply. But statements of total quantity in an area may be misleading, since the algae are often sparsely scattered, making the cost of collection high. For example, popular fiction describes ships caught in great masses of weed in the Sargasso Sea. The quantities of seaweed there are indeed great; it has been estimated that this part of the ocean contains 4 to 10 million tons of sargassum, but the density is only two to five tons per acre—too thin for profitable exploitation.

But what is uneconomic today may become profitable tomorrow, when technology improves and needs increase.

Seaweeds will probably be produced for nonfood substances, since most nations are not likely to follow Japan in developing a liking for it. Over the centuries the Japanese have established it as a regular part of their diet—not merely an accessory but an essential item of food. The Australian botanist Ferguson Wood relates how the Japanese strenuously resisted efforts of American Occupation officials to divert supplies of *Laminaria* from use as food to the production of potash, which was in seriously short supply after World War II. Japanese fishery and prefectural officials agreed that the seaweed had little food value but felt that the psychological effect of depriving the people of this traditional food was worse than the shortage of potash. By comparison with other kinds of food, seaweeds are really of small significance even to the Japanese: the production of algae totals less than 3 per cent of their rice harvest, and the percentage of nutrients contributed is even smaller.

Utilization of seaweeds as sources of extracted gels has increased during the last two decades. With research and improved technology, this trend will continue and probably accelerate. Thus it is to be expected that the harvest of red and brown algae will be large in future years, until eventually—many years from now—the seaweed forests will be fully exploited. But it is apparent that they will not solve the world's food problem. Unless much more progress is made during the next several decades than during the last few, seaweeds can be ignored in our accounting of the resources of the sea that will make a strong contribution in the fight against hunger.

[63]

6   *Farming the Sea*

In the eighth decade of the twentieth century man still gets most of his food from the sea by hunting—he catches fish by dangling hooks and floating nets beneath the surface. On land hunting was abandoned as an important method of producing food at least a thousand years ago; it is far more expensive and less efficient than farming. This transition is considered to be one of the key steps in man's rise to civilization. It is time we learned to farm the sea.

One of the reasons for man's slowness in learning marine farming is that he himself is a land animal. He understands the land environment and his fellow air-breathing creatures, and he can supply them with the things they need to thrive and multiply because these are the same things, in general, that he himself needs. The creatures of the waters are inhabitants of another world, most of them getting their oxygen differently, eating different foods in a different manner, producing their young, and carrying on a great many other life functions differently from man himself. He does not understand these creatures nearly as well as he does the animals he has subdued and cultivated on land. The hostile environment of the ocean prevents man from making the same frequent and intensive observations of sea creatures that have made him master of many land animals. And the lives of many water creatures are bewilderingly complex, so that even longer and more careful study is required to understand them than is necessary for cows or pigs or turkeys. A salmon, for example, may move through hundreds of miles of river and lake during its babyhood and adolescence, and additional thousands of miles of open ocean during its adult phase. Fishery scientists only dimly apprehend how it passes its time and what conditions are ideal for its survival and growth in this variety of environments, and the great shadowy areas of ignorance are being lighted with painful slowness.

A shrimp, for another example, starts life in the open ocean as a pinpoint of protoplasm. Before it reaches the rich feeding grounds of mangrove-swamp shallows at the edge of land it has passed through a dozen or more stages, each different, and the early ones unlike the adult in such an extreme fashion that only a biologist would recognize that the two were both phases of the same creature. What forces take the small larvae of the shrimp from their oceanic spawning grounds to the estuarine nursery grounds? What kinds of food, sustained by what conditions of temperature, saltiness, acidity, and chemical content, support them in their youth? What stimuli take them out of the brackish waters back to the spawning grounds again? What weakness in their chain of life makes it necessary for the female shrimp to produce hundreds of thousands, perhaps millions, of eggs in order to be sure that an average of two of her progeny survive a terribly perilous existence to maintain the population? Until men understand such complex matters, they cannot farm sea animals successfully.

Some aquatic farming has been carried out for many years. Several species of fish are raised in fresh water, and some of these operations—with carp, trout, catfish, and other species—are true farming. In salt water, fish culture has been conducted for a century or more in the United States, with hatcheries turning out millions of cod, shad, salmon, lobsters, and many other marine creatures. But most of these latter operations are decidedly not true farming, which involves full control over the animal from birth to slaughter. And the overwhelming majority of them have been a waste of time and money.

The United States hatcheries were established before the turn of the century to supplement the natural production of young, usually for species whose catches had declined. It was recognized, then, as now, that the most vulnerable phase of the life history of a marine animal is its youth, when lack of food and heavy predation commonly reduce the numbers of any species to a small fraction of 1 per cent of the eggs laid. Hatchery enthusiasts criticized nature as being woefully inefficient, requiring the helping hand of man. They hoped to build up the stocks of particular species by raising young fish in protected environments and then releasing them into the ocean. In 1885 the United States Commission of Fish and Fisheries put the *Fish Hawk* into service to survey fishing grounds, and in particular to carry out fish-culture operations; in effect the ship was a floating hatchery. Millions of shad fry were distributed, and additional millions of the young of lobsters and other

[65]

FIGURE 6.1. *U.S.S.* Albatross *at Woods Hole. The* Albatross *was the first ship built expressly for marine research, and she had a long and distinguished career.*

Bureau of Commercial Fisheries

species. Few people doubted at the time that the addition of millions of young fish to the sea would result in larger catches of adults. In 1898 George M. Bowers, United States Commissioner of Fish and Fisheries, expressed the commonly held view this way: ". . . fishing by effective means must be allowed, and a due proportion must be taken from their spawning grounds so that sufficient ova may be touched by the magic wand of protected propagation to provide for future crops." In 1904 Bowers said, "In order to keep pace with the increased catch by commercial fishermen and anglers, the establishment of additional hatcheries from time to time is demanded, and larger appropriations are required to operate existing hatcheries to their full capacity." Year after year the fish commission asserted stoutly in its annual reports that culture activities were successful. To quote Bowers once more: "The practical value of the Commission's work of artificial propagation has long since been removed from the realm of doubt, and is appreciated and conceded by all persons qualified to express an intelligent opinion thereon." The commissioner exaggerated the extent of his support by "persons qualified," but he certainly was backed by general opinion, at home and abroad.

The American effort in this field was applauded in other parts of the world. In the Berlin Fisheries Exhibition of 1881 the United States fish culture exhibit won prizes and acclaim. After the turn of the century the Woods Hole Laboratory became mainly a hatchery. By 1916 more than a hundred federal hatcheries and large numbers of state hatcheries were in operation. European countries followed the United States' lead.

The theory of hatcheries is that by providing protection against predators and by supplying ample food, the terrible attrition of young fish can be reduced and far higher survival achieved. In many cases this expectation has been realized. In 1917, to take only one year, three United States Atlantic coast hatcheries produced 236 million cod fry, 1,474 million pollock, 6 million haddock, and 1,814 million young flounders, and it is likely that these numbers were higher than they would have been if the same eggs had been hatched in nature. In a plaice hatchery at Port Erin in Britain a survival rate of 6.6 per cent from egg to three-month-old fish has been achieved—40 per cent higher than normal.

But fish culturists have made another assumption, which has

FIGURE 6.2. *Mackerel were among the many kinds of fishes cultured in the golden age of hatcheries, from the 1880's to the 1920's. Hatcheries have been revived in recent years, but with the difference that present methods usually attempt to raise the animals all the way to marketable size. These six-month-old mackerel were raised from eggs at the Bureau of Commercial Fisheries Laboratory at La Jolla, California.*

Bureau of Commercial Fisheries

proven to be false in nearly every case. This is that if the fish are released they can be recaptured in numbers large enough to make the culture effort pay its way. Hatchery men in the past have measured their "success" by the numbers of young animals they released, ignoring the real criterion, which is whether fishing was actually improved as a result of these operations. Few reliable tests have ever been made of this, partly because satisfactory ones are difficult to perform. It is not enough to say that a hatchery is successful because fishing improved after fry were released, as has sometimes been the case; fishing success is notoriously variable, following natural changes in the abundance of wild stocks from year to year. Only carefully designed experiments, carried out for many years under rigid mathematical controls so that the effects of natural variations are discounted, can show the effects of planting fish from hatcheries. In the few cases in which such experiments have been conducted it has been concluded that the hatcheries were useless. For example, in British Columbia, hatcheries for salmon were closed when Dr. Earle Foerster showed that the number of sockeye salmon returning to the Cultus Lake system in the Fraser River as a result of natural spawning was as large as when culturists collected the spawning fish and protected and fed them in hatcheries. Critical examination of the effects of cod hatcheries in Norway, shad hatcheries in Maryland, lobster hatcheries in Maine, and other similar operations have failed to show that catches increased because of the liberation of fish into the sea. As a result of such studies, the hatchery movement slowed down in the 1930's and came to a virtual standstill after World War II.

The reasons for the failure of hatcheries are not difficult to find. In the first place, hatchery-raised fish and invertebrates are less able to fend for themselves after they have been released. Conditioned to being fed, they often do not learn to seek their food; having been protected from enemies, they fall prey to predators more readily; weakened by the artificial existence of the hatchery ponds, where they are often stunted or afflicted by disease and parasites brought on by crowding, they are less capable of survival in the fierce world of nature. More importantly, even if the hatchery animals are fully as vigorous as those surviving the struggle in nature (and some hatcheries are able to produce vigorous young), there are not enough of them to make a significant contribution to the total population in the sea. In most fisheries the numbers of animals caught are numbered in the millions—sometimes the billions. These millions or billions are the survivors of enormous numbers of young—numbers that are so large that by contrast the millions of hatchery-reared young represent but a small drop in a huge bucket.

Finally, hatcheries have failed because they do not eliminate hunting; fishermen must still chase the fish released into the sea. It is as though cattle ranchers were obliged to turn their beef animals loose in a vast and nearly impenetrable forest, to be pursued by hunters before the meat could be brought to the table—an expensive and inefficient procedure.

The hatchery concept, nevertheless, is being revived in some places. The Port Erin plaice hatchery of the English Whitefish Authority is rearing plaice to a small size and releasing them into the sea. In 1964, 200,000 were turned loose in Port Erin Bay. They were less than half the size of wild fish of the same age, and 92.9 per cent of them were abnormal in color. Within five days the hatchery fish had disappeared, "apparently being eaten by (larger) plaice and dab at a much higher than normal rate." Plaice hatcheries may some day prove profitable, especially if the young are released into nearly enclosed bays, but the prospects are still poor. Dr. J. E. Shelbourne, who is in charge of the program, has said that 20 million young plaice would have to be released in a single year to increase the catch 5 per cent four years later. The goal of the Port Erin hatchery is only 1 million young per year. And, of course, the recovery rate assumes that the hatchery fish will be as hardy as the wild young, which is now far from the case.

Thus, despite decades of experience, most hatcheries fall far short of nature in their ability to stock the sea. A ray of hope is provided by the results obtained by coho salmon hatcheries on the Columbia River in Washington and Oregon. Excellent sport fishing in recent years, apparently on hatchery-raised fish, may mean that improved diets and culture techniques are producing enough salmon to increase oceanic stocks. Perhaps the pattern of hatchery failures has been broken. But other species of salmon have yet to be cultured successfully, so this is still an isolated case, if indeed the present indications are proven by time. For the moment, then, fish culture involving the release of young back to the ocean will probably not increase harvestable quantities of the vast majority of useful marine animals.

The ultimate aim of fish farming should be to achieve control over the animal during every phase of its life. Brood stock should be maintained in captivity and spawning controlled; techniques should be available to feed and protect not only the young but the larger animals, right up to the time they are ready for harvest. Natural selection should be possible, so that brood animals can be chosen for size, flavor, rapid growth, hardiness, resistance to disease, and other desirable characteristics. The modern trend in fish culture is to strive for this kind of complete control.

We are a long way from such control over the vast majority of aquatic animals; in fact it has been achieved only for a few freshwater species such as trout and (very recently) oysters and clams; it may be in sight for some kinds of shrimp. Meanwhile, as man strives for this ideal through research into the life histories of the animals, he must be content in most cases with a less firm control, depending on natural reproduction to produce young for pond stocking. Fish farming at this level involves the protection and feeding of young on leased or owned land until they are of marketable size.

Of course, many, perhaps the great majority, of marine animals eaten by man are not suitable for farming of any kind. Tuna, for example, are fish of considerable size, requiring large quantities of food and a great deal of ocean for maneuvering; they probably could not be raised in aquatic farms, no matter how large. Such is the case with most of the open-ocean fishes. It is hard to imagine mackerel or herring and their swarming allies—sardines, menhaden, anchovies—penned up in saltwater farms. Fictional accounts of submarine-mounted "cowboys" herding whales will probably remain fiction. It is unlikely, in fact, that the open sea will ever be fenced or farmed—it is simply too unmanageable an environment, even if the knotty problems of ownership are solved.

And yet the open sea is by far the greatest part of the ocean, in area and especially in volume. The continents are rimmed by shelves that extend beneath the oceans to depths of about 400 feet; the terrain then dips steeply into the abyss. The total shelf area constitutes only a small fraction, some 3 per cent of the ocean's surface, and it is unlikely that aquaculture can ever be conducted beyond the shelves; in most cases it would only be possible to farm areas very much shallower, probably less than 100 feet. Thus the idea that man may some day cultivate the whole of the vast ocean is completely unrealistic; he is, in fact, restricted to a thin band around the shore. Furthermore, not all shorelines will be hospitable to the water farmer, either because they are rocky or otherwise untillable, or because they are in cold climates.

But even after subtracting these regions, there are still enormous acreages available for the production of food. These are the marshy edge-of-the-sea "wastelands." Contrary to a commonly held misconception, which regards marshes and half-drowned areas at the edge of the sea as useless, these regions are extremely rich. An unpracticed eye may easily be forgiven for regarding a mangrove swamp as unpromising, but such swamps in Java have been made into fish farms producing hundreds of pounds of protein food per acre each year. In the Philippines fish ponds yield 300 pounds per acre annually; in the Celebes, over 600; in Sumatra, 750; on the Malabra coast of India, 900 to 1,500; in Formosa, up to 950. By comparison, the land farmer, after centuries of practice, using the most modern scientific techniques and the most carefully balanced and lavishly applied fertilizers, produces 800 pounds of beef per year on the best land available. With help from scientists, who are only beginning to turn their attention to his problems, the sea farmer should be able to improve on his present yields very substantially. The shallow-water farm can be a richly rewarding area, promising returns beyond the best from land farms.

The production figures quoted, all from fish ponds in the Orient, are not from farms in the strict sense defined earlier in this chapter. Nearly all the Oriental and other estuarine fish ponds omit the first important step, that of producing the young from captive brood stock. Instead, the young animals are caught in the ocean, or are trapped when they are swept into the ponds with the incoming tides. The farming consists in the protection and feeding of the growing fish or invertebrates, followed by their harvest or sale. Such operations are handicapped by the inability to control the supply of young. If nature does not complicate matters by making the supply variable and all too often scarce, the fish farmer has to contend with the whims of the fishermen who supply him with fry.

There are a few cases in which farming of marine animals is conducted on a more sophisticated basis—pioneer operations that undoubtedly will be the ancestors of multitudes of aquatic farms in the future.

FIGURE 6.2A. *Oyster culture in Hong Kong. The spat collectors (materials set down to serve as a substrate for the attachment of the oyster larvae) are hung from rafts instead of thrown on the bottom, as in the past.*

Copyright C. F. Hickling

Oyster culture is one of these. Oysters have been farmed in many parts of the world for a long time, and the necessary techniques are well established. The ancient Romans raised oysters and the Japanese have done so for centuries. The long history and the success of this activity result from the fact that oysters are well suited to culture. Since the adults are fixed firmly to the bottom there is no need to build enclosures for them. They grow rapidly, providing a quick crop, and their high market value provides the necessary economic incentive.

Oysters produce enormous numbers of young—sometimes more than 100 million eggs by a single female during one spawning. In the commonest species fertilization is external. The resulting larvae swim weakly for two or three weeks and then settle as "spat" to the bottom, where they fix themselves to a hard surface. Traditional oyster culture starts with the collection of the spat by suspending old oyster shells, special tiles, or some other hard, clean surface in shallow bays just before natural spawning takes place. The spat are separated to prevent crowding and thus produce larger, better-shaped adults. They are scattered evenly over the bottom in brackish estuaries, where they feed on phytoplankton and grow for varying periods, up to two or three years or longer, depending on temperature and availability of food. Commonly, areas suitable for spawning or for the growth of the younger stages do not induce the best growth of larger oysters, and the culturist may move them once or more before they are harvested. Control of predators is one of the harder tasks of the oysterman. Starfishes are removed by chemicals or by dragging "mops" over the bottom. Oyster drills—small, voracious snails—are killed by chemical or mechanical means.

Oyster culture has adopted a number of specialized techniques in various parts of the world. In the western United States the industry depends almost entirely on the importation of the spat of the big Japanese oyster *Crassostrea gigas*. These are planted on tidal flats. In France oyster culture is centered in the Bay of Arcachon, from which 400 to 500 million oysters are exported each year. In some areas in France highly esteemed green oysters are produced in specially prepared fattening ponds, or "claires." A particular kind of algae flourishes in these ponds and oysters placed there in the last phase of their life grow rapidly, taking on the color of their food.

Japanese oyster culture is highly advanced. A major industry exists merely to grow seed oysters, which are sold to growers in Japan and are exported to Canada and the United States. The most successful Japanese oyster culture involves raising the animals off the bottom, either on sticks thrust into the mud or on ropes hanging from rafts. Besides reducing predation and increasing growth rates, this technique allows deeper waters to be used than is possible with the bottom culture common in most parts of the world, enormously extending the coastal areas available for oyster raising.

By land standards, even the most advanced oyster farming is a crude business, with the oysterman having very little control of his "herds." He does not know the parentage of the young, and he has no way of selecting the progeny of big, well-shaped, flavorful, or otherwise desirable parents. He is at the mercy of highly variable times and places of production of young, and there are many years when spawning is poor or even totally absent. The oysterman has no way of controlling the kind or quantity of food for his crop. He is plagued by many kinds of diseases and predators.

But great advances have been made in recent years in oyster culture, especially in Japan and the United States, and true farming is close to becoming a reality. In hatcheries and growing grounds at Northport, on the north shore of Long Island, New York, brood stock is maintained permanently in shallow plastic trays through which natural seawater is kept running. The parent oysters have been chosen for their size and shape, and gradually, generation by generation, selective breeding is improving their growth rate and quality.

FIGURE 6.3. *Oyster culture in Australia. Sticks bearing two-year-old oysters are nailed to racks in George's River, New South Wales. They were raised to this size in Port Stephens, 160 miles north. The transfer of oysters from an area favorable for growth of the young stages to another area more suitable for later development is common over the world in the more advanced methods of culture.*

W. Brindle, Australian News and Information Bureau

Instead of guessing when spawning will take place, and being forced to depend on wild stocks for the young, the modern Long Island farmer can make his oysters reproduce "on command." This is possible since spawning is affected by water temperature, and it can be delayed by keeping the temperature below about 28°C. (83°F.) until a brood is required. When the temperature is allowed to rise above the critical point millions of eggs and sperms are released in the water. The fertilized eggs hatch quickly and the larvae are transferred to large tanks. During the time the larvae are free-swimming they are fed with microscopic planktonic plants. These are prepared in pure cultures in carefully controlled nutrient media at a precisely maintained temperature. The water used for culturing the phytoplankton is centrifuged at high speeds to remove most of the detritus and suspended plant and animal material, filtered again, sterilized, and then inoculated with a pure culture.

After the first day the oyster larvae are transferred to fifty-gallon opaque glass fiber-polyester cylinders with conical bottoms, where they are fed with measured amounts of the cultured phytoplankton. Air is bubbled into the water to supply oxygen and to keep the plankton and the larvae in suspension.

The tanks are emptied every day, the water being drained through fine filters of decreasing mesh so that the growing oyster larvae are sorted by size. Each size is kept separate, and the smallest are thrown away; selection for rapid growth is accomplished in this way. The larger larvae are returned to freshly prepared tanks, at controlled densities.

After about ten days, the larvae are transferred to five-by-ten-foot tanks filled with three feet of water maintained at 28°C. Eight to ten bushels of clean oyster shells are placed on the bottom, and the larvae settle on these. Now the shells with the small oyster spat are placed in black polyethylene net bags, ten inches in diameter and two feet long, which are suspended in large concrete nursery tanks in a translucent-roofed room. Centrifuged water, carrying only the small phytoplankton that make the best food for juvenile oysters, is supplied to these tanks, the temperature being gradually reduced until it corresponds with that of the water of the adjacent bay.

In the nearly ideal conditions of the culture room, the oysters grow to about half an inch in diameter after only three weeks. Still in the plastic net bags, they are put into the water of the bay. For a while they are vulnerable to damage and predation, so they are kept suspended from polystyrene rafts floating in the bay alongside a pier. Tides bring them planktonic food and carry away wastes. But mussels and barnacles quickly foul the small oysters, so they cannot be left indefinitely suspended from the rafts, as is the practice in some places in

FIGURE 6.4. *Suspended culture of oysters. The shellfish grow faster and are less subject to predators and pests if they are suspended on ropes or other material rather than being left on the bottom, as they normally are. But this method requires more labor, and the shells of the oysters are thinner. Methods of overcoming these problems are being sought.*

Bureau of
Commercial Fisheries

Japan. Furthermore, oysters raised all their lives off the bottom have abnormally light shells, which lowers their market value. So, after about a month they are taken from their bags and put on the bottom of the bay to continue their growth.

The bay bottom is carefully prepared before the oysters are put down. It is dragged or harrowed, then vacuumed to free it of silt; it is treated with calcium oxide to kill starfishes and with a chlorinated benzene to kill oyster drills.

The oyster beds are inspected by scuba divers about twice a week. Each diver checks the growth of the oysters and looks for disease, predators, and silting . He reports conditions by phone to a man in a boat above him and his observations are plotted on a grid chart. If starfishes or snails have invaded the beds, or other dangers are seen, action is taken.

The oysters may be moved once more to take advantage of good growing conditions. Eventually those of proper size are harvested and sent to market.

Another interesting wrinkle is being tried in the Long Island oyster culture. This is to make use of heated water from a nearby power plant. There is rising concern in the whole United States about the threat to marine ecology from power plants, which discharge heated

[75]

water that has been passed through the condensers to cool them. It is feared that the shallow areas will be spoiled for recreation and their biological productivity damaged. Controls are being designed for this threat, and uses are being devised for the heated water. In Long Island the water from the power plant is about 20°F. above the temperature of the bay. Now the heated lagoon is used to replace the inside nursery, providing a low-cost production of juveniles.

This promising scheme of oyster culture is a big step forward in seafood farming. Such farming still has a long way to go before it catches up with the sophistication of land farming—but after all it is 10,000 years behind. Already, however, sea farming promises to deliver fat, prime oysters on the half shell in less than two years, compared to four or more years by the old-style culture.

The same general techniques used to farm oysters can be applied to the production of clams and scallops, and similar ones can probably be developed for some species of fish.

Perhaps the most extensive culture of a marine fish is that of the milkfish, or bango, *Chanos chanos*. It is farmed in shallow-water areas in many parts of the world, especially in the Philippines and Indonesia, where the practice is at least eight centuries old. During this long period the milkfish farmers have developed a complicated and highly effective procedure for wresting protein from the sea.

FIGURE 6.5. *Large outdoor hatching or holding tanks are used to test feeds and other variables in the culture of shrimp, crabs, and fish at the University of Miami.*

C. P. Idyll

In 1962 it was estimated that there were 217,500 acres of milkfish ponds in the Philippines and 317,500 acres along the shores of Indonesia. An additional total of approximately 100,000 acres of ponds was being farmed in Pakistan, Formosa, India, Hawaii, and Hong Kong.

The milkfish is somewhat like a plump herring in appearance. Its delicate, firm, white flesh is a favorite food of Far Eastern peoples. In addition to having an established place on the daily menu, it constitutes the principal food of many ceremonial and holiday feasts, especially in Indonesia. The Indonesian expression "Makanikan bandeng," meaning "eating milkfish," is synonymous with feasting; wedding parties, circumcision feasts, and other joyful occasions are not conceivable without a meal of steamed rice and fried milkfish. At New Year's the Chinese part of the population is willing to pay three to four times the usual price for milkfish in order to celebrate the feast according to tradition.

The fish that has so firmly established itself in the culture of many Asian peoples is of minor occurrence in the local commercial catch. It is of value only because it is peculiarly suitable for artificial culture. It consumes plants directly—blue-green algae in its youngest stages and filamentous green algae a little later. It is like a steer or a pig, converting vegetable material into protein in a single step, with a minimum loss of substance.

Milkfish culture has four phases. These are the capture of wild fry for stocking the ponds, the rearing of the fry to fingerling size, the growing of the fingerlings to market size in different ponds, and the transport and marketing of the finished product. Sometimes one man performs all of these duties; sometimes he leaves one or more of them to specialists.

In the clear water along the coasts of the Indonesian islands of Java and Madura, the small milkfish fry appear in hordes during October and November. As they swim over the gently ascending sand beaches, the fishermen wait for them with some of the strangest tools of any trade in the world: a rope, an unglazed earthen pot, bamboo stakes, a small-meshed net on a triangular frame, and a white clamshell. The rope, made of grass and closely strung palm leaves, is tethered to stakes set in a row at right angles to the shore. This serves as shelter or a barrier to the milkfish fry. As they accumulate against the palm-leaf rope the fisherman sweeps his net back and forth along and under it. From the net the little fish are transferred to the earthen pot by means of the clamshell. The white shell is used to sort out the valuable milkfish from the fry of other species, which may be useless or even harmful, since their presence in the farm ponds would make them competitors for food or predators on the milkfish.

[77]

The little milkfish fry are now raised to market size in ponds called "tambaks," one to five acres in extent. Tidal flats with little or no vegetation are the easiest places to build these ponds, but mangrove forests are more commonly used.

Under the water a tremendous bustle of biological activity takes place. The growth of a complicated matted mixture of algae, bacteria, worms, crustaceans, and many other creatures is the key to the high productivity of the ponds. In properly handled ponds a culture of this mixture, which goes by the name of 'lab-lab," grows naturally after the water is allowed to enter. It is a mat of brown, dark green, or yellowish material, covering the bottom of the pond with a jellylike, soft mantle. Sometimes it coats the bottom like newly applied shellac. In the unicellular and filamentous matrix of the blue-green algae live bacteria, diatoms, small amounts of green algae, protozoans (one-celled animals), copepods, and ostracods (small crustacean relatives of the shrimp), flatworms, round worms, and multitudes of the larval forms of mollusks (clams and snails) and of higher crustaceans such as shrimp and crabs. This incredible biological community provides highly nutritious food for the little milkfish, allowing two and a half acres of good pond to support 300,000 to 500,000 fry.

The fry are released into the carefully prepared ponds in the relative coolness of morning or evening. A magic formula or a blessing is pronounced while the jars of little fish are slowly tipped. As many as 55,000 are planted in a 1,000-square-yard pond, the operator watching carefully to detect signs that the fish are short of oxygen, which would make it necessary for him to put the excess in another pond.

After a month or six weeks, during which the fry have grown from about half an inch to two inches or more, they are transferred to bigger ponds, where they are fed green algae. They may be sold any time after they are five to twelve months of age, at sizes ranging from four ounces to two pounds.

Nearly halfway across the world from Indonesia another ancient kind of fish culture is carried out. In northern Italy, in the Adriatic, fish have been raised since Roman times in ponds called "valli da pesca." These are lagoon basins, associated with river deltas, especially that of the River Po. The valli of the Lagoon of Venice are among the most interesting and ancient, having been in operation for considerably more than a thousand years.

Italian valli vary in size from a few hundred acres to several thousand. Their operation depends on the trapping of fish entering the lagoons with the tide. Thus protected, the fish grow and are harvested and sold. When shortages of small fish entering the ponds make culture unprofitable, pond managers seek supplies from fishermen who catch the fry in other areas. Thus a special fishery has grown up to supply the valli.

Mullet (*Mugil* spp.) is the most important species in these ponds; eels, sea bass (*Morone labrax*), and other species are also raised to a lesser extent.

The annual mean production of about seventy valli in the Italian Adriatic was 3,000 tons in the 1950's, with an average of about 125 to 130 pounds of fish per acre.

The principal defect of the valli culture is that the system depends largely on the capture of small fish entering the ponds with the tides, or in more recent years on the somewhat more reliable but still chancy capture of fry in the ocean. Thus the valli farmer is at the mercy of the vagaries of natural fluctuations in abundance of the fry.

The shrimp is one of the marine animals most suitable for farming. It has a high market value and it grows rapidly on materials very near the bottom of the food pyramid. Shrimp are cheerfully indiscriminate eaters. They nibble on algae and bacteria; they take quantities of mud, apparently deriving sustenance directly from it as well as from a multitude of small animals and plants that it contains, including worms, small crustaceans and mollusks, larval fishes, diatoms, bacteria, and algae. Shrimp are scavengers and cannibals.

Shrimp culture is important in the Philippines. Here the young of the shrimp called "sugpo," *Penaeus monodon*, are caught as they appear in shallow water near shore and are transported to specially prepared ponds, where they are fed and carefully protected from predators until they become big enough to sell.

The capture of the sugpo is the weak link in the culture chain. The Philippine fisherman pursues them with unlikely tools, including clumps of weed called "bons-bons," white porcelain dishes, and earthenware jars. He takes advantage of the fact that the sugpo likes to cling to sticks, seaweed, or other material floating in the water. He sets out bon-bon lures consisting of bundles of twigs or grass attached to lines, and ties these to poles set into the bottom in shallow, brackish water where the tide runs. Tiny plankton creatures such as copepods and worms attach themselves to the weeds, and they, along with the shelter the weeds offer, attract the shrimp to the lures. Sculling among the lures in a small dugout, the fisherman visits them two or three times a day, shaking the little shrimp from the bundles of grass into a fine-meshed dip net and transferring them to his porcelain dish; the dark bodies of the young sugpo show up plainly against the brilliant white of the porcelain. The little shrimp are dumped into an earthenware jar, whose porous sides allow water to pass through and evaporate, keeping the shrimp cool despite the tropical heat.

The pond owner is at the mercy both of the fisherman who supplies him and the vagaries of nature, and often he is not provided with enough small shrimp to satisfy his needs.

Whatever shrimp he does get the farmer now places in the ponds with their crusts of lab-lab. As many as half a million little sugpo per hectare (about 200,000 per acre) are held in the nursery ponds for about six weeks. Care during this period includes occasional renewing of the water through the sluice gates, maintenance of the all-important lab-lab, and sometimes supplemental feeding with rice bran. At the end of six weeks the shrimp have grown to nearly two and a half inches in length, and they go now to the rearing ponds. In about three more months —a total of six since they were first captured—they are ready for market. Now they are six inches or so in length and weigh about three quarters of an ounce. If left in the pond for a full year (as they sometimes are), they reach a length of nine or ten inches and a weight of three and a half ounces.

In Indonesia and Singapore there are no special fisheries for the capture of the young shrimp; instead the ponds are stocked by opening the flood gates and letting post larval shrimp enter with the tidal current. Of course, many other creatures enter at the same time, including many pests and predators. This keeps the productivity of these ponds at a lower level than those in the Philippines.

Shrimp culture of the kinds just described has been carried on in Japan for centuries. A major advance in recent years, however, involves the farming of shrimp at a more sophisticated level: females are allowed to spawn in captivity, the eggs are raised through numerous young stages, and the adults are fattened, collected, and shipped to market. The shrimp providing the greatest profits to the culturist is "kuruma-ebi," the "wheel-shrimp" (*Penaeus japonicus*), used in the preparation of the traditional dish "tempura." This is in such great demand that in Tokyo alone there were 110 large and 500 smaller restaurants specializing in tempura in 1960. In addition there were 5,700 smaller restaurants in the city that included tempura on their menus. To meet the immense demand for kuruma-ebi, Japan imports considerable quantities of shrimp.

The man responsible for the development of kuruma culture is Dr. Motosaku Fujinaga, formerly director of the Research Bureau of the Fishery Agency of Japan, and beginning in 1954, president of the Kuruma Shrimp Culture Company.

In the first years of his work for the government his operation consisted of the collection of young in the manner of the Philippine culture.

But in the meantime he worked to raise shrimp from the egg on a commercial scale, and thus to carry out true farming.

The problem was formidable: the shrimp passes through twelve very small and delicate larval stages, and the larvae died at first for lack of proper food and environmental conditions. Only after the most patient and skillful labor was Dr. Fujinaga able finally to raise shrimp from eggs to marketable adults.

The farming operation begins with ripe females six to seven and a half inches long (occasionally nine inches or even more), which are bought from commercial fishermen and put into big spawning tanks in a hatchery. The females carry a third to half a million eggs—occasionally up to 1,200,000. About 200,000 are cast in one spawning. It is not necessary to purchase males since copulation has already taken place in the ocean, the male having transferred a packet of sperm to the underside of the female. As the eggs are cast into the water they are fertilized from this packet. The female spawns while she is swimming, and at night, usually around midnight.

Before long the water swarms with tiny bits of life that are the nauplius larvae, one fiftieth of an inch long. In the biggest tanks several million of them start life together.

Three days after the shrimp hatch, they have gone through six nauplius stages and become protozoeal larvae. During this time their food has been carried with them in the yolk sac. But now, at a length of about one thirtieth of an inch, the larvae must begin to feed. Their food consists of diatoms, one-celled plants so small they can scarcely be seen without a microscope. These are cultured in a tank illuminated night and day.

As the larvae grow their appetite increases and their taste changes. Sometimes the same little diatoms are fed to the protozoea, but the latter flourish better if "meat" such as oyster eggs and larvae, copepods, brine shrimp (*Artemia salina*), or ground clams is offered. These brine shrimp are the same little creatures used extensively by aquarists over the world to feed tropical fishes; they are especially valuable food for the shrimp, both now and in the next series of stages, the mysis. Brine shrimp are easy to handle because they are shipped as eggs, which can be hatched as needed by placing them in water. The eggs are obtained in San Francisco and other places, but they are expensive—$25 a gallon in Japan. A young kuruma shrimp consumes about 20 to 75 brine shrimp per day.

The three protozoeal stages, lasting a total of about three days, are followed by three mysis stages, each lasting about one day. The postlarval stages (variable in number but about five altogether) follow in a series lasting about a week or ten days. Now the little shrimp become actively cannibalistic if they are not supplied with ample food, so the delicate balance between food supply and consumption becomes even more difficult, with the farmer facing the threat of thousands of little shrimp becoming one big one. The postlarvae are usually fed clams.

A month or so after the last mysis stage the shrimp drop to the bottom. Under favorable conditions survival from the eggs to this stage has been recorded at a high of 50 per cent—far better than in nature. At this point the shrimp are taken from the tanks where they were born and begin an outdoor existence.

October-spawned shrimp take about ten months to reach market size; those spawned in April are ready in about seven months. There is an important difference between the shrimp market of the United States and the kuruma-shrimp market of Japan. In the latter, medium-sized shrimp (about three quarters to one ounce in weight) are most valuable, while in the U.S.A. the price rises steadily with size. The Japanese preference for medium shrimp is because they are most easily handled on chopsticks when prepared in the traditional way. This is fortunate for the grower, since costs rise rapidly if shrimp are raised to a size bigger than about an ounce.

When they reach marketable size the shrimp are taken from the ponds and transferred to a chilling tank in a nearby building. Here the water is kept in active turmoil, bubbling and rolling as compressed air is forced through it. It is kept dark, covered by a removable trapdoor.

FIGURE 6.6. *Farm-raised kuruma-ebi (wheel-shrimp) ready for market. Their attractive appearance and fine flavor make them the most highly priced shrimp in Japan, where they are used to make the traditional dish tempura.*

C. P. Idyll

Most important, it is cold, about 50°F. This is necessary since the metabolism—the body chemistry, and therefore body activity—must be slowed as much as possible, short of immobilization, so that the shrimp can be sent alive to market.

One of the most remarkable parts of this whole operation is the manner in which the shrimp are shipped. They are packed live in small cardboard boxes (about eight by twelve by eight inches) in *dry* sawdust, two boxes to a case, and sent by rail (or less often by air) to distant cities. The sawdust is carefully chilled beforehand to match the temperature of the shrimp coming from the cold water, and the live animals are rapidly packed about 65 to 100 individuals to a box, lined up side by side. The function of the sawdust is to insulate the shrimp against a rise in temperature, so that their life processes are barely ticking, like the idling motor of a well-tuned car. It would be reasonable to expect that moisture would be required for respiration, but the small quantity of water trapped in their gill chambers when they are taken from the tank is enough to supply them with the greatly reduced amounts of oxygen needed in their cold-induced torpor.

Shrimp shipped in this remarkable way survive for as long as four days in winter, and half that in summer. Most of the year, when cultured shrimp must compete with those caught by trawlers in the Inland Sea of Seto, the price is about $2.80 per pound of tails (the edible part of the shrimp—it takes about thirty-five kuruma to make up a pound of tails). In winter, when kuruma are otherwise unavailable, the price is about $3.50 per pound, and if people are really hungry for tempura, and must have it, scarcity or no, the price may rise as high as $4.40 per pound. In the United States, by contrast, shrimp cost about $1.30 to $1.70 a pound retail.

The live kuruma-ebi are in such demand because Japanese epicures insist that the one indispensable ingredient of tempura be made from absolutely fresh shrimp—so fresh that they are kept alive until just before they are cooked.

A very special dish called "odori" is sometimes served. This consists of a single large and especially fine shrimp, served with its legs spread so that it is presented in a natural upright position. Its abdomen has been cut into sections for the convenience of the chopstick-wielding diner. Since kuruma-ebi are handsome, black-striped animals, this presents an interesting and attractive dish. What makes it remarkable, however, is that the shrimp is *still alive* when it is brought to the table—its severed head is thrust high and its mouth parts are moving! For this extraordinary delicacy the cost is equivalent to $1.50 for the single shrimp.

The costs of shrimp culture are high, and the total production in

[83]

1967 was only 404 tons. The shrimp culture procedure of the Japanese is still dependent on fishermen to supply egg-carrying females, although their biologists are reported to have raised several generations of shrimp of a few individuals each. Eventually it will probably be possible to close the circle completely and raise parent shrimp, opening the door to selective breeding.

Shrimp culture of the same kind is being tried experimentally in the United States. Since Japan's eager demand and resulting high prices are missing in the United States, an American shrimp farm can be made to pay only by reducing costs far below those of the Japanese process. Some reduction can certainly be made by using labor-saving devices and by finding cheaper food. To be a success the process must include methods of growing high numbers of shrimp per unit area of pond without encountering suffocation, disease, or cannibalism. Experiments in commercial shrimp culture are being conducted at the Institute of Marine and Atmospheric Sciences of the University of Miami and other institutions.

A few other species of marine or brackish water animals have been cultured with some success. In Japan the young of eels, *Anguilla japonica,* are caught at the entrances of rivers and transferred into ponds. On a diet of cheap fish (e.g., sardines) and the chrysalids of silkworms they grow to marketable size in one year. Eels are a delicacy in Japan, and the whole crop is sold to the better restaurants.

The yellowtail, *Seriola quinqueriadiata,* a fish related to the tuna, is also extensively cultivated in the Inland Sea of Japan. Fry three quarters of an inch to two and a half inches long are caught in coastal waters and held in net cages until they are big enough to be put into larger pounds. The latter are constructed of wire mesh or netting and are placed in protected areas with high tidal exchange, where the young fish are fed crushed mussels and inexpensive small fish. Yellowtail put in the pounds in early spring can grow to marketable size (about four and a quarter pounds) by November or December.

Clam culture is conducted in several places in Japan, but it depends on the spawning of wild parents. Trials are being conducted there with other mollusks, notably scallops, abalones, and octopuses.

The mussel *Mytilus edulis* is farmed in France, Holland, Spain, and Italy. This shellfish is abundant in the United States and could be farmed here if there were a demand for it. The methods of cultivating mussels are similar to those used for oysters. Some astonishing yields have been reported from raft culture in Spain—to 500,000 pounds of meat per acre. Of course this cannot be extrapolated very far, since such production is only possible in the best areas, and the addition of more

FIGURE 6.7A. *In the foreground ropes are covered with young mussels, which will be used to replace the adult crop harvested from poles.*

raft colonies in a bay would result in forced sharing of available food by the mussels, and hence in reduced yields. Nonetheless, with markets to absorb the crop, and the improved techniques that will come with experience, mussels are one of the most promising kinds of marine animals for culture.

In the United States, clams, principally the quahog or hard clam (*Mercenaria*) of the Atlantic coast, can be conditioned to spawn in hatcheries at any time of the year, and controlled culture similar to that of the Long Island oysters is possible on a commercial basis.

There is great interest in the United States in the possibility of "farming" lobsters. As early as 1865 French biologists succeeded in hatching northern lobster eggs (*Homarus*) and bringing the larvae through several stages. In the early part of this century the United States government established lobster hatcheries in Maine, Massachusetts, Rhode Island, Connecticut, and New York. In such hatcheries lobsters can be raised in large numbers to their fourth or fifth stage, when they change from a swimming to a bottom existence. Culturists usually release them at this point. This is probably a useless exercise, and the evidence is so firm against any benefit to the fishermen that most

[85]

FIGURE 6.7. *Mussel culture in Arguenon Bay, near St. Malo, France.*

John Ryther

of the northern lobster hatcheries have been closed. Large-scale attempts to raise them from the egg to marketable size in confinement have also been failures.

Spiny lobsters (*Panulirus*) are even harder to culture. They have a series of strange-looking leaflike larvae called phyllosomas. These drift in the sea for considerable periods—weeks or perhaps months—before they drop to the bottom in shallow water. Serious attempts at the Institute of Marine and Atmospheric Sciences to raise spiny lobster larvae to the bottom-dwelling stage have failed.

It might be profitable to catch the young of either *Homarus* or *Panulirus* and protect and feed them in enclosures until they are big enough to sell. This is apparently being done successfully at Ibusuki in the far south of Japan. The keys to a profitable industry here are efficient operation and abundant, cheap food suitable for fast growth and high survival. Trials in the United States on a carefully controlled basis would be worthwhile, but in the meantime lobster farming is not feasible. About the same situation exists concerning crab culture, whether it be the blue crab of the East Coast (*Callinectes*), the stone crab of Florida (*Menippe*), or the Dungeness crab of the Pacific (*Cancer*).

The pioneer sea farmer will find himself faced with a variety of problems for which no solutions will be immediately available. These will include attacks on his stock by disease and parasites, whose detection

[8 6]

and control will be made particularly difficult because he will have little experience to guide him. Indeed, the problem will never be fully solved. One has only to contemplate the proportion of the land farmer's time spent in providing diets to prevent deficiency-diseases and in discovering measures to combat pathogenic diseases to realize that after thousands of years of experience this is still a substantial problem. Salmon and oysters, for instance, have been cultured for many years, but disease problems seem no less troublesome than they were in the beginning. Thirty diseases have been identified in oysters, and no fewer than fifty parasites are known to attack sockeye salmon.

All animals, including those that will be cultured in sea farms, carry pathogenic organisms and parasites, probably as many as those found on the oyster and the sockeye. These organisms are usually kept in balance in nature, with some weak and heavily infected individuals succumbing while the general population flourishes. This nice balance can be upset when animals are crowded into ponds, and the sea farmer will face the danger of seriously reduced growth rates, poorer quality products, or even of having his whole stock wiped out. On relatively rare occasions an epidemic will kill a substantial part of the population.

The artificial raising of marine animals has an extra dimension of difficulty because the food of the young individuals is often difficult to obtain. It is characteristic of fishes and even more so of marine invertebrates that they pass through a number of juvenile stages that differ considerably from the adult, so that several kinds of food may be necessary. The young stages may require not only unusual kinds of food, but living food. Unlike the land farmer, who can provide milk or easily prepared and stored dry diets to his young animals, the sea farmer must set up one or more extra culture operations to raise the food for his crop.

An important task of the land farmer is to renew the minerals of the soil. This is done either by adding fertilizer, or by plowing to bring to

FIGURE 6.8. *Protozoan parasites, like those shown under the skin of a pinfish, will be among the many diseases to be faced by aquaculturists.*

Wm. M. Stephens

the surface deeper soils into which nutrients have leached. Sea farming might be able to employ these procedures too.

The several ways in which the sea "plows" itself to bring mineral-rich water to the lighted surface were described in Chapter 3. It is at least theoretically possible to supplement these natural methods by producing artificial overturns of deep water, bringing minerals to the surface where plants can make use of the sun's energy in manufacturing protoplasm.

Artificial plowing of the sea will be much harder than plowing the land. In the soil the nitrates and phosphates are carried only a few inches below the surface; in the sea they sink hundreds or thousands of feet in the bodies of dead plants and animals.

Deep water containing nutrients might be brought to the surface either by pumping or by warming. To move a sufficient volume of water to make a significant change in the amount of nutrients would require thousands of huge pipes, at the cost of billions of dollars. And enormous amounts of heat would be required to warm a large quantity of deep water sufficiently to bring it to the surface. In addition to the problems raised by the large scale of such activities, there are many other complications. In the first place, the choice of the ocean area would be important. It would have to be one where surface waters lacked sufficient nutrients to produce a large harvest, yet where deep waters were rich. There would have to be populations of useful fishes already there, or the possibility of introducing new species—a difficult and chancy procedure. The water would have to be shallow enough so that reactors (probably the best heat source) could be placed on the bottom and serviced. The currents would have to be so small that the nutrient salts carried up from the depths, and the plants and animals produced by the enrichment, would not be swept away.

The amount of energy required would be very great. This method of warming deep water was never seriously considered until the development of modern nuclear reactors. Dr. David A. Farris of San Diego State College has made calculations of energy requirements and probable costs. He has assumed that about forty square miles of sea would be the minimum area required to be affected if any useful harvest of fishes were to result. Using the region off the Virgin Islands in the Caribbean as a possible test area, Farris calculated that if water were raised from about 2,600 feet (the depth at which a sufficient store of nutrient salts exists) about 7 million kilowatts of power would be needed. This would employ the capacity of hundreds of the largest nuclear reactors, at a cost of $200 billion a year.

And even if the technology were easier and the costs less, there are a great many other problems: How could the scientists guarantee that the

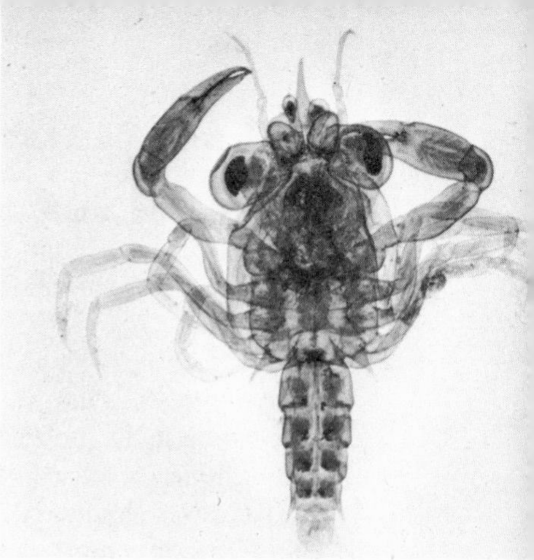

FIGURE 6.9. *The megalops larva of the blue crab,* Callinectes sapidus. *After one more molt the abdomen will be tucked under, the body proportions will change, and the larva will assume the familiar shape of the adult crab. Blue crabs have been carried successfully through this stage to marketable size, but it has still to be established whether this can be done on a large scale, and at a profit.*

Virginia Institute of Marine Science

added nutrients would eventually produce useful materials in the form of edible fish? What assurance would there be that the whole ecology of the area would not be ruined—clear water made murky with plankton, coral reefs destroyed, beaches changed, even climate altered? Who would decide which fishermen of what nations would be allowed to harvest the catch?

Yet despite the knotty technological, political, and economic problems involved, the possibility of producing artificial plowing of the sea on a massive scale is extremely intriguing, and it must have further serious examination.

There does not seem to be much point in adding fertilizers to the sea as the farmer does to the land, except in very limited areas of semi-enclosed bays. The open sea is far too immense for this technique to have any effect. Whatever amounts of fertilizer might be added would be diluted and swept away so rapidly that pouring money down a rathole would be a paying proposition by comparison. It might work in certain very special places, where small arms of the sea are enclosed so that the fertilizer and the fish could be prevented from escaping.

But most trials so far have not been encouraging. During World War II Scottish biologists tried fertilizing two inlets of the ocean to increase fish production. The smaller of these, Loch Craiglin, is eighteen acres in extent. It was fertilized with considerable amounts of nitrates, ammonium salts, and phosphates. The productivity of everything in the food chain increased remarkably—phytoplankton, zooplankton, seaweeds, and fishes, including the valuable plaice and flounders. The population density of bottom animals increased in the summer by 750 per cent and in the winter by 300 per cent.

But no extra fish harvest was won. Much of the added nutrients were taken up by the bottom-living plants—weeds that contributed nothing and would be hard to remove in a farming operation. Weed fishes also flourished—useless species such as gobies and sticklebacks that ate eighteen times as much food as the marketable plaice and flounders. And when natural circulation was impeded by a dam across the mouth of the bay to prevent the fishes from escaping, a layer of warm, relatively sterile water formed across the loch, spoiling it as a fish farm.

The other arm of the sea in which experiments were made, Loch Kyle Scotnish, is larger than Loch Craiglin, with an area of 180 acres. Two and a half tons of fertilizers were added each month, and the plants and animals increased remarkably. Plaice grew three to five times faster than normal, flounders four times faster. But Kyle Scotnish has no barrier across its mouth, and the fish produced simply swam away, so that they could not be harvested. It might be possible to construct some kind of barrier to prevent this, to devise means of providing well-mixed water, and to weed out useless plants and animals, thus overcoming the difficulties encountered by these pioneer experiments.

Yugoslav scientists have succeeded in significantly increasing the growth of oysters and mussels by fertilization of a bay, and there is no doubt that other trials in the future will add to our ability to manipulate the sea to our advantage. Yet the regions where this technique could work are so few, and the areas so proportionately tiny, that very little real impact is promised on the food supply of the world from artificial fertilization of the sea.

It should now be clearer why aquaculture is many centuries behind agriculture. It should also be apparent that aquaculture by itself cannot solve the human hunger problem.

The food production by sea farms has been trivial: in 1964 the world produced only 10,000 tons of plants by farming and 600,000 tons of animals by "herding" in the sea, compared to 2 billion tons of plants and 520 million tons of animals on land farms. (The United States produced no plants and only 10,000 tons of animals by ocean cultivation.)

The record of ocean farms will improve greatly in the future, since this is an activity in which a great deal of interest has been aroused recently, and in which skills are rapidly being improved. But sea farms will always be restricted to shallow areas of the world, and for many years they will raise only expensive animals.

It is not realistic, therefore, to expect aquaculture to produce really substantial quantities of food for the hungry now or in the near future. Instead sea farms will probably prove to be profitable operations for some investors, and they will supplement the production of fish, shrimp, and other seafoods that are in high demand.

[90]

7   *Transplantations*

One possible method of increasing the yield of human food from the sea is to transplant a useful species into an area where it does not occur naturally. Such transplantations have a special kind of emotional appeal, since they fit the image man has of himself as master of the world and the other creatures that live in it. And they offer what appears to be a facile and logical method of increasing the larder. As we shall see, they are usually not at all easy, and often by no means logical or wise.

Transplantations have many times led to unfortunate and even disastrous results. All too often the introduced animal has taken hold of the new environment with such enthusiastic ferocity that desirable native creatures have been shouldered aside. Diseases and pests commonly come with transplanted hosts too, to cause expensive and sometimes permanent damage.

Perhaps the classic example of transplantation gone awry is the introduction of the rabbit into Australia. This can only be described as a catastrophe. It has resulted in the destruction of millions of tons of food, the ruin of thousands of acres of land, and the waste of thousands of tons of materials and hundreds of thousands of man-hours of effort.

The European wild rabbit, *Oryctolagus cuniculus,* was introduced into Australia to serve as a source of food. In 1859 Thomas Austin released thirteen of them on his estate, Barwon Park, near Geelong on the southern coast of Victoria. In the presence of a favorable environment—ample food and cover and the absence of natural enemies such as weasels and stoats—the rabbits prospered astonishingly. Within three years they were already regarded as pests; within six years Austin had

[9 1]

killed 20,000 on his grounds and believed another 10,000 remained.

Of course the rabbits did not stay in the woods of Barwon Park. They spread rapidly over the adjacent countryside of western New South Wales, and by 1928 they had invaded nearly two thirds of the vast Australian continent, devouring crops and despoiling the land. The estimated rabbit population in 1953 was between 500 million and 1 billion.

Australians have tried desperately to control this pest, and the cost of these attempts adds enormously to the economic losses. Traps and poisons have been used; the burrows and nests of the rabbits have been destroyed; dogs have been used in huge community drives to stampede the rabbits into killing yards. For a time the great Nullarbor Plains desert was regarded as an effective barrier against the westward spread of the rabbits. When it was found to have been breached, the State of West Australia began to construct an enormous fence to block their migration into the wheat fields of the region. Not long after construction started it was discovered that the rabbits were already past it. A second fence was begun seventy-five miles west of the first. This structure, built at a cost of $1 million and stretching over the continent from sea to sea, some 2,000 miles, was not effective.

In fact, none of the methods used to wipe out the rabbits, so painfully and expensively carried out, have been successful. Enormous numbers of rabbits have been killed, but the population springs back vigorously after every attack.

In the early 1950's it was thought that the problem had been solved. A virus disease, infectious myxomatosis, was inoculated into some rabbits, spreading by direct contact and by mosquitoes and fleas. The results were spectacular, and 80 to 90 per cent of the population was destroyed. Australians rejoiced in an apparent victory. But the rabbit was not to be beaten. A common biological phenomenon occurred: the victim of a parasite recovered from a reeling blow and adapted itself to the new menace. Now a population of rabbits immune to myxomatosis has increased rapidly, while the virus itself is producing mutants with greatly reduced virulence.

A report by the Department of Agriculture in 1928 stated, "The cost of the rabbit to the State of New South Wales in the forty-five years since the animal first began to be reckoned a serious pest, is beyond all calculation." And now, many years and many millions of dollars later, Australians are bitterly resigned to the fate of never seeing the end of the rabbit.

The introduction of mongooses into the Caribbean Islands was another calamity. These bloodthirsty little rodents (*Herpestes auropunctatus*) were brought into the Caribbean from India in the nineteenth century to control rats and the deadly snake, fer-de-lance, in the sugar-cane fields. At first the rats suffered severe declines; then the familiar pattern appeared. They found strength to resist the effects of the depredations of the mongooses, and they are now as strong as they were before their enemies appeared.

Meanwhile, the mongooses are regarded as the worst of all pests. They destroy domestic fowl and wildlife, and they are suspected of being a reservoir of the virus of canine rabies. They have resisted all attempts to eradicate them.

There are dozens of other examples of unfortunate or even disastrous effects of introducing land animals into a new environment. These greatly outnumber introductions showing a balance of benefit against harm. And the percentage of successes is not likely to improve in the near future because not enough is known about the ecology of the animals involved to exert any useful measures of control or to predict the effects of a given introduction.

The introduction of fishes or other marine animals is fraught with even more than usual danger, because of our relatively poor knowledge of them compared with that of many land mammals and birds. In the sea, some species of great value in their native area have proved to be plagues when moved to new habitats.

The blue crab of the eastern seaboard of the United States, *Callinectes sapidus,* is a valuable commercial species in its native waters, since it supplies tons of popular food and supports a multimillion-dollar industry. But in Egypt, where it was accidentally introduced in 1942, it is a hated pest. Millions of individuals swarm in shallow waters of the Nile Delta, damaging nets and devouring tons of fish. Commercial fish catches from the Delta lakes of Manzala and Edku fell so disastrously in 1964 that Egyptian authorities sought desperately for means of controlling the invasion. Efforts to establish a commerical fishery failed, since the Egyptions consider the taste of the crabs repulsive.

The diseases and parasites that have hitchhiked with oysters are examples of the common undesirable side effects of transplantations. The oyster industry of the Pacific coast of the United States and Canada depends largely on supplies of Japanese oysters, *Crassostrea gigas.* Spat, or small oysters, are shipped each year from Japan and planted in the waters of Washington and British Columbia. Here they are fattened and sold, and this activity supports a valuable industry. But there has been a price to pay in the form of unwanted immigrants. A small snail, *Ocenebra japonica,* is an example. Paul Galtsoff, American authority on oysters, found this devastating predator on beds in Puget Sound, Washington, in 1928, among oysters imported from Japan. He warned

FIGURE 7.1. *The drill,* Uro-salpinx cinerea, *on an oyster shell. The white urns are the egg cases of the snail. This pest kills oysters by drilling holes in the victim's shell and scooping out the meat with its long "tongue," or radula. The snail was introduced into Europe with shipments of North American oysters.*

P. J. Warren,
Fisheries Laboratory,
Burnham-On-Crouch

oystermen and state officials about the dangers of buying infested seed oysters, but in vain. In a few years mortalities due to this snail were estimated at 15.4 to 22.6 per cent.

Unfortunately the United States industry has itself contributed to the sorrow of oystermen in other countries. Perhaps the most notorious contribution to such international ill will is the introduction into Europe of the slipper shell, *Crepidula fornicata,* with transplanted American oysters. This curious little shell is not a predator on oysters, and in the United States it does not usually present a major nuisance. But as is so often the case, in the new environment of the oyster beds of England, the Netherlands, Germany, Denmark, and elsewhere, it burst forth with such exuberance that it has become a serious problem. In the German and Dutch Wadden Zee and the Danish Lim Fjord, *Crepidula* became so numerous that its larvae took up all the available space on clean shell and rock, leaving no place for the oyster larvae to settle, and they deposited so much mud and silt on the bottom that it was spoiled for oyster planting.

If there is peril in the too hasty or unthinking shift of a species of animal from its native haunts to an area where it is unknown, another kind of transplantation, involving a milder alteration of natural circumstances, may be safer. Transplantations of species into areas where they already occur, but where populations are held below the natural carrying capacity of the region for one reason or another, offer what Professor Walter Garstang of Great Britain termed an "unimpeachable method" of increasing the yield of fish from the sea. Garstang was director of the famous Lowestoft Laboratory from 1902 to 1908. During this short period, he oversaw a series of highly productive studies in fishery biology, which form the basis for our understanding of many important food fishes of the North Sea and assist in their rational exploitation. One of his most interesting programs of research involved experiments on plaice. He tested the idea that catches could be improved by the transplantation of small fish from crowded nursery grounds, where food and living space were scarce, to better-endowed grounds, where the numbers of inhabitants were fewer, and where, consequently, survival and growth rates might be higher.

The plaice, *Pleuronectes platessa,* is a flatfish, allied to the halibut. It is one of the two or three most important food fishes of the North Sea, ranking with herring and whiting in importance for several European nations exploiting those waters. It spawns offshore in relatively deep water, principally in the Flemish Bight, about halfway between the Thames estuary and the coast of Holland. The eggs are carried toward the coast of continental Europe by the prevailing currents. The tiny fish, about a quarter of an inch long, emerge to a perilous existence, the first part of which is spent on shallow nursery grounds along the coasts of Holland and Denmark. If the current pattern is favorable, and if the supply of food for the larval fish is abundant, the nursery swarms with countless millions of baby plaice. The struggle for existence is hard when an individual has to compete for food with so many relatives. Growth is slow, and when the time comes for the plaice to leave the shallows and move back into the deeper waters of the open North Sea—an event that occurs when they are two years old—they are the relatively stunted and underprivileged products of a watery slum. The idea of transplanting baby plaice from their nursery grounds to the Dogger Bank, a famous fishing area in the North Sea, was first proposed in 1894 by R. Douglas,

FIGURE 7.2. *Tile collectors for spat (young oysters) on grounds at Arcachon, France. The picture was taken at low tide; when the water submerges the tiles, the swimming larvae of oysters as well as of many kinds of pests may settle on them, to infest areas where they may be transplanted.*

H. A. Cole

a citizen of Grimsby, England. In 1903 Walter Garstang urged the International Council for the Exploration of the Sea to undertake experiments leading to possible commercial transplants. A series of trials gave encouraging results.

The Dogger Bank is a raised area on the floor of the North Sea where the depth of water is about sixty feet. The Bank is large—about twice the size of Puerto Rico—and is rich in the kinds of bottom animals that plaice find appealing as food, especially a little clam called *Spisula subtruncata*. But the currents that carry the eggs do not run in the right direction, so that the newly hatched fish are denied the use of this favorable nursery. Later in their life many plaice find the Dogger Bank as they range farther and farther from the coastal nursery grounds, but Garstang believed that it could support many more plaice than it does naturally.

To test this theory a research trawler of Lowestoft Laboratory was equipped with live wells to carry fish from the Dutch nursery grounds to the Dogger Bank. Thousands of young plaice about eight inches long were measured and tagged with numbered disks. Half of them were liberated on the same grounds where they had been caught, and the other half were carried to the Bank and freed.

Remarkable differences in growth were noted for the Dogger fish compared with that of their fellows on the original nursery grounds. The transplanted fish showed growth in length from three to six times as fast, and increases in weight (which is what most concerns the fishermen) were even more spectacular.

After such encouraging results had been confirmed by several more experiments, Garstang was convinced that it would pay to cultivate "the Great Fish Farm," as he dubbed the Dogger Bank. In 1930 he urged the commercial fishing industry of Britain to follow up the scientific findings and institute a transplantation scheme, advice that was backed very strongly by a committee of fishery scientists appointed by the International Council for the Exploration of the Sea. The committee concluded that the operation would result in a yearly profit of £3,440 to £6,000 ($17,000 to $29,000) after allowance had been made for all contingencies, and recommended that the plan be put into effect on a large scale.

But it wasn't. And the reason is not too far to seek, even in the face of the committee's convincing estimates of probable profits. The problem was then, as it is now, to ensure that whoever went to the trouble and expense of transplanting the fish would reap the rewards of his effort. The Dogger Bank is open to fishing by any fleet and any nation. Control of its fishing by a single country is far from being fully

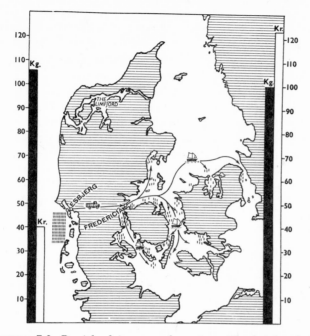

FIGURE 7.3. *Danish plaice transplantations. The height of the black bar on the left indicates the weight of plaice from near Esbjerg in the North Sea at the time they were transplanted, that on the right the weight of fish caught in the Baltic; similarly the white bars show the values of the fish at transplantation and capture. As the chart indicates, the plaice were trucked across the narrow neck of the peninsula, then carried by boat to various fishing grounds in the Danish Baltic. The map also shows the complex "broads" of the Lim Fjord, where another successful plaice transplantation was carried out.*

R. S. Wimpenny, *The Plaice*

effective, and international control among the many countries that exploit this part of the sea has proved to be impossible.

The Danes appeared for a time to have avoided this problem, in a series of interesting plaice transplants, by restricting their operations to national waters. But quarrels among groups of Danish fishermen eventually nullified this effort too. C. G. J. Petersen, a sagacious and resourceful Danish fishery biologist, was an early twentieth-century pioneer in moving young plaice from nurseries to other areas where crowding was less intense. The earliest transplantations of plaice carried out before those of Petersen seem to have been tried by the Danish fishing industry in 1892, when fish were transported from waters of the western part of the Lim Fjord to some of the sparsely populated broads, or lakes, further to the east. The Lim Fjord, a series of saltwater lakes joined by narrow channels, joins the North Sea to the Baltic across Jutland, the narrow neck of Denmark. Plaice do not spawn in the Lim Fjord but move from the west into the inner broads, becoming progressively sparser in numbers as they go east, and showing increasingly faster growth rates as the farthest-ranging fish share rich food supplies with fewer and fewer companions.

Petersen picked up the early, tentative work of the fishermen and instituted an effective program of transplantations. In Nissum Broad, the westernmost part of the Lim Fjord, the density of plaice was very high—about 400 to 2,000 fish per acre—and growth rates were slow. About 80,000 of these stunted fish were tagged and transferred to the inner areas of the Fjord. It was discovered that they had benefited considerably by the move: individuals less than ten inches in length and a quarter of a pound in weight increased as much as five times in a matter of six months. Between the world wars the Danes stocked some parts of the Lim Fjord at an average annual cost of kr. 9,000; fishermen reaped an average annual yield of kr. 37,000. The transplantation was a resounding success.

With this encouragement, the Danes tried another imaginative experiment. The valuable fishery for plaice in the Belt Sea, the water area between the Baltic and the Kattegat around the islands of eastern Denmark, began to show severe declines in the 1920's, landings falling from 3,000 to 1,000 metric tons a year. The first transplantations were in 1928. For many years, from .5 million to 2 million small fish from Horns Reef in the North Sea were loaded into trucks in Esbjerg and carried across the narrow neck of Denmark to Fredericia and to various grounds in the Kattegat, and the Belt and Baltic seas. The growth of the transplants was twice as fast as that of the native fish. Stunted by overcrowding in their original nursery grounds, they flourished in their new homes where heavy fishing had reduced the native stocks, thus providing room for the immigrants. The value of the catch of transplanted fish was estimated to be three times as great as it would have been on the original fishing grounds, and the operation was credited with 100 per cent profit.

But the program has been discontinued—largely for social reasons. In 1957 complaints from North Sea fishermen caused transplantations to the Lim Fjord and the Belt Sea to cease. They objected to their plaice being carried away to be caught by other boats. In 1964 and 1965 the movement of plaice was resumed as a result of demands from the Belt Sea fishermen, but these transplantations may be the last of such attempts, since opposing pressures are high.

Thus, despite the success of so many experiments, plaice still cannot be successfully transplanted because the social and political problems remain unsolved. But if these knots can be untied there are other grounds in European waters to which these valuable fish might profitably be moved. They include some of the Swedish and Norwegian fjords and certain grounds in the English Channel. The technique of transplantation merits the most careful study by fishery scientists and social scientists, not only for plaice, which has benefited, but for other valuable species, even those that have been the object of hitherto unsuccessful efforts.

During the last three decades of the nineteenth century, fish conservation in the United States was very heavily oriented toward the transplantation of useful fishes from one part of the country to another. It seemed eminently reasonable that if the waters of one part of the land had valuable fishes which another part lacked, the oversight on the part of nature should be emended by man. Enthusiasm and optimism swept over the pioneer fish people like waves, washing the shores of a large part of the world as American fish culturists sought to share their more highly valued species not only with their countrymen but with the rest of humanity, and to receive in exchange species from other areas. Fish eggs and young shuttled back and forth between the United States and dozens of countries.

This aspect of fish culture was a waste of time in the great majority of instances. There were some exceptions; for example, the transplantations of shad and striped bass from the Atlantic seaboard to the Pacific were resoundingly successful. But in our present context of examining the prospects of increasing the yield from the sea, even these two famous examples appear less successful than their general reputations. Striped bass are not caught commercially anywhere on the Pacific coast; shad are landed only in small quantities in Oregon and Washington, and not at all in California, where it is illegal to fish them commercially.

To fish culturists in the last decades of the nineteenth century the transplantation of shad (*Alosa sapidissima*) appeared to be highly desirable. It was the view of the U.S. Commission of Fish and Fisheries that "the pride fish of the East Coast" should be shared by the whole country, and a long series of transplants was initiated.

Some of these transplantations were made without any thoughtful planning and without—it is now realized—the slightest hope of success. For example, between 1873 and 1892 millions of shad fry were trans-

[99]

planted to the bitter, highly saline waters of Great Salt Lake. The little fish must have curled up their tails and died very soon after they were released. Probably those set free in the Gulf of Mexico in the late 1800's lived a little longer, although, as in the vast majority of such plantings of dozens of species in thousands of places, the fish never became established as residents.

But if the Great Salt Lake and the Gulf of Mexico failed to provide satisfactory habitats for shad, the waters of the Pacific suited them excellently. In 1871 some 10,000 fry were carried from the Hudson River and released in the Sacramento River in California. They took hold with a vengeance. Commercial fishing started in the 1870's, and at times catches outran market demand. In 1902 Charles A. Vogelsang, chief deputy of the California fish commission, reported that "shad have increased so enormously that the principal dealers restrict the catch, and they are sometimes sold for 25 cents per box of about 75 pounds." In 1926 California returned the original compliment by shipping approximately 2 million pounds of shad back to the home of their ancestors. In the words of Maryland's slightly miffed Conservation Commissioner, they "were solemnly sold as a great and rare delicacy of the Atlantic waters."

The species began a rapid spread over the whole Pacific coastline of the United States. By 1961 it occurred from San Diego to the Aleutian Islands, and across to the Kamchatka Peninsula of the Soviet Union. In 1927 commercial landings rose to 5,946,000 pounds, 4,104,000 of this total being contributed from California. Landings never reached this height again: the catch from 1928 to 1945 was from 1 to 2 million pounds a year, and it fell to between 300,000 and 700,000 pounds in the period 1946–1957.

In California the great success story of the shad has now lost its meaning. This fish offers very little sport, but to protect more popular game fishes, in 1957 anglers persuaded the state to outlaw commercial fishing in the region where shad can be caught.

A successful fish transplantation can be every bit as puzzling as a failure—witness the case of the striped bass. Whereas hundreds of transplants involving billions of salmon, lobsters, and other species have failed to establish permanent populations, two tiny plants of striped bass in California, totaling something over 400 fish, produced large populations that have persisted for nearly ninety years.

The striped bass, or rockfish, *Morone saxatilis,* is a big, handsome fish of the Atlantic coast. It is one of the most popular of the game fishes of the region, being pursued avidly by anglers along its whole range, from Florida to the Gulf of St. Lawrence. In addition it supports an important commercial fishery of about 2 to 5 million pounds a year.

The first introduction of striped bass to California took place in 1879, when Livingston Stone, a fish culturist of the United States fish commission, carried a mere 135 little stripers across the country by rail. These fish, from the Navesink River, New Jersey, were released into the Carquinez River at Martinez, in the delta area of the Sacramento River in San Francisco Bay.

This small plant, which modern fish culturists would not dream of attempting, was successful. Eleven months after the fish were released some of them had attained a size of twelve and a half inches and a weight of one pound, and they were described as being in the "best condition."

The second, and only other, introduction of striped bass into California was made in 1882. J. G. Woodbury of the California fish commission carried a little more than 300 five-to-nine-inch fish from the Shrewsbury River, New Jersey, to Suisun Bay at Army Point in San Francisco Bay, about three miles from the original plant.

In 1889, only ten years after the first transplantation, a commercial fishery existed for striped bass. In another ten years the catch in the delta area had risen to a remarkable 1 million pounds, and the fish had spread at least to southern Oregon. In 1902 the commercial catch in San Francisco Bay was 2 million pounds, the fish frequently reaching thirty to forty pounds and occasionally attaining a size of fifty pounds. By 1914 the species was abundant enough in Oregon to support a commercial fishery in Coos Bay.

Meanwhile a big sport fishery had developed, and anglers had become so fond of their new toy that they exerted increasing pressure on the California Fish and Game Commission to outlaw commercial fishing. This was done in 1935, and there have been no legal sales of striped bass in California since that year. Sport fishing for this species continues to be excellent, and it is one of the most important game fishes of California. Each year about a million and a half fish weighing 6 to 10 million pounds are caught by a quarter of a million anglers, who spend $20 million on their fishing trips.

Striped bass are tolerant of moderately wide ranges of temperature, and this may account in good measure for their successful establishment in California by the mere flick of a fish-cultural wrist, while the salmon, more finicky about their temperature requirements and more likely to roam far from home, have proven distressingly difficult to transplant.

It is not surprising that among all the scores of fishes and other aquatic animals involved in transplantations, the Pacific salmon should

[101]

FIGURE 7.4. *The U.S.S.* Fish Hawk, *a floating hatchery, at Woods Hole, Massachusetts. This pioneer ship of the United States Commission of Fish and Fisheries was put into operation March 12, 1880, to conduct research on the commercial fisheries of the Atlantic coast. Some of her chief jobs were to hatch marine fishes and invertebrates and to transport valuable species from one area to another.*

Bureau of Commercial Fisheries

be the most popular. Many people consider them the noblest of all fishes: beautiful to see, exciting to catch, flavorful to eat. And in some areas they are extremely abundant, supporting rich commercial fisheries. Before the turn of the century salmon thronged in unbelievable numbers up the rivers of Alaska and the Pacific states. The accumulation of sexually mature fish in streams where they can easily be caught, the large size of the eggs (about the size of big peas), and the ease of fertilizing the eggs and of hatching the young are other factors that made the salmon popular for culture and transplantation operations. The techniques for the process of raising salmon and trout in captivity were developed independently by several men in the 1860's. Probably the first fish hatchery in the United States was in Mumford, New York, started in 1864 by Seth Green.

The new skills were quickly put to use, and in the 1870's an ambitious plan for salmon transplantations was started with the establishment of an egg-taking station on the McLoud River, a tributary of the Sacramento River in California. The place chosen was twenty-five miles from Reddington, in an area still wild enough to make it necessary for Livingston Stone, the expert of the U.S. fish commission in charge of the operation, to begin his task by persuading the Indians that his cause was good. The Baird Station, named for the great first Commissioner of the U. S. fish commission, operated vigorously for a great many years. But Baird and his dedicated assistants would be bitterly disappointed to know that all their efforts, and those of hundreds of others over nearly a century of time, resulting in billions of eggs and young salmon being sent to hundreds of distant areas, have not produced a single commercially important salmon run in a marine area!

Baird and the early fish culturists would not be alone in their bewilderment. The failure of marine salmon transplants is still a puzzle, and it shows how far men are from understanding the complexities of the ocean well enough to control its yields.

In the first twenty years of salmon transplantation there was a heavy concentration on one species, the chinook or king salmon. The first shipment of chinook eggs was made from the Baird Station in 1872. In the years 1873–1876 several thousand fry were carried to the Hudson River, New York, and in 1891 chinook fingerlings were planted in a Vermont tributary of the Hudson. Results were zero. Argentina received chinook eggs in 1905–1908, but there were no returns. The same lack of success followed plantings in Italy, Mexico, Nicaragua, Chile, the Hawaiian Islands, England, Australia, Holland, Germany, France, Ireland, and Finland, and several other attempts in the United States. Enthusiasm ran so high in New Zealand in favor of the introduction of Pacific salmon that twenty "acclimatization societies" were formed by 1887, all clamoring for eggs. One New Zealand observer noted that some of the rivers proposed as future homes for chinooks "are entirely unfit for salmon to thrive, or, even to live in." He could have been describing streams into which many millions of benighted salmon eggs and young were dumped, not only in New Zealand but in all too many of the far-flung places of the globe.

The one partial success in transplanting salmon, like the success in transplanting striped bass to California, is just as puzzling as the many failures. The successful salmon transplant was made in New Zealand at the time when fish culture was an extremely inexact science and culturists relied more on enthusiasm than skill and knowledge.

Chinook eggs were first taken to New Zealand in 1875, but for many years there was no success. In 1900 the government decided to "make a vigorous and systematic effort" to introduce chinooks (or quin-

[103]

nat salmon, as the New Zealanders prefer to call them), and a station was set up on the Hakateramea River, tributary to the Waitaki, on the South Island. In 1901 the Baird Station supplied half a million eggs, a gift of the United States Commission of Fish and Fisheries. By 1907 five shipments totaling about 2 million eggs had been made to New Zealand.

In 1905 the first adults were caught by anglers in the tidal area off the mouth of the Waitaki River. Excitement among fish people must have been very great that year. And it probably increased in 1906 when quinnat salmon were found spawning in the Hakateramea River in May and June. Perhaps the most remarkable fact was that the fish were winter spawners, just as their California ancestors had been, but they had somehow managed to surmount what must have been an enormous biological barrier by adjusting to the reversal of the seasons in the Southern Hemisphere. The April, May, and June spawning season in New Zealand corresponds to the November, December, and January period in their native California.

By 1908 enough fish were produced naturally in streams of the South Island that a New Zealand fish culturist could "fairly claim that they are established." Chinook runs have maintained themselves through reproduction over a great many years, and small populations still exist in rivers of the Canterbury Plain of the east coast of the South Island.

The continuing presence of chinook salmon in New Zealand has had great influence on fish culture. The early success appeared more remarkable as the years passed because it was the only one that persisted. In 1937 Frederick Davidson and Samuel Hutchinson, biologists of the United States Bureau of Fisheries, reported that of the scores of salmon introductions over the world only four had been successful. But three of these supposed successes later turned out to be failures, and this left the New Zealand case as the sole triumph. In the face of these failures, fish culturists returned to their task battered, but spurred on by the assurance that "it could be done."

Whether the New Zealand transplantation was really a success depends on definition. If success requires that a self-perpetuating run be established large enough to support a significant commercial fishery— and this was the intent of the fish culturists—then the Waitaki introduction was not a success after all. By 1923 reports stated that "many" salmon were taken. But this is a relative term. In most seasons a North American purse-seine skipper would count it a bad day if he caught only 1,000 salmon. Yet there seem to have been only six times in the entire history of New Zealand salmon fishing that the entire commercial fishery caught more than this in a whole year! The largest amount of commercial gear fishing for salmon in New Zealand in any one year was eight beach seines, plus a few rods.

In 1928 sport fishermen protested loudly against commercial salmon fishing. Four nets took 2,514 fish (apparently the largest catch ever made), and the Marine Department of Fisheries received bitter criticism in the newspapers. The department's report for that year struck back: "In view of the fact that the original object of the Government in acclimatizing this fish was for commercial purposes, it is clear that anglers, who have been enjoying quite gratuitous benefits from this fishery, have no grounds for complaint." But the anglers' point of view eventually prevailed, because in 1960 commercial fishing was outlawed.

So, at its "height" the commercial fishery for salmon in New Zealand was insignificant, and now it does not exist. The transplantations have been failures in terms of establishing a run of food fish of economic value. Their limited success in supporting sport fishing in some New Zealand streams is gratifying, but this falls far short of the original dream of the fish culturists.

If this seems discouraging, it is as close as any marine transplantation of any salmon species has come to permanent success.

As a food fish the sockeye or red salmon (*Oncorhynchus nerka*) is considered the finest of all the five species, and it has been involved in many of the attempted transplantations. In the 1920's the Canadian Federal Department of Fisheries transferred sockeye eggs from spawning runs near the mouth of the Fraser River, at Cultus Lake, British Columbia, to depleted areas in Shuswap Lake, many miles upstream in the interior of the province. The Shuswap had once been a principal spawning area for the great Fraser River runs, but enormous slides in the river, caused by blasting for the construction of the Canadian National Railway in 1913 and 1914, had blocked the free migration of the fish at a narrow place in the river called Hell's Gate. Populations of sockeye salmon spawning upstream from the slide had been severely damaged, and the rich Shuswap run had been one of those whose loss was most serious. From 1922 to 1924, 1.1 to 2.3 million eggs were transplanted each year from Cultus Lake to the Shuswap, and in 1925 and 1926 eggs were taken from the Birkenhead River system, a spawning area closer to the Shuswap than Cultus Lake. None of the efforts of these five years had any effect on the Shuswap runs.

And in the case of the Cultus fish, at least, surely none should have been expected. The culturists put too much of a burden on fish taken from spawning grounds only seventy miles from the area in expecting them to rehabilitate populations of very different kinds of salmon 375 miles up the Fraser system. It is true that they are all the same species, but there are many races among the sockeye, and the Cultus race is one of the most inferior—small, and low in the vital fat that sustains the fasting fish during its struggle up the river. In addition, the normal time of passage upstream for the Cultus fish was much later in the season than that of the original Shuswap runs.

Many unsuccessful trials at establishing sockeye salmon populations had been made before the Cultus-Shuswap introductions, and some were made afterward. In the years 1902 to 1936 there were seventy-nine failures. Then, starting in 1947, a series of carefully planned and executed sockeye transplantations were performed by the International Pacific Salmon Fisheries Commission. The commission had been established in 1937 by the governments of Canada and the United States to rehabilitate the dwindling runs of sockeye in the Fraser River. The two countries were involved because the fish spawn in the streams of the Canadian Fraser River system but some of them approach the river through United States waters and American fishermen share in the harvest.

The commission has had a brilliant record of restoring the sockeye fishery, both by careful regulation of fishing intensity and by building fishways at Hell's Gate, where the great slide had blocked spawning runs. The commission hoped that the upstream populations could be restored by transplantations. Its biologists were well aware of the failures of the past, but they thought that most of these were a result of neglecting to meet the ecological requirements of the fish with sufficient care. It seemed clear that introduced fish should come from stocks spawning in grounds about the same distance from the sea as the new area, so that donor streams would be as nearly identical as possible to recipient streams, especially in respect to water temperature at the times of spawning and incubation. The Upper Adams River was one area where very large runs had once existed, but as a result of the Hell's Gate slide and a logging splash dam at the outlet of the lake, the populations had disappeared. The planting of eyed eggs (fertilized eggs whose development was far enough advanced that black specks of the eyes of the embryo salmon could be seen through the transparent shell) showed exciting possibilities, and two early experiments were declared to be "eminently successful." But by 1956 the commission was expressing grave doubts about its rehabilitation program, declaring that while hatcheries produced nine times as many fry from a given number of eggs as survived naturally, mortality of these fry was far higher than in nature, wiping out the initial advantage. In 1960 commission biologists were forced to state that returns of their transplantations were "disappointingly small."

[106]

Thus, despite some of the most careful culture work done by any fishery organization, the International Salmon Commission has not been able to match the success it has had in other areas of conservation. So far no proven permanent run has been established in a barren area as a result of transplantation. In 1963 the commission gave up, for the time being, its efforts to transplant sockeye salmon.

Some of the most interesting attempts at transplantations have taken place with the pink salmon, *Oncorhynchus gorbuscha*, the most abundant of the five species. One characteristic of the pink salmon marks it apart from the other species. This is its age at maturity, which is invariably two years. In the other species of *Oncorhynchus* maturity is later, and there is considerable variation among individuals within the species.

This curious inflexibility in the spawning age of pink salmon has an interesting corollary. In some areas they spawn in the even years but not in the odd; in others areas the opposite is true. For example, in Washington and southern British Columbia there are pink runs in the odd years but the even years are barren; in the Masset Inlet and other areas in northern British Columbia there are runs only in the even years. In central British Columbia and in most streams in Alaska pink runs occur every year.

It is one of the many mysteries of salmon biology that the barren years occur in certain streams but it is clear that if the salmon are wiped out in an area they can not reestablish themselves the following year. Since pinks invariably return as two-year-olds, no fish are available to establish the missing runs.

If that is the case, then it should be possible to start off-year runs of pink salmon by the simple expedient of transporting fish from an even-year area to an odd-year area, and vice versa. Perhaps by now the reader will know enough about the perversity of salmon to have guessed that the task is not as easy as it might seem. No persistent off-season run of pink salmon has ever been established.

Earnest attempts to establish pink salmon runs in the barren years took place in British Columbia and in Washington State. In 1918, 15 million eggs were taken from the Oyster River on the east coast of Vancouver Island, B. C., to Seton Lake in the Fraser River system. There were no returns.

On Graham Island, British Columbia, attempts to establish odd-year pinks a mere thirty miles from the place of origin were failures three years running. Later, in Jones Creek, a tributary to the Fraser River in British Columbia, the expensive addition of an artificial spawning channel (with controlled water flow) gave no better results. Other

[107]

spawning channels may help salmon transplantations in the future but there is no proof of this yet.

Similar lack of success followed pink salmon transplantations in Washington State. Starting in 1914 and continuing intermittently until 1932, pink eggs were brought from Alaska to Puget Sound. There were no results. In 1948 trials were resumed, with the aid of new techniques, but these were no more successful than the others. Attempts ceased in 1956.

It is no accident that the Soviet Union has leapfrogged over the United States and other countries in recent years to become the third fishing nation of the world. Russia works at it, with massive research and the development of huge, modern fishing fleets. Among the vigorous activities to develop the Soviet fisheries have been large-scale transplantations of many kinds of fish. In the decade of the 1950's there were 2,621 transplantations of forty-nine species, involving 1,353 bodies of water. Most of these were freshwater introductions and are not of interest here. But the Soviets have also carried out very large scale transplantations of salmon from Asiatic Russia to the White and Barents seas in the arctic region.

From 1933 to 1939 more than 10 million eggs, resulting in more than 9 million fry, were involved in these experiments. In 1936 and 1937 a few adult chum salmon were caught, but all the plants ended in failure.

Transplantations were resumed in 1957, and for the next several years a great deal of effort was put into this enterprise, especially with pink salmon. At first results were encouraging.

The fish were taken in streams in the Sakhalin and Kamchatka regions of the Soviet Union, and were planted as eyed eggs. In the cold arctic regions the plantings sometimes had to be made under ice covering the streams.

The plants of fry in 1959 (from eggs of the 1958 brood year) were the first to show signs of success, and the results were spectacular. Adult pinks began to appear along the coasts of the Barents and White seas in 1960, some to be caught by fishermen and others to enter streams to spawn. And not only were Soviet fishermen rewarded; pink salmon were caught or were seen spawning in north and central Norway, in Iceland, and in Spitsbergen; one was even caught as far south as Aberdeen, Scotland. Altogether about 80,000 adults were counted in 1960. Great excitement among fish culturists over the world followed this fine result.

In 1960 fry from the 1959 brood year were brought from the Pacific and planted as fry. As before, returns in 1961 were widespread, but this time not in anything like the great numbers appearing in 1960.

But after these two successes—one spectacular and the other good —the depressingly familiar sequel occurred. There were almost no survivors of fry from the spawning of the 1960 migrants, and few from the 1961 fish. This was attributed by Soviet biologists to unusually severe cold, which killed many eggs in the gravel. Some of the fry were misshapen or had watery yolk sacs. But one wonders, in view of the often-repeated failures of salmon transplantations, whether the most favorable conditions on the spawning grounds would have had any other result.

It is chastening to realize that man has so little understanding and control over his environment that nearly a century after the first trials, no commercially valuable, self-sustaining run of Pacific salmon has yet been established through transplantation. Clearly there is something special about the sea-run populations of these fish that makes them difficult subjects for manipulation.

Firmly rooted populations of Pacific salmon have been established in land locked areas—most spectacularly, silver salmon in Lake Michigan in recent years—and hundreds of flourishing stocks of brown trout, rainbow trout, and other close relatives of the Pacific salmon have been built up in streams and lakes. These successes, achieved when knowledge was far less than today, make it all the harder to account for the fact that without half trying, in the very infancy of the art, fish culturists were able to establish flourishing runs of anadromous shad and striped bass in a completely new and distant environment.

The lessons to be learned from the ninety-odd years of disappointing experience with fish transplantations suggest that redoubled effort must be made to understand the ecology of the areas where the introductions are to be made, and the biology of the stocks proposed to be used as donors. Close matching of the requirements of the fish with suitable conditions is a minimum requirement for success.

It seems eminently worthwhile to try again to transplant salmon and other desirable species. The high value of these fish as sources of food and wealth (and in some cases, as objects of sport) makes a great deal of trouble worthwhile, and the suggestions from the recent experiments that biologists are missing the mark by smaller and smaller margins encourage further attempts.

8 *The Great Fishing Nations*

Six of the 150-odd nations existing today dominate world fishing. In 1968 these nations—Peru, Japan, the USSR, Mainland China, Norway, and the United States—caught 57 per cent of the total production. Japan, Norway, and the United States have been engaged in ocean fishing on a large scale for centuries; Peru and the USSR are newcomers in the field. The remaining nation, Mainland China, is something of an enigma. Statistics for Communist China are hard to get, the most recent available being for 1960. And these figures apparently combine production from fresh water with that from the ocean. Certainly the boats of Communist China are encountered less frequently in the world ocean than those of Japan, the USSR, and the United States. This suggests that Red China is ranked too high in FAO statistics, a proposition with which most experts on world fisheries agree.

A large proportion of the fish harvested over the world is still caught within sight of the shore, but impressive increases are being made in catches on the high seas. Fishing operations by the successful nations are on a global scale, often half a world away from home port.

This new flurry of activity on the high seas has resulted in many boats scraping across one another's bows and many a skipper's temper being rubbed raw from interference by a vessel bearing a foreign flag. The international problems that have been a minor irritation in past decades are magnified now, and competing fleets and governments face new, vexing problems.

Ocean fishing may be the first—so far, perhaps the only—truly international industry. It exploits a resource freely open to everyone, and society has not yet developed rules for the orderly conduct of this exploitation. It is here that some of the most difficult problems arise concerning the better and fuller use of the sea. They will have to be solved, however, or mankind will destroy a vital source of wealth and food.

TABLE 3

CATCH BY COUNTRY, 1968 [a]

Rank	Country	Catch in Metric Tons
1	Peru	10,520,300
2	Japan	8,669,800
3	USSR	6,082,100
4	China (Mainland)	5,800,000 [b]
5	Norway	2,804,100
6	United States	2,442,000
7	Africa and South-West Africa	2,115,900
8	India	1,526,000
9	Spain	1,503,100
10	Canada	1,490,300
11	Denmark	1,466,800
12	Chile	1,376,100
13	Indonesia	1,175,800
14	United Kingdom	1,040,300
15	Thailand	1,088,800
16	Philippines	944,600
17	Korea (Republic of)	841,100
18	France	793,600
19	Germany (Fed. Republic)	682,300
20	Iceland	600,700
21	Portugal	559,800 [c]
22	China (Taiwan)	527,300
23	Brazil	419,400 [c]
24	Pakistan	424,000

[a] Information from Food and Agriculture Organization
[b] 1960 figure
[c] 1967 figure

Considerable light can be cast on the character of modern world fishing by an examination of the activities of Japan, the USSR, and Peru, the three nations now leading in the exploitation of the sea. The United States' position is a not-too-happy contrast.

For many decades Japan was the leading fishing nation of the world. Forced by a scarcity of arable land to feed her enormous population from the sea, she has become exceedingly skillful at the game. Waters off the home islands are strained and re-strained by a bewildering variety of fishing gear. Everything edible—and a great many things that most Westerners regard as not edible—is caught. In 1968, 55 per cent of the animal protein consumed by the Japanese came from the sea, making per capita consumption of food fish five times that of Americans.

Gradually more distant waters have been exploited. The Japanese salmon fishery on the eastern coast of Russia started in the 1880's and crab-canning mother ships were operating off Kamchatka in the early 1920's. In the 1930's there were enough Japanese fishing boats off the Pacific coast of the United States to arouse the anxiety of American fishermen, and in that same decade refrigerated Japanese trawlers fished in the South China Sea and off the coasts of Australia, Mexico, and Argentina. Japan's antarctic whaling began in 1934. World War II interrupted the expansion of Japanese fisheries, but only temporarily. After the war vessels were rebuilt swiftly—bigger, better and more efficient than before. By 1952 the fishing industry had surpassed prewar levels. Aggressive, intelligent, well-planned programs of expansion have put Japanese fishing boats in every major sea of the globe, and shore establishments and marketing systems in a great many foreign lands.

Starting about 1954 the Japanese fishing industry began another round of expansion. The new gains were made mostly in the high-seas fisheries: tuna long-lining (miles of baited hooks are dangled on vertical lines fastened to horizontal lines floating between buoys), trawling (conical nets are dragged over the bottom to scoop up fish), and salmon gill-netting (slack-meshed nets entangle fish trying to force their way through). The Japanese dominate tuna fishing, which now takes place over the whole of the tropical and subtropical world ocean. In 1965, 64 per cent of world tuna landings came to shore in their boats.

Japanese trawlers have long worked home and middle-distance waters—their own insular shelf, the East China Sea, and the South China Sea. Now they are busily scraping the bottoms of the Bering Sea, the Gulf of Alaska, the Grand Banks off Newfoundland, and the shelf off west Africa. In the open Pacific their offshore gill-netting of immature salmon spawned in North American and Asian streams has raised a storm of protest from United States and Canadian fishermen, and has created a difficult international fishery problem of the sort that the world will face more frequently in years to come.

In 1968 Japanese trawling fleets caught a little less than 480,000 tons of fish in the Bering Sea and the Gulf of Alaska—far more than the United States trawl catch of 750 tons off these parts of her own shores. In 1966 Japan sent fourteen fleets, consisting of more than 200 catching vessels, into the Bering Sea. Their main target was pollock, destined to become fish cake and sausage.

Tuna are among the most popular fishes in Japan, and new grounds are constantly being sought. Following World War II Americans became interested in the possibility of catching the big schools that had been observed in the mid-Pacific during naval operations, and oceanographic research revealed a good deal about their occurrence and availability. But because of fishing costs, United States vessels were unable to take advantage of this knowledge, and American tuna fishing was restricted to waters of the eastern Pacific. The Japanese, however, were able to exploit the tropical Pacific offshore stocks, and they made good use of American research, backed by more of their own.

In 1957 Japanese long-line boats began fishing off Brazil and other parts of the tropical Atlantic. They based their ships in such ports as Las Palmas in the Canary Islands, and covered vast areas of ocean with their floating gear. They are still there (and sporadically in the Caribbean Sea as well), but fishing success is lower now, and some species of tuna may already be overfished in these new areas. In 1966 there were an estimated 200 Japanese long-liners in the Indian Ocean; here, too, lower catches suggested that overfishing had occurred.

In October 1962 the *Aoi Maru #2* appeared off St. Pierre, Newfoundland—the bellwether of the Japanese fleet in the North Atlantic. Japanese trawlers are now a common sight on the Grand Banks, an area dominated for centuries by American fishermen to the extent that they had come to regard it as their private fishing pond. The Japanese sent a big new stern trawler to St. Pierre in 1965 to strengthen the Grand Banks fleet.

Japan was not a factor in the early days of whaling, which was dominated by the Yankees out of New Bedford and Nantucket. But the Japanese must certainly be reckoned with in the modern era, since their whaling ships take a high proportion of the world catch and are seen wherever whales can be caught—especially among the ice floes of the Antarctic.

The Japanese have pointed the way to most of the rest of the world in efficient exploitation of the sea, but they have also illustrated the danger of overdoing it, since many of the stocks that they have exploited with such enthusiasm show signs of depletion. Heavy fishing on the whales by the Japanese and other nations has placed several species in desperate jeopardy, with the strong possibility of actual extinction in some instances. The once-rapid rate of expansion of the Japanese tuna fisheries has slowed down markedly, and the boats are searching with urgency for new areas of the ocean where the former profits can be

[113]

made. The world's biggest fishing company, Taiyo Gyogyo, showed an overall profit of 110 billion yen ($333 million) in 1965 but lost 300-400 million yen ($0.8-1.1 million) on their tuna operations. The second largest Japanese tuna firm, Hoko Suisan, lost more than 500 million yen ($1.4 million) on tuna fishing and failed to pay stockholders a dividend for the first time in many years.

Besides lower abundance of fish, some segments of the Japanese industry are troubled by a tightened labor supply, caused by high wages on shore as the Japanese economy improves. Men who were forced by economic circumstances to go to sea now take jobs in shipyards and other shore industries at higher wages. In 1964 I was aboard a Japanese long-line fishing vessel in Port of Spain, Trinidad, where it was unloading tuna caught in the tropical Atlantic. The men had been away from home two years. They were soon to sail for the Pacific, where they would fish off the coast of Peru for one more load, and they expected to be home in another six months! It is no wonder Japanese shipowners have had a difficult time manning their vessels, and it is not surprising that all nations have had the same trouble. Fishing, besides being dangerous, is one of the hardest and lowest-paid trades in the world. It is ironic that Japanese fishermen, famous for their efficiency and for the low wages and the hardships that they tolerated, should now find themselves replaced to an increasing extent by Koreans and Formosans, who will accept the poor conditions many Japanese now disdain.

The answer of Japanese fleet owners is to conduct more research in finding fish and in developing gear that will catch them more cheaply. For example, improvements in mechanization of the long-line tuna gear have permitted a reduction in the size of the crews from twenty to fifteen men, considerably reducing the cost. Japan is not to be counted out of the world fishing picture by a long shot, but her experience should be carefully examined by other maritime nations.

Japan is a successful veteran in the game of global fishing; the Soviet Union is a successful newcomer. The firing of *Sputnik* in 1957 jolted the United States into the realization that the USSR was its technological equal in some important respects. This event spurred the United States to much greater activity in space exploration and led to a rivalry that has proved so expensive that many Americans now doubt the wisdom of the investment.

In the long run the Russian challenge on the sea may be far more significant than the challenge in space. The USSR is well launched on a scheme to dominate world fishing; in 1968 she surpassed the United States in total production and (assuming that Red China's production is overestimated) ranked third among all nations. This challenge has

FIGURE 8.1. *A Soviet trawler in the ice of the central Bering Sea. Russian vessels caught nearly 850,000 tons of fish off North American shores in 1967.*

Bureau of Commercial Fisheries, Alaska

received far less attention than *Sputnik,* partly because it has been heralded by no one spectacular event; instead Russia has advanced in this area in a steady but highly effective manner.

In 1917, the year of the Communist Revolution, nearly all the fish in the country came from fresh waters. In 1922 only about a fifth of Russia's half-million tons came from the sea, and right up to World War II Soviet boats fished close to land. But after the war agricultural development lagged, especially in the production of animal protein, and the Soviet planners turned their attention to the prospects of food from the sea. Their conclusions are of great significance not only to the Soviet Union but to the rest of the world as well.

It is often said that the USSR operates its industry without regard to economics, but in fact its decisions are based as much on the ratio of input to output—that is, to considerations of return on investment— as those of capitalist nations. It is only the level at which the profit or loss occurs that is different: the state, rather than the individual or private company, is the gainer or loser from a well-planned or a poorly planned operation.

Comparing the cost of protein from the sea with its cost from land,

[115]

FIGURE 8.2. *The* Konstantin Sukhanov, *a Soviet factory ship. This 532-foot vessel, and several others of similar size, operate off Alaska in the herring, shrimp, and king crab fisheries. They have complete canning, freezing, and fish meal factories aboard and have complements of about 640 men and women. Twenty or more large trawlers and varying numbers of smaller boats supply the factory ship.*

Bureau of Commercial Fisheries, Alaska

Soviet economists concluded that the sea is more efficient by a significant margin. S. C. Mikhailov, a Russian economist, calculated that to produce 100,000 tons of beef and pork on Soviet farms required a capital investment of from 2 to 2.5 million rubles; to produce the same tonnage of fish required an investment of only 1.5 to 1.7 million rubles. After the capital costs were paid the production cost for the meat would be 600 million rubles; for the fish, 200 million. The advantage on the side of fishing was even more striking in terms of expenditure of labor: it required 5.4 million man-hours to produce the meat, compared with 1.35 million man-hours to produce the fish equivalent. With this kind of information before them, the Soviet planners were easily convinced that Russia could satisfy its vast and rapidly increasing needs for animal protein better from the sea than from the land.

Having arrived at this conclusion, the government proceeded to make a detailed plan for an all-out assault on the sea. It became national policy to expand the fishing industry, and meticulous planning was backed by undeviating conviction and successful execution.

By 1948 the Soviets began building large trawlers for exploratory fishing. These were followed quickly by vessels of the newest design—boats of the *Pushkin* class of stern trawlers, 277 feet long, based on the British experimental *Fairtry*. By 1959 the USSR had at least 150 factory ships of this design, capable of fishing in nearly any weather and of operating in every ocean of the world. Later, scores of even more modern stern trawlers were put into operation.

Soviet activity in ocean fishing began to attract some notice starting in the early 1950's, largely because it involved the appearance of Russian vessels off foreign coasts, and this made the natives nervous.

In 1954 Soviet fishing vessels turned up on the American side of the Atlantic, off Newfoundland, operating in waters that the United States and Canada had regarded for centuries as their preserve. In 1958 there were ships off Labrador. On March 4, 1961, Russian vessels were reported off Cape Cod, on the grounds where United States fishermen had operated for centuries. Late in 1962 Russian fishing vessels were seen off the coasts of North and South Carolina, and they were soon observed passing along the coast of Florida, apparently to and from an impressive new fishing port built with Soviet help in Cuba. By 1964 Soviet fishermen were operating on nearly all the important grounds of the North Atlantic, and their research was leading their fishermen to the richest stocks.

On the other side of North America, Soviet trawl fleets began operating in the Bering Sea in 1959, first on flounders and cod, later on ocean perch, king crabs, herring, and shrimp. In that year their catch off the Pacific coast of North America amounted to about a thousand tons. Early in 1962 two Soviet exploratory fishing vessels appeared off the coasts of Washington and Oregon, pursuing hake. They were the harbingers of big fleets, numbering at least 300 vessels by 1966, fishing practically within sight of shore. By 1965 their catch off the American coast had zoomed to nearly 850,000 tons. Russian ships entered the Alaskan shrimp fishery in 1962–1963 and were soon catching large quantities from the eastern Bering Sea and the Gulf of Alaska, a resource that American fishermen have had a hard time exploiting profitably despite an estimated annual potential of 1 billion pounds.

Soviet fishing vessels have appeared in Queen Charlotte Sound off the coast of British Columbia. They operate off Ghana, Togo, and other west African countries. Two of their research vessels, belonging to the Pacific Research Institute for Fisheries and Oceanography, appeared off Ecuador, Peru, and Chile in the spring of 1967.

[117]

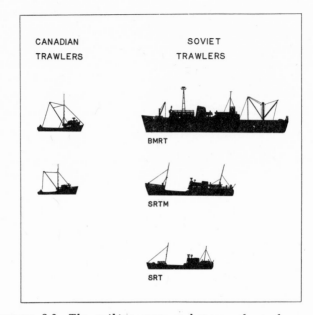

FIGURE 8.3. *The striking contrast between three classes of Soviet trawlers operating off British Columbia and the newest and largest Canadian trawlers is shown in this drawing. The difference in size between Russian and United States vessels would be even more marked.*

Trade News

Much has been said about the political activities of Soviet fishing vessels, and the claim has been made that fishing is merely a blind for spying. The Russians may be using these fleets incidentally for espionage, but fishing is their primary task and they are doing a thoroughly good job of it.

An important characteristic of Soviet fishing is that nothing is wasted. Unlike American fishermen who usually select the high-priced species and discard the rest, the Russians sweep the ocean for everything that can be reduced to protein. They are more interested in fish that can be caught in great bulk, such as herring in the North Atlantic, the bottom fishes of the Bering Sea, and the small shrimp of the Gulf of Alaska, than in higher-priced but often scarcer species usually sought by American fishermen. Soviet factory ships are equipped to handle anything live that comes aboard. There are machines to freeze whole fish, to cut and freeze fillets, to can fish, to reduce to meal and oil species that are too small or too soft to be used otherwise. The Soviet Union is the world leader in the frozen fish trade. The factory ships are huge. The *Professor Baranov*, for example, is 543 feet long. It processes the catch of a fleet of twenty to forty SRT-class catcher boats 130 to 180 feet long. In one day it can salt 200 tons of herring and store it at 23°F.; process 150 tons of fish into meal; fillet and freeze 100 tons of bottom fish; and manufacture 5 tons of fish oil, 20 tons of ice, and 100 tons of distilled water. Even bigger factory ships, such as the *Sovetskaya Ukraina* (715 feet long), are equipped to handle sixty-five whales a day with a crew of 510 men and usually (as on other Soviet ships) some women. A helicopter is carried on the stern.

The Soviets' "vacuum cleaner" type of fishing has alarmed American fishermen, and there may be real cause for such concern in the case of some stocks. But in many cases stocks have not been overfished, and this all-embracing use of all kinds of fishes and invertebrates is good conservation. There is evidence that more harm is sometimes done by selective exploitation, whereby desirable species are withdrawn from the ecological complex, leaving the field to the less desirable species, than by taking everything—removing predators and competitors of the prime species at the same rate as the marketable fishes.

Exploitation must be carried out with due consideration for the total amount of fishing that the complex of stocks can stand. American fishery scientists do not have enough biological information to be sure what level of fishing is proper for most species, and it is highly doubtful that the Soviets do either.

Meanwhile, the Russians are pursuing their national policy with

FIGURE 8.4. *A purse seiner near the end of its set off Iquique, Peru. Here the fishermen are competing for the anchovies with enormous flocks of guanay birds.*

Instituto de Fomento Pesquero

determination. In a little over a decade the USSR more than doubled its fish production, from about 1,627,000 metric tons in 1950 to approximately 3,616,500 in 1962. Since then the pace has quickened even more, and in 1968 the Soviet catch was over 6 million tons. The catch of American fishermen, by contrast, has declined. It was 2,508,800 tons in 1950 and 2,442,000 tons in 1968.

The increase in fish production in the Soviet Union has been accomplished through research and hard work. Among the Russian oceanographic research vessels is the 359-foot *Vitiaz,* converted to its present purpose in 1948. The 337-foot *Mikhail Lomonosov* (named, along with the University of Moscow, for the famous Russian chemist of the eighteenth century) was built in Rostock, East Germany, in 1957 specifically as an oceanographic research vessel. She carries a sixty-two-man crew plus sixty-eight scientists, and is reported to have more oceanographic gear than any other research vessel in the world. This distinction may have been taken over by a still more impressive Soviet research ship, the *Akademik Kurchator,* built in 1966. She is 407 feet long, carries eighty-five crewmen and eighty-one scientists, and is equipped with twenty-two laboratories and a helicopter.

One of Russia's other specially interesting research vessels is the *Severyanka,* a converted Soviet Navy W-class submarine. She is soon to be replaced by a smaller but more useful submarine, designed especially for fishery research.

The first step in Soviet fishing reconnaissance is to scour a particular section of the ocean with exploratory fishing boats. Good results lead to commercial operations. Instead of sending individual vessels, whole fleets move in to exploit the new area. A fleet may include 100 modern stern trawlers of several classes, ranging from 240 to 278 feet in size; smaller trawlers (like the biggest of American fishing boats), ranging from 130 to 170 feet; and perhaps seiners and other kinds of boats. Mother factory ships, up to 571 feet in length, are likely to go along too. Accompanying the fishing boats are fuel tankers, salvage tugs, refrigerated transports (to 515 feet long), and repair ships such as the *Neva,* which carries eleven different kinds of repair shops aboard. This whole immense navy-type operation is controlled by a commodore aboard a command ship. He receives twice-daily reports of the catches of individual boats; comparing these with the catches of scouting vessels and their reports of weather, water temperature, and other information, he deploys his fleet to best advantage.

The Soviet equipment, planning, and effort are paying off in immense hauls. In the Bering Sea, for example, single trawls have made catches of Pacific ocean perch estimated to be more than 40,000 pounds; American fishermen regard 5,000 pounds as a very good catch. With equipment and instrumentation superior to that on American boats, Soviet ships fish on grounds that American fishermen consider untrawlable.

Officials of the Soviet Union have stated publicly that Russia intends to surpass other nations in fishing. Plans for the 1966–70 five-year program included about $650 million to expand fishing activities —two thirds more than was spent in the previous five years. The plan called for 1,500 new fishing vessels, including 250 big stern trawlers, and 145 refrigerated fish carriers and factory ships. With the kind of determination Russia is exhibiting, and with the effectiveness of her operations, she may very well achieve her announced goal—and soon.

The present leader in world fishing is Peru, whose recent and spectacular entry into this industry holds important lessons for a world trying to increase its supply of food from the sea.

Before World War II Peru nearly ignored the fish off her shores. In 1938 the industry was barely above subsistence levels, with a catch of 23,400 tons. Twenty-five years later she landed more than 10,000,000 metric tons—about a fifth of the world's catch, and more than triple the landings of the United States.

What makes this accomplishment the more amazing is that a single species, the anchovy, *Engraulis ringens,* accounts for virtually the entire Peruvian catch. Immense concentrations of anchovies have existed off the coast of Peru since time immemorial. Men paid little attention to them, but great populations of sea birds owed their existence to these fish. Peru's people benefited indirectly from them by way of the birds, since the droppings produced thick deposits of guano, which were scraped off the rocks and used for fertilizer. The guano industry existed in pre-Columbian times and it provided Peru with considerable wealth. In the 1840's and 1850's the Castillo administration used the proceeds of this industry, one of the few providing export revenue, to finance economic and social advances of great importance to the country, including a railroad across the Andes. In the quarter-century beginning in 1850 Peru exported 2 million tons of guano worth $2 billion.

Peruvian anchovies are edible but small—four to five inches in length—and their size makes them difficult to use as food for humans. But another way of using small fishes has become important. This is to reduce them to meal by cooking, drying, and grinding. A surge in demand for fish meal resulted from the discovery that a small amount in the diet of poultry and other farm animals was of great nutritional value. Over the whole world the market rose rapidly.

[1 2 1]

As a consequence of this stimulus Peru began to use the anchovies for reduction after World War II. In 1946 there were two fish meal plants in the country, and for the next decade growth was very slow. This was partly the result of the uncertainty of Peruvian officials, who feared that fish meal reduction might destroy the guano industry, so profitable and so anciently rooted in the history of the country. But the government was eventually persuaded that the anchovies could probably feed a great many birds and still support a fish reduction industry.

In 1955, after a decade of inching upward, anchovetta production began to soar. In that year Peru landed 58,707 metric tons of anchovies; twelve years later the total was 10 million tons! In 1963 Peru surpassed Japan in fish landings.

Peruvian anchovy production rose steeply each year until 1964 and then fell for two years. It rose again in 1967, but it may be that the populations have reached about their maximum yield. If so, the fishermen cannot take much larger catches of *Engraulis ringens* without damaging the stocks.

Peru's experience has important implications for world effort to obtain more food from the sea. Of greatest significance is the fact that 10 million tons of new protein has been made available for world consumption. It is true that most of this is not used directly by humans, but is cycled through poultry and other animals; however, the conversion efficiency of these animals is high, and the contribution of the anchovies to human feeding is of great importance. Secondly, the anchovy fishery is operating on a trophic level (a layer of the food pyramid) lower than most fisheries of the past. This is of great theoretical and practical interest, since it avoids the loss occurring from one trophic level to the next.

The last lesson to be learned from the Peru story is that a stock of fish can be brought to a state of full exploitation in a very short time: from a nearly virgin condition in the years immediately before World War II, and an almost unexploited condition as late as 1955, the anchovies have been fished so hard for a mere dozen years that full exploitation may already have been reached. The Peruvian government has had the wisdom to anticipate this possibility: in 1960 it established a fishery research institute, with the help of a sizable grant from the United Nations Development Programme. Scientists of the institute are determining what conservation measures will be necessary to maintain the country's immensely valuable resource.

While Japan, the USSR, and other countries raised their fish production rapidly after World War II, the United States failed to do so. Fish remains an important food in this country, but Americans are now becoming increasingly dependent on foreign fishermen for their supply.

This was not always so. The profit to be made from catching the fish in American waters was a major incentive for the early settlement and development of this country, and fishing has continued to be an important industry in many coastal areas to the present time. Well before Columbus, fishermen from Europe regularly made the long and perilous voyage across the Atlantic for cod, whose teeming numbers and high quality as a dried and salted product made them profitable objects of pursuit. Commercial fishing was the first industry of the New World, and cod made the original fortunes of many a New England family whose name is still famous. Later, when whale oil began to light the houses of the world, Americans plunged into the whale fishery with an enthusiasm that is legendary. Yankee whalers dominated this industry for years, and their impact over a great part of the world was political and social as well as economic.

TABLE 4

LEADING FISHING NATIONS, 1938–1967 [a]

Rank	1938	1948	1958	1960	1962	1966	1967
1	Japan	Japan	Japan	Japan	Peru	Peru	Peru
2	USA	USA	China [b]	Peru	Japan	Japan	Japan
3	USSR	Norway	USA	China [b]	China [b]	China [b]	China [b]
4	UK	USSR	USSR	USSR	USSR	USSR	USSR
5	Norway	UK	Norway	USA	USA	Norway	Norway
6	N. Korea	Canada	India	Norway	Norway	USA	USA

[a] Source: Food and Agriculture Organization of the United Nations
[b] China's landings and position are uncertain

From these strong beginnings the fishing industry of the United States burgeoned over the years. Cod remained important for decades but gradually lost its grip on the market as seafoods more appetizing than salted fish became available. Oysters achieved popularity and were produced in millions of pounds in the nineteenth century. Salmon had been eagerly sought from the beginning, and after their preservation by canning began in 1864 that industry shot into prominence. America's sardine catch at its peak amounted to 750,000 tons in a single year.

Until the end of World War II this nation was second only to Japan in fish production. In the next few years the world catch rose rapidly, but the harvest by this country has remained nearly the same from year to year—or has actually declined slightly. In 1968 the total production was 2.4 million metric tons—except for some war and depression years the lowest total in four decades. From the rank of second among world fishing nations, the United States has fallen to sixth —behind Peru, Japan, Mainland China, the USSR, and Norway.

This slide down the ladder does not mean that the United States dislikes fish. On the contrary, this country consumes 10 per cent of the total seafood available in the world while possessing only 6 per cent of the population. For many years the per capita consumption of fish used directly as food has remained stable at ten to eleven pounds. But this figure is misleading; the actual consumption is more than sixty pounds per person (one of the highest in the world) when the quantities used indirectly (through the consumption of poultry and other farm animals fed fish meal), as well as the quantities used for pet food, are included.

The relative overall decline in United States fisheries is not due to a shortage of fish in American waters. This is perhaps emphasized best by the willingness of vessels of foreign nations to come thousands of miles to fish off these shores. Japanese and Soviet trawlers took 3 billion pounds of fish from the Bering Sea and the Gulf of Alaska in 1966; boats of these same nations caught more than 3 million king crabs in Alaskan waters that year; Soviet trawlers off the coasts of Washington and Oregon have thrown American fishermen into panic by their activities barely outside the limits of United States territorial seas; the vessels of more than a dozen nations are fishing on the Grand Banks and other rich grounds off the northeast coast of the United States— grounds that are far closer to New England ports than to those of any foreign boats, except those of Canada.

Despite the melancholy loss of the California sardine resource (from a combination of overfishing and changes in the ocean environment) and the severe drop in productivity of other valuable fisheries, the United States has not even come close to tapping the full reserve of the resources off its own shores. With good management and the cleaning up of polluted and damaged habitats, many of the depleted stocks could be restored. These include salmon, oysters, menhaden—perhaps even sardines and others whose fate seems nearly sealed. And contrary to common opinion there are still rich underexploited resources. In fact, it is estimated that waters close to United States shores are capable of producing 48 billion pounds of fish and shellfish a year, about nine times this country's present catch.

The United States fishing industry has remained static, not from lack of fish but because of the high cost of production. An aspect of this factor is the lack of government support: the industry is not considered to be important to the nation. Consequently, other nations, whose governments do provide them with a variety of economic assistance, are able to deliver fish to the American market (sometimes caught in waters closer to America than to their own ports) more cheaply than American fishermen can. As a result, fish imports have zoomed to the point that Americans eat three times as much foreign seafood as that caught by their own boats.

Efforts in Congress to create a national policy of support for fishing have run afoul of the enormous diversity of the American industry. Different parts of the industry are so divided among themselves that they have been unable to present a solid front, with the result that the necessary laws have not been enacted.

The biggest schism within the industry exists between the producers —fishermen and fleet owners—and the processors. Frustrated by inability to fill the heavy demands of their customers from American boats, processors have turned increasingly to foreign suppliers. Importers are able to buy foreign fish cheaply because of the free-trade policies of this country, and they naturally fight vigorously against any change. Manufacturers of frozen fish sticks and fish steaks in the New England area are eager to maintain their present supply of cheap Canadian and Scandinavian groundfish; California canners show the same enthusiasm for the free entry of Japanese tuna.

Then, many of the principal United States producers have conflicting interests. For example, a great number of American tuna and shrimp boats fish off foreign shores, and it is in their best interest to have narrow territorial waters so that as much as possible of the sea is open to their activities. Other producers, such as the salmon fishermen of the Pacific and the groundfish trawlers of New England and the Pacific Northwest, want foreign boats pushed out as far as possible from their shores. They are loud in their complaints about Soviet, Japanese, and other vessels fishing on the Grand Banks and off the coasts of Alaska, Washington, and Oregon. Thus, with major segments of the United States industry bringing opposing pressures to bear on Congress it is little wonder that action is difficult.

Another factor of significance is the United States Constitution, which gives the states the right and responsibility to control their fisheries and prevents the federal government from regulating fishing except outside territorial waters or in waters under international control. Unfortunately, fish pay no attention to artificial political boundaries, and piecemeal regulation of fisheries by various states of a given fish stock is not effective. A common pattern is for states to regulate a fishery by deliberately reducing the efficiency of capture—in many cases without convincing evidence that reduced catches are necessary. Of course this raises the price of fish, and puts the industry in an unfavorable position in relation to the prices of competing foods.

And when a fish stock is being overexploited it is common for one or more states harvesting the resource to neglect to control its fishermen, frustrating regulations by its neighbors. Attempts to coordinate control through interstate commissions have not been very effective. As a result many valuable seafood resources—oysters, salmon, sardines, menhaden—have gone down the drain or are seriously damaged.

The United States should not blindly follow other nations in attempting to cure the stagnation of its fishing industry. For example, it does not need the big fleets of costly freezer trawlers or factory ships operated by the Soviet Union. Russia is forced to use this particular technique because 90 per cent of its deep-sea fishing is done too far from home to allow fresh fish operations, and thus big floating bases and shipboard processing are required. To a much greater extent the United States can fish close to home, and it can thus use more economical ships and shore bases for supply and processing.

To revitalize the American fishing industry it would be necessary first for the nation to adopt the philosophy that commercial fishing is worth encouraging. This would require the making of controversial political and economic decisions involving subsidies to the industry (for example, for vessel construction), tax relief, import duties, and quota protection against foreign fish. In the face of the assistance competing nations give their operators, American fishermen and fleet owners in large segments of the industry are helpless to revitalize their activities.

Some better ways of managing fish stocks must also be used. In particular, the widespread policy of controlling fisheries by imposing inefficiencies on production should be changed. Gear such as purse seines should not be outlawed because they are efficient, and the sizes of vessels should not be restricted; instead vigorous encouragement should be given to methods that catch fish as quickly and cheaply as possible. Contrary to the fear of many, this does not prevent conservation regulations. Where stocks are known to be overexploited, conservation measures should be imposed to ensure that excessive total catches are not made, but the optimum catch should be harvested as efficiently as possible. States should examine their regulations with a cold eye, to root out those that have a false rationale.

The present state-by-state system of regulating fisheries has been shown to be inadequate, and resources will continue to be damaged or destroyed until changes are made. The federal government performs much of the research but its findings are left to the states to apply— or not. The results are a hodgepodge of overregulation of some stocks, so that their full, rational exploitation is prevented, or a patchwork of conflicting and sometimes unworkable laws controlling other stocks, some of which may be seriously damaged as a consequence.

It may be impossible to alter this pattern, since the states are touchy about their rights, and they have shown little inclination to submerge differences with other states let alone vacate their prerogatives to the federal government. But some hard thinking has to go into the question of whether common regulation should be imposed, and whether federal regulations should be used if states are unable or unwilling to act.

Industries flourish only when money can be made by their participants. The nearly universal pattern is for ever-increasing numbers of boats to engage in a successful fishery, dividing the catch so many ways that the return on investment is marginal. This can only be prevented if there is some government control, which is lacking in the United States. Japan fixes the number of boats she allows to operate in a particular fishery, and Canada has made her first essay in this direction in the Pacific salmon fishery. Sooner or later the United States probably will have to do the same if it wants to rebuild a successful fishing industry.

If, as experts have asserted, the United States has nine times as much fish off its shores as it is now using, a rich opportunity to capture fish and dollars is being lost—especially when the resource is renewable and is thus permanent if wisdom is employed in its use. Much of this potential is already being exploited by foreign boats, and much of the remainder consists of unfamiliar and presently unmarketable species— hake, anchovy, saury, thread herring, lanternfish, squids. Deliberate efforts should be made by government and private fishery agencies to encourage their use. Processing methods and new products (such as fish protein concentrate) should be developed and sold to the public to bring this about.

The shape of world fishing has changed dramatically in recent years, with old actors and new ones playing successful roles. The United States has been edged toward the wings, but it still has the capacity to move stage center again, if it makes the deliberate choice to do so.

9 *Fish Meal and Fish Protein Concentrate*

In recent years world fish landings have increased twice as fast as human population (in contrast to the trends for other kinds of food), and from 1958 to 1964 fully 60 per cent of this increase consisted of varieties made into fish meal—species such as sardines, anchovies, and hakes.

For many decades fish meal was used largely as fertilizer and was referred to as "fish guano." Useful as it is for fertilizer, fish meal is now far too valuable to be used for this purpose. Instead, its enormously increased popularity is a consequence of the remarkable things it does in increasing the growth rates, the vigor, and the general health of farm animals at a cost much below that of most other supplements.

Farmers have known for centuries that their livestock relish—and thrive on—fish. In 325 B.C. Nearchus, one of Alexander the Great's generals, attacked a town on the Persian Gulf to restock his larder. According to the account given by the Greek historian Arrian, "the natives showed freely their flour, ground down from dried fish. . . . Even their flocks are fed on dried fish so that the mutton has a fishy taste like the flesh of sea birds." In the fourteenth century Marco Polo reported that some Asian peoples "accustom their cattle, cows, sheep, camels and horses to feed upon dried fish . . . of a small kind which they take in vast quantities during the months of March, April and May; and when dried they lay up in their houses for food for their cattle." Farmers in such far-flung places as Malaysia and the Shetland Islands of Scotland learned long ago to feed fish to pigs and sheep. The first bulletin issued by the United States fish commission in 1881 contained a letter from Isaac Hinkley describing the fish-eating cows of Provincetown, Massachusetts, which crowded around fishermen cleaning their catch to browse on the offal. Ling or blennies of three pounds and more were "freely eaten." Farmers taught cows to accept fish by mincing it and including it in their rations.

The use of fish meal for farm animals picked up momentum when its high content of nitrogen and phosphorus compounds was noticed in the early decades of this century. Feeding experiments met with remarkable success. Fish meal began to have general use as animal food in Europe, but this trend lagged in the United States until after World War I.

The American poultry industry has grown enormously with the aid of fish meal. More than a third of the United States broiler production can be attributed to it. More than half the fish landed in the United States goes to feed farm animals, and in 1968 this enormous bulk (more than 200,000 tons of fish meal) was supplemented by imports of 855,000 tons for the same purpose. In America turkeys and pigs also benefit from fish-supplemented diets. In Europe more meal is fed to swine than to chickens; in Germany, for example, 70 per cent goes to pigs.

For all farm animals—and for humans too—growth, vigor, and general health are dependent to a very important extent on the amount and quality of proteins available. These are the substances making up the muscle and other parts of the body mass. In addition, the minerals that are essential components of the skeleton and the vitamins that control the chemistry of the body are other important food constituents. Fish, whether fresh or reduced to meal, is one of the world's best sources of all three of these food groups.

Proteins occur in many kinds of foods, including plants: cereal grains, fruits, soybeans, and many more. They occur also in foods of animal origin: meat, milk, eggs, fish. The ruminants—cows and sheep—flourish with proteins derived from any of these sources. Other animals, including chickens, pigs, and man, may be undernourished on a diet high in protein if the sole source is cereals or other plants. The difference is related to the composition of the proteins from the two food sources.

Proteins are among the most complex of chemical substances. Their large molecules are made up of networks of smaller molecules of various amino acids. There are about eighteen amino acids, occurring in varying proportions in different kinds of protein. Nine or ten of these, called the essential amino acids, must be supplied already manufactured, since most animals cannot synthesize them. Foods containing these essential amino acids are more nutritious than others in which some or all of them are deficient or out of balance.

Of all the essential amino acids three are likely to be missing in the grain rations of poultry. These are lysine and two sulfur-containing amino acids, methionine and cystine. For swine rations, lysine and tryptophan are those likely to be deficient. Cereal grains are low in all of these, so that chickens fed only with corn have to be fed larger amounts of grain to achieve optimum growth rate, maximum size, survival, and general health than if a better balance of amino acids can be supplied. Soybean meal does a better job than the grains, having ample quantities of lysine and tryptophan, but it is low in methionine and cystine. Sesame and sunflower meals, used increasingly in feeds in recent years, are rich in the sulfur amino acids but are low in lysine.

The rapidly rising use of fish meal for animal feeds has taken place because it is rich in all of these essential amino acids. One of the great strengths of fish meal is that only small amounts are required to supplement the essential nutrients available in cereal grains. Fish meal has by no means replaced the grains or soybean meal in animal feeds but instead has been used as a feed supplement. Soviet scientists have discovered that a metric ton (2,204 pounds) of fish meal added to the ration fed to pigs increased the yield of pork by 700 to 800 kilograms (1,540 to 1,760 pounds). When the same amount of fish meal was added to poultry feed, production of eggs increased by 25,000. In addition the meal replaced three tons of vegetable feeds. In Norwegian experiments, 7 per cent of fish meal added to the diet of chicks during their first six weeks increased their growth 11 per cent over that of animals fed only vegetable food. Pigs given a fish meal supplement to only their diet of grains increased in weight an extra 5 to 12 per cent by the time they reached market size. In Denmark the number of eggs per hen in ten months of production was 153 for birds fed 15 per cent fish meal compared to 126 for those on vegetable protein only. Soybean meal produced a 45 per cent hatch of eggs, but when the ration was supplemented by condensed fish solubles (the dissolved and suspended materials from fish reduction) the percentage rose to 74.

In the United States small proportions of fish meal—ordinarily about 2 to 3 per cent but sometimes as much as 10 per cent—are used in the diet of chickens. More fish meal gives better results, but the cost rises when the fish replaces grain.

Meat, eggs, or milk fed to farm animals would give the same desirable effects as fish, and chemists have learned to synthesize methionine and other amino acids, as well as vitamins, in the laboratory. Hence it is possible to formulate fully balanced rations without fish meal. The modern poultry farmer lets a computer tell him what to use. The computer juggles the amino acid content of various components and comes up with a formulation that may include fish meal one day but exclude it the next because a cheaper protein source may be available. But fish meal is usually the cheapest source of high-grade animal protein.

Fish meals are rich in minerals, especially calcium and phosphorus, which are essential to the formation of bones. All such meals include iodine, copper, manganese, zinc, iron, and cobalt; they contain large quantities of the B vitamins, including B_{12}, riboflavin, niacin, and choline, all necessary for proper nutrition.

Finally, there is an air of pleasant mystery to the nutritional qualities of fish meal. After all the beneficial effects—the high protein content, the good amino acid balance, the high mineral and B vitamin content— have been accounted for, an additional value has been reported by some investigators. This has been called the "unidentified growth factor." It makes fish meal unique in nutritional value and has helped push it to its present heights of popularity.

There are a number of ways of making fish meal, but the largest quantities by far—some 95 per cent worldwide—are manufactured by the "wet reduction process." This is used when large volumes of oily fish are available. The fish are cooked with steam to denature the protein and break the cell walls to release the oil. The cooked mass is squeezed in a continuous screw-type press to remove water (up to 80 per cent of the raw fish) and oil (up to 20 per cent). The resulting "press cake" is dried and ground, an antioxidant is added, and the meal is bagged. Fish meal has a moisture content of 6 to 10 per cent, a fat content of 5 to 12 per cent, a protein content of 60 to 75 per cent, and an ash (mostly mineral) content of 10 to 20 per cent. It takes five pounds of raw fish to make a pound of fish meal; the difference is the water and oil removed.

This removal has two important results: it reduces the weight (and hence the shipping costs) to a fifth of the original fish weight, and it reduces spoilage, since bacteria must have moisture to operate. Hence fish meal can be stored at room temperature in simple containers such as bags, and can be shipped without expensive refrigeration.

Two other products, oil and solubles, result when fish meal is made this way. The oil-water mixture, called press liquor, is centrifuged, and oil and stickwater result. The stickwater is centrifuged again, to produce solubles. The market for these products is poor at present.

Fish oils are relatively unsaturated, meaning that their molecules are capable of picking up hydrogen atoms. This is of importance in human nutrition—and presumably for farm animals as well—and consumption of unsaturated instead of saturated fats may be a factor in the prevention of heart disease. Fish oils also have ready markets as ingredients for soap, paint, linoleum, lipstick, table and cooking fats, ink, and a surprising variety and number of other products.

Stickwater (or gluewater in Europe, both names describing its most obvious physical characteristic) is the residual liquid from the pressing of the cooked fish. It contains soluble and suspended materials —protein, minerals, and in particular, large amounts of the water-soluble B vitamins. Stickwater, once discarded, is now evaporated to about half its original volume to produce "condensed fish solubles." It is a valuable supplement to animal feeds, sometimes being added back to fish meal to produce "whole meal."

TABLE 5

WORLD PRODUCTION OF FISH MEAL IN METRIC TONS [a]

1938	627,000
1948	571,000
1952, 1953, 1954 average	995,500
1955, 1956, 1957 average	1,198,400
1958	1,396,000
1960	1,955,800
1961	2,496,000
1962	2,885,000
1963	2,890,000
1964	3,660,000
1965	3,549,000
1966	4,196,500
1967	4,500,000
1968	4,802,000 [b]

[a] Source: Food and Agriculture Organization of the United Nations
[b] Estimate

There has been a phenomenal rise in the use of fish meal throughout the world in recent years. From a production of 571,000 metric tons in 1948, production increased eight and a half times by 1968 to about 4.8 million tons. The proportion of the world fish catch used for meal in 1948 was less than 8 per cent, rising to 14 per cent eight years later and to a level of about a third of the total catch in 1966. The price of fish meal before World War II was $30 to $40 per ton. By

1948 this had risen to $125, and in 1969 it ranged from about $150 to $195 per ton, depending on season and market.

This worldwide surge in demand for fish meal has been made against strong, sometimes bitter opposition. That this opposition should exist in the face of the obvious benefits in making better use of the desperately needed resources of the sea and in the creation of new food and new wealth, is only one more illustration that man is the world's most baffling and inconsistent animal.

Opposition to the use of fish for reduction to meal often takes this tack: By transforming fish into meal, costs are raised. More important, fish meal is fed to chickens and pigs, and only a fraction of the food value is passed on to human beings. It is cheaper and more efficient to feed fresh fish to people. Hence it is immoral and it should be illegal to manufacture fish meal.

This argument is a complex mixture of the truth and of blind sentimentality. It is true that costs are raised when fish is processed, and that there is loss of energy, protein, and other nutrients when it is cycled through chickens and pigs on its way to the human belly. But most of life's goals are reached by zigzag paths. The day will never come when mankind can use all fishes just as they come from the sea, wasting nothing by processing or by transforming the fishes to other kinds of flesh. The manufacture of fish meal permits the utilization of fishes that cannot be used in any other way at the present state of our skill.

The efficiency of conversion of food value by farm animals is already good and it is increasing as agricultural research progresses. When fish meal is added to a hen's ration, it lays eggs or grows to a plump broiler more rapidly, and with a recovery of food value higher than the rule-of-thumb 10 per cent usually used in calculations of transfer from one trophic level to another. A hen's recovery of energy from fish meal ranges from about 20 to 25 per cent of the calories; for proteins it is a high 40 to 50 per cent; and for the all-important essential amino acids it is even greater. Turkeys, pigs, and other farm animals also do good jobs of conversion.

It was pointed out earlier that more than a third of the broilers produced in the United States can be attributed to fish meal. In 1964, for example, fish were responsible for some 720,425 broilers on American tables; to this should be added substantial numbers of turkeys, pigs, and other food animals. Similar results are produced in Germany, in Japan, and in many other countries. In the face of such figures the argument that fish should be fed to humans instead of animals, implying that beasts are being fed at the expense of people, misses the point.

Humans probably will continue indefinitely to benefit from feeding

FIGURE 9.1. *Laboratory-scale production of fish protein concentrate at Belts-ville, Maryland. Storage kettles hold isopropyl alcohol, used as a solvent to remove fat from the groundfish—one of the principal steps in the manufacture of FPC.*

Bureau of Commercial Fisheries

fish to farm animals. Yet, in the face of a desperate and worsening shortage of food throughout the world, men should learn to use directly as human food as much as possible of the fish now fed to livestock. We may be on the threshold of such a development. It is possible now to produce high-quality fish meal and tasteless, odorless (or suitably flavored) fish protein concentrate (FPC) acceptable to many palates.

There are two principal barriers to rapid and widespread use of edible fish meal and FPC. The first of these is technological and economic: methods available are still relatively costly for most markets. The second barrier is psychological: they are unfamiliar foods, and therefore, in the minds of many people, unacceptable. Both of these situations can be changed—the first relatively easily and quickly, in direct proportion to the amount of effort put into research and development; the second only slowly and painfully, since human prejudice is far less amenable to manipulation than machines or chemicals.

Fish meal can be made for human food by the same methods as those used to make the meal now sold by the millions of tons for animal feed. But so much more care must be taken in its manufacture, and the cost is therefore so much higher, that this approach is probably not feasible. The raw material must be delivered fresher to the plants than is now usually done; the work must be conducted more hygienically and at a lower temperature than is common. Such edible fish meal is highly nutritious, but it has very little appeal to most palates, since its odor and flavor are strong. In the future it may be possible to improve the manufacture of fish meal sufficiently and to conduct energetic campaigns to persuade people to eat it. This would be a cheap and satisfactory method of improving the nutrition of mankind, but it will be long in coming, if it ever does.

A much more likely possibility is that the use of fish protein concentrate, or "fish flour," will be greatly increased. This is a whitish powder with high animal protein and mineral contents, a nutritionally well balanced amino acid composition, and a low fat content. It can be made tasteless and odorless if this is required by its consumers; it can have a fish flavor if this is preferred. It must be made with a process different from and more expensive than that used for fish meal.

FPC has some exceptionally weighty credentials as food for humans. It is nutritious and wholesome; two ounces contain as much animal protein as a twelve-ounce steak. It can be shipped and stored in cheap containers without refrigeration; in Canada herring flour has been stored in polyethylene bags for three years without noticeable change in flavor. It is acceptable in a variety of foods in many parts of the world. It is already moderately cheap and it will become cheaper.

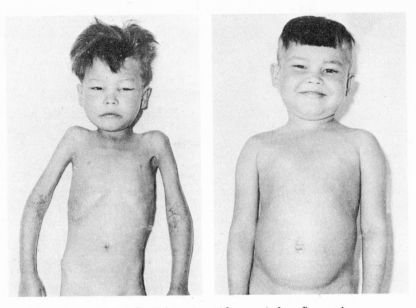

FIGURES 9.2A & B. *Dramatic evidence of the effects of protein deficiency on the health of children, and of the beneficial results from relatively small additions of protein to the diet. This eight-year-old boy at the Hospital for the Society for the Protection of Children in Guatemala suffered from kwashiorkor, a widespread protein-deficiency disease. The boy made the dramatic recovery shown here after eight weeks of a diet of Incaparina, a vegetable-protein mixture. Animal protein, including fish protein concentrate, has equally favorable results and in fact supplies some of the essential amino acids lacking in many plant proteins.*

UNICEF Photo

At least 500 million people throughout the world are short of proteins, but 5 million tons of FPC could supply them with enough animal protein for a year. Made into fish protein concentrate, the unharvested fish of the United States coastal waters alone could raise significantly the nutritional standard of 1 billion people for 300 days.

Despite all this, there is no substantial commercial production of FPC anywhere in the world. This is largely because it is a new and unfamiliar material, and men are afraid of strange things.

FPC has had a difficult youth in the United States. Perhaps this is because ours is a country, unlike a considerable portion of the rest of the world, with very little need for new, cheap sources of animal protein.

The opposition of greatest consequence has been to the sale for human food of fish protein concentrate manufactured from whole fish. This opposition has been important because it came from the United States Food and Drug Administration, whose word on such matters is law and whose edicts produce repercussions in the rest of the world. The Food and Drug Administration has served the people of the United States well by protecting them against unscrupulous or careless manufacturers of drugs and processors of food; it has undoubtedly saved countless lives and dollars. But in the case of FPC made from whole fish the FDA has been wrong. Until early in 1967 it argued that such a product, containing as it does scales, fins, and entrails of fish, as well as the muscles and other parts of the body, would be "aesthetically unacceptable" and could not be sold in this country for human consumption. But the American public eats canned sardines and other fishes, entrails and all; it greedily swallows oysters and clams without cutting out any parts of them; it consumes a great many other foods that are truly "unaesthetic" if they are viewed in a detached and dispassionate manner. FPC, on the other hand, is wholesome and no more objectionable to the unprejudiced palate than a chicken leg or a spoonful of boiled spinach. The FDA came under heavy fire from nutritionists, biologists, members of Congress, and government groups for its stand, and it eventually retreated.

Research by scientists of the Bureau of Commercial Fisheries confirmed FPC's low level of toxicity (content of fluoride) and high nutritive value. These results were important in persuading the Food and Drug Administration to change its position, as was a strong stand taken by the Advisory Committee on Marine Protein Resources of the National Academy of Sciences.

One reason that FPC is more expensive to make than fish meal is that a greater proportion of the fat must be removed. Fat and its decomposition products are the principal causes of objectionable odors and flavors, and the length of time the product can be stored before use depends heavily on low fat content to prevent it from becoming rancid. Thus, in the manufacture of FPC, processes must be employed to remove nearly all the fat. For example, the pioneer VioBin process uses ethylene dichloride, and the method developed by the Bureau of Commercial Fisheries (BCF) in its laboratory at College Park, Maryland, employs isopropyl alcohol. The fish used by the BCF is red hake, *Urophycis chuss,* a cheap and abundant species caught on the Atlantic coast of the United States. It is sold only in small amounts in this country, since it is too small and too soft to fillet, freeze, or can.

[137]

To make FPC by the Bureau process, whole fish are minced and treated three times with separate batches of isopropyl alcohol, once cold and twice hot. The alcohol extracts water as well as fat, and the residue of fish is dried, ground, and packaged. One hundred thousand pounds of raw hake yield 15,000 pounds of fish protein concentrate— a ratio of about 6 to 1. The concentrate is a white powder with a yellowish cast. It contains 80 per cent protein, 13.5 per cent ash (mostly calcium, phosphorus, and other minerals), and has virtually no odor or flavor. If the fish were bought for 1 cent a pound, a plant with a daily capacity of fifty tons of raw fish could probably produce this flour at 13.9 cents a pound and sell it at a profit for 20 cents a pound. If two extractions instead of three were sufficient (that is, if the market would accept a small residue of fat in the product and thus a faint fish taste) the selling price per pound would be about 13.5 cents. Canadian technologists estimate that FPC from herring would cost 15 cents a pound to manufacture in their country. In other parts of the world the selling price would be about the same as for dried skim milk, and in most countries fish protein concentrate could probably be produced more cheaply per unit of protein than any other animal material.

Fish protein concentrate is already highly acceptable to many people, especially children. Adults, with the usual stubborn adherence to the ways and tastes developed in youth, take to it much less readily, as they do to any other new product. But the Food and Agriculture Organization and the Children's Fund of the United Nations have carried out tests in thirty or more countries—often with encouraging success.

FPC can be used in a great many ways: in breads, pastas (that is, macaroni, spaghetti, and similar products), cakes, cookies, sauces, cereals, pastries, candy, soups, baby foods, and beverages. If a neutral bland product is required, without taste or odor (for markets in Europe, the Americas, and India), it can be produced; various strengths and kinds of fish flavors can be added for markets in central and southern African countries and those in Southeast Asia. With additives, fish flour can even be made to taste like cheese or beef.

Chile started testing FPC as early as 1958. Children in Santiago schools like bread made with an FPC content of 7 to 10 per cent. At the upper limit the color of the bread was affected, and above that the flavor was noticeable, but it will be remembered from the experiments with poultry that amounts of fish meal considerably less than 10 per cent were remarkably effective in improving nutrition, and with children similarly small proportions had beneficial effects.

In Kuala Lumpur, Malaya, children fed a standard diet enriched with skim-milk solids showed twice the rate of gain in growth as those without the milk; better still, those fed a standard diet supplemented with cookies made of FPC, cereal, sugar, and flavoring showed a *triple* gain. Moreover, the children (but not their parents) liked the cookies. In Senegal foods containing fish protein concentrate were successfully fed to children. In Burma it has been incorporated into soups, sauces, and vegetable dishes with high acceptability. In the Belgian Congo and in Ghana FPC was in good demand when the price was kept low by subsidy; later it was commercially successful at competitive prices.

In Mexico Dr. Federico Gomez carried out several years of experiments in the Hospital Infantil in Mexico City, and in Tlaltizipan, with impressive results. In 1960 he declared that "10 to 15 years after supplementation with 30-40 grams [about 1 to 1.5 ounces] of animal protein in the form of fish flour to the daily Mexican diet of corn, beans, and chili, the characteristics of Mexican people will change physically, mentally, and emotionally."

Sweden and the Union of South Africa have FPC plants in operation. The United States established a pilot-scale plant in Grays Harbor, Washington, in 1969.

The U.S. Agency for International Development (AID) has launched a vigorous campaign to persuade people in developing countries to eat FPC despite their reluctance to try strange foods. The first step in this program is to get an insight into consumer psychology in several countries (including Brazil, the Philippines, Korea, Thailand, and India), then to launch a campaign that will encourage voluntary use of FPC on a scale sufficient to support a profitable industry.

When the world is ready to accept it, immense amounts of FPC can be manufactured. A great proportion of the fish now landed and consumed in various fresh or processed forms is suitable for this purpose. Obviously no one is going to close the salmon canneries of British Columbia and Alaska, or the fillet and fish stick freezers of New England, and convert them into FPC factories, and highly regarded species such as halibut, sole, red snapper, shad, and others will continue to be marketed in their present forms. But more than a third of the world fish catch is now used to make fish meal, and all the same fish could theoretically be made into fish flour.

It is unlikely that all fish meal plants will be converted for fish protein concentrate, but once a demand is created and handling methods are improved, such huge stocks as the Peruvian anchovetta (now harvested at the rate of 22.5 billion pounds a year) would be suitable for making fish protein concentrate. Next door, Chile has pro-

FIGURE 9.2C. *Anchovies concentrated in the bunt of a purse seine off the coast of Peru. This enormous catch will be scooped aboard the boat, taken to plants nearby, and transformed into fish meal, Peru's leading export item.*

Pesca

duced 22 million pounds of anchovettas. At its peak the California sardine fishery produced 1.5 billion pounds. Whether it will ever do so again apparently depends on whether the ocean off California and adjacent areas warms up again to the sardines' liking, and whether they can shoulder their way back into a living space lost to the anchovies when their numbers dwindled. But if the sardines do come back, they would make millions of tons of good FPC. The menhaden industry of the United States Atlantic and Gulf of Mexico waters has produced as much as 2.25 billion pounds of fish. The Alaska herring populations produced 261 million pounds at their peak, and even this may have been less than the stocks could sustain. The British Columbia herring fishery peaked at 96 million pounds. In South Africa 880 million pounds of pilchard are landed in some years for the fish meal plants; in South-West Africa the peak amount has been nearly 1.5 billion pounds; in Angola, 238 million pounds. And so the roster grows.

These figures are taken from maximum catches of fisheries exploited now at varying levels: some fully exploited like that of the Peruvian anchovy, some overexploited like that of the California sardine, some underexploited to various unknown degrees. Of course, it is mis-

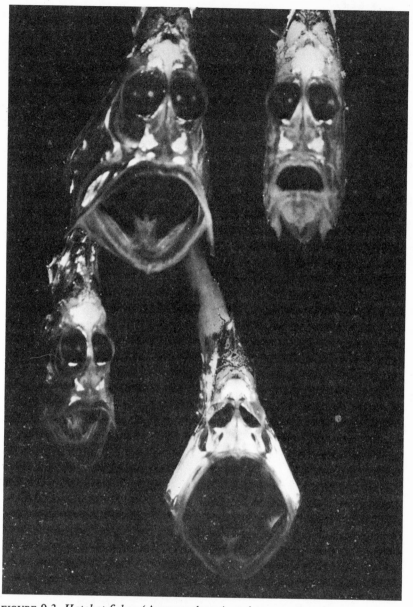

FIGURE 9.3. *Hatchet fishes* (Argyropelecus) *and many other deep-sea species could be made into fish protein concentrate if methods of catching them economically could be devised.*

Photograph by Paul A. Zahl, © National Geographic Society

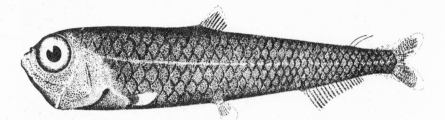

FIGURE 9.4. *The blacksmelt* (Bathylagus euryops) *is one of the numerous deep-sea fishes not presently used by man that would make good fish meal and FPC.*

Fisheries Research Board of Canada

leading to quote maximum catches as though these were the amounts available every year from their respective areas, and greatest catches may represent unusually favorable years instead of average years, or years when overfishing occurred. But some inkling of the immense total potential is gained in this way, and by no means all the fishable stocks have been included in the list above.

There are also stocks of fish whose existence is known but whose size can only be guessed, since fishing has not tested them. Estimates here may be very inaccurate, but judging from previous experience, assessments are more likely to err on the conservative side than otherwise. This is to be expected, since what is not seen is not counted.

In California alone there may be 30 billion pounds of anchovies, hake, lanternfishes, deep-sea smelt, and other species now unused. From one quarter to one half—probably closer to the latter—of this quantity of fish is available on a sustained-yield basis. There are millions of pounds of hake and smaller but substantial quantities of other species to be taken off the coasts of Argentina and other southern South American coasts. West African nations are just beginning to exploit the fish off their coasts, and there are millions of pounds to be had there on a sustained basis. The total for these and dozens of other fish stocks over the world is impressive.

Another enormous resource, the squids, might also contribute great supplies of fish meal or FPC. Less is known about squids than about many other sea creatures; because relatively few people eat them, they have not been studied sufficiently. But it is clear from a few isolated fisheries and from limited scientific investigations that the sea contains enormous quantities of them.

Squids are popular food in some parts of the world, notably

Japan and southern Europe. Fisheries exist in waters off Hokkaido (the northern island of Japan), off Newfoundland, in the Mediterranean, and in a few other places. Japan landed 14.4 billion pounds in 1963, and its stocks of squids may be no larger than some others in various parts of the world. It is certain that vastly greater quantities could be caught worldwide. This is largely a matter of developing markets. One large market would be created by the manufacture of meal and protein concentrate from squids.

The protein of squids is of high quality, nearly equal to that of fish. They have a strong advantage over many other animals in the large proportion of edible parts of the whole body: 80 per cent compared to 40 to 70 per cent for fish. The water content of squid flesh is about the same as that of white fish meat, ranging from 70 to 80 per cent. The oil content of the flesh is low, ranging from 1 to 1.5 per cent.

On my desk I have meal made from squids by the American Vio-Bin process, containing 77.6 per cent protein, 10.2 per cent ash, 9.0 per cent moisture and 1.9 per cent fat. It is a tan powder, like very fine beach sand, with a faint fishy odor. There is no reason to doubt that it would be an excellent supplement to either animal or human diets deficient in animal protein.

Of course, there is an eventual limit to the amount of fish, and even squids, that can be brought to shore. At that point the only place to go, if mankind is to get more food from the sea, is down one or more steps in the oceanic food pyramid, to exploit zooplankton. The quantities available are enormously larger than those of the nearly untouched squids, or even of the swarming little fishes that have formed the basis

FIGURE 9.5. *A deck-load of menhaden, following extraordinarily successful fishing. The vessel is steaming toward the fish meal plant, followed by flocks of birds seeking their share of the catch.*

Edw. W. Renneberg & Sons Co., Baltimore

FIGURE 9.6. *A large catch of Pacific hake in a floating trawl. These very abundant fish are not used by North American fishermen to any great extent, although the Russians and the Japanese prize them. They could be made into fish meal and FPC.*

Bureau of
Commercial Fisheries

for the greatly expanded landings of recent years. The chance of harvesting plankton was discussed in detail in Chapter 4, and the conclusion was reached that although it looked unlikely that man could soon make use of most of these resources, some of the larger animal-plankton organisms, notably the antarctic krill and the red crabs of the eastern Pacific, seemed promising. Fantastic totals of millions of tons of krill may be available in far-southern waters, and the Soviets have shown that nutritious meal can be made from this raw material. Enormous quantities of red crabs are likewise available for capture off California and northern Mexico.

Thus we are not short of raw material for fish meal and fish flour. If we have the skill to produce acceptable products and to catch the animals cheaply, we have the opportunity to supply immense quantities of human food.

10 *The Worldwide Outlook For More Fish*

The ocean as a whole can be made to yield far more food than at present, but the potential increase varies substantially from region to region. Some areas are already so heavily fished that any increase in production can only come in the form of minor species for which no market yet exists or through the restoration of stocks that have been depleted by overexploitation. In other areas, where natural productivity is poor due to unfavorable hydrographic conditions, the increase in catches will be small no matter how heavily they are fished. But not a single area is yet being exploited to the limit of its potential, and in many instances much larger catches are possible.

Whether these potentials, great and small, are ever realized depends on the demand for food from the sea and the consequent development of technology to harvest, process, and distribute it. While it is impossible to predict the exact shape of the future, it seems certain that substantial and perhaps startling technological improvements will be made. It is also impossible to predict just how large the potential increases may be, since surveys for most parts of the world ocean are either incomplete or totally lacking. Nevertheless, enough trustworthy data have been accumulated to permit fairly confident predictions of which areas are most likely to provide the largest increases in fish production.

Some areas have been exploited heavily for a long time, and consequently have approached the limit of their productivity more closely than others. These include the northeast Atlantic (the traditional fishing grounds of Europe), the northwest Atlantic (including the Grand Banks and other areas off the North American continent), and the northwest Pacific (principally the well-strained waters off Japan). Other regions of the sea offer rich potentials for increased fish production because of their high productivity and because they have so far been lightly exploited: these include the eastern North Pacific, the western coasts of South America and Africa and parts of the Indian Ocean. The southwest Atlantic, the Caribbean Sea, the deep sea, and the Antarctic offer unknown but perhaps substantial promise.

Since prehistoric times Europeans have fished with ever-rising intensity, especially in areas like the North Sea, close to ancient centers of population. Over the centuries the landings from the northeast Atlantic have risen steadily except for two breaks during the World Wars, when military activity prevented full-scale fishing. Following World War II landings increased sharply, mostly because of the Soviet Union's entry into the field. Between 1938 and 1955 total catches rose from 2.6 million metric tons to 7 million metric tons, but there the increase stopped, despite an uninterrupted rise in the amount of fishing, which was seven times as high in 1966 as in 1946. Species that are probably overexploited, at least in parts of the area, include cod, haddock, and ocean perch. Several other popular fishes may be at or beyond the level of maximum sustained yield, and no stocks of large bottom-living fishes are still unexploited.

But even in the northeast Atlantic, where many observers have suggested that little increase in production can be expected, yields may be even richer than in the past. Some additional increase in the size of catches will come from relaxation of overzealous fishing pressure on such species as plaice and cod. And there are still species of fishes that are under-used because no satisfactory means of processing and consuming them has been developed. The Norwegians have recently greatly increased their catches of mackerel and capelin. Other species promising greater production include saithe, whiting, argentines, skates, sandeels, and squids. The potential catch from the region of all species combined is perhaps 15 million tons, compared to a 1966 catch of 9.25 million tons. Most of the increase will come in catches of pelagic (mid-water) species.

Across the Atlantic Ocean, in waters off the North American continent and around Greenland, fishing was carried out by European nations before the history of the region commenced. There is good evidence that Basque fishermen visited the Grand Banks before Columbus

FIGURE 10.1. *Lobster fisherman at Canso, Nova Scotia, leaving in early morning to haul up his traps, like those stacked on the dock in the foreground. This fishery is one of the oldest and most valuable in the waters of eastern Canada and New England.*

Department of Fisheries and Forestry of Canada

came to San Salvador Island in the Bahamas. And when the French explorer Jacques Cartier sailed past St. Pierre near Newfoundland in 1536, he passed "many ships" of the fishermen of France. European fishermen have found it worthwhile to make the long voyage across the ocean ever since—first to catch the cod, which salted well; later to catch haddock and ocean perch, which froze well, and herring and other species, all in great abundance.

Landings in this area have risen steadily, and in the last decade fishing effort has increased between two and three times. This has put great pressure on some favored species, to the extent that most haddock stocks are fully exploited or overfished, as are those of cod, ocean perch, silver hake, halibut, salmon, and others. In the early 1960's the Soviets began to fish herring and silver hake, and as a result landings in the Gulf of Maine more than doubled in five years. From the southern end

[147]

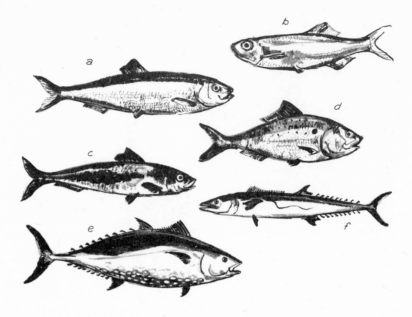

a. Herring (1/4)	c. Pilchard (1/4)	e. Tuna (1/15)
b. Anchovy (1/2)	d. Menhaden (1/6)	f. Pacific Mackerel (1/7)

Pelagic species (fractions give ratio of drawing to average life size).

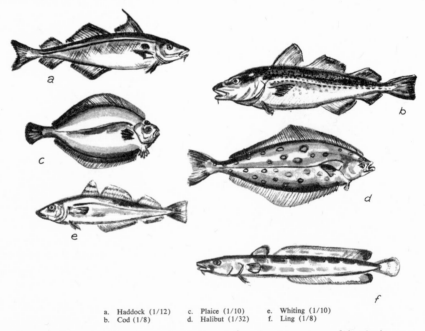

a. Haddock (1/12)	c. Plaice (1/10)	e. Whiting (1/10)
b. Cod (1/8)	d. Halibut (1/32)	f. Ling (1/8)

Demersal species (fractions give ratio of drawing to average life size).

FIGURE 10.2. *Some of the many species of commercially important fishes, mostly from the North Atlantic region.*

C. H. Blair and W. D. Ansel, *A Guide to Fishing Boats and Their Gear* of the Nova Scotia shelf to the Hudson Canyon it has been estimated that there are 1,373 million pounds of spiny dogfish, of which 400 million pounds could be caught annually on a sustained basis. There are also several species of skates, which in sum constitute a population of 1,438 million pounds. At present there is no market for these fish, so they are ignored. Nor is there a market for squids, whose standing crop is estimated at 700 million pounds. If demand were developed these animals could provide vast sources of protein.

Three kinds of fishes—the capelin, the lantern fish, and the sand lance—offer promise of greatly increased catches. Lantern fishes live mostly in the deep sea and have been inaccessible to fishing gear; their harvest will be difficult and their demand is nonexistent at the moment. But capelins and sand lances are already caught in some parts of the world. Sand lances (*Ammodytes*) in particular are enormously abundant, and they would make a good fish meal or FPC. Their larvae are more than one hundred times as abundant as those of the cod and more than two hundred times as abundant as those of the haddock, the species supporting the largest and the fourth largest fisheries of the region. The potential catch of sand lances may be millions of tons a year.

Thus, while the familiar fishes in the northwest Atlantic may be capable of only slight expansion in catches, altogether a doubling of production may be possible by using the neglected species.

The northwestern Pacific is a third area of the ocean that has been subjected so long and so hard to fishing that it may be approaching the limit of yield. Japan, the USSR, South and North Korea, Mainland China, and Taiwan are the major exploiters of the fishery resources in this area. These nations include some of the giants of world fishing, and their activities have made the region one of the most thoroughly exploited parts of the sea. Around the Japanese home island, for example, almost nothing that lives has escaped the fisherman's gear and the cooking pot. The Japanese eagerly consume all the fish that the Western world regards as acceptable—salmon, flounders, mackerel, tuna—but in addition they eat species that many Westerners hardly use at all: sharks, sauries, and hundreds of others. Squids and octopuses are regarded as repugnant by most North Americans but the Japanese consume over a billion pounds of them in some years. In addition they eat shrimplike creatures so small they can just be seen, slimy sea cucumbers that Westerners throw away in disgust, barnacles, seaweed, moray eels—nearly everything that the sea produces.

The long and vigorous fishing pressure has resulted in some of the most valuable stocks in the western North Pacific being overexploited: most of the salmon, all the whale, and many of the groundfish popula-

FIGURE 10.3. *The fishing boats of Taiwan are becoming more numerous and more successful each year. Here a small harpoon vessel searches for spearfish, sharks, skates, and other large fishes.*

Taiwan Information Office

tions. Herrings and sardines have shown distressing tendencies to decline. Most of the groundfish and tuna stocks are probably being fished to their full capacity.

In this area the list of species whose populations might support heavier catches is not a long one. In the north, more pollock and rockfishes might be caught; the sand lance is nearly unexploited, and could support a fish meal industry. Pomfret (*Brama*) and some other species from subarctic waters might yield moderate catches. The deep-sea lantern fishes and the squids offer possibilities for the future.

Dr. Hiroshi Kasahara, the Japanese expert on the staff of the United Nations Development Programme, says, "I believe the overall picture in this general region is fairly close to one of full utilization—the potential resources available for future expansion of the fisheries are rather limited."

In other parts of the world ocean there is more room for expansion. For example, the eastern North Pacific off the United States, Canada, Mexico, and Central America includes some of the richest areas of the world ocean, waters that have not reached their full potential.

North American fishermen in the North Pacific have been choosy in the past about the kinds of fish they were willing to catch, partly because certain species (especially salmon) were in such abundance that there was no need to spend time on anything less valuable. Other species caught traditionally have been halibut and herring in British Columbia and Alaska, sardines and tuna in California. In recent years king crabs, shrimp, and other species have been taken in Alaska, and within the last decade Japanese and Soviet trawlers have caught enormous quantities of demersal fishes in the Bering Sea: flounders, pollock, and ocean perch.

The stocks of many North Pacific species are underexploited. These include anchovies, hake, and jack mackerel in the south; flounders, sablefish, pollock, cod, rockfishes, pandalid shrimp, and tanner crabs in the north; sauries, sandeels, and squids over the whole area. Other species are capable of expansion in greater or lesser degree.

Landings by American fishermen on the Pacific Coast dipped from 1,010,000 tons in 1940 to 550,000 tons in 1968. A considerable part of this drop was due to the disappearance of the California sardines that for many years had supplied the highest landings of any fishery of the nation. This tragedy has given nightmares to fishermen, scientists, and lawmakers throughout the world, who fear their own fisheries might suffer a similar fate. Massive studies have been carried on to probe the causes of the collapse of the sardines, and out of a complicated situation an answer is emerging. It appears that cooling of the surface waters in which the sardines live combined with very heavy fishing pressure to reduce their numbers to a fraction of their former strength.

The fall of the sardine population has been coincident with a rise in the abundance of anchovies. These occupy the same ecological area as the sardines, competing with them for food. And since the virtual disappearance of the sardines there are even more anchovies—an estimated 4 to 6 million tons—in the waters off California and adjacent Mexico. This huge population might support a sustainable catch of 1,400,000 tons or even higher. At the present time the catch is fixed by law at a maximum of 5,000 tons. It is not certain that the disappearance of the sardines and the rise in prosperity of the anchovies are cause and effect, but if this is so there is a good possibility that a vigorous fishery on the anchovies would help restore the stocks of sardines.

Hake constitute a second vast population of unexploited fish off California. A standing crop of 3 million tons of this species, scarcely touched by Americans, is estimated to exist in these waters. Hake are small soft fish that have little demand in the United States market, but an Atlantic species forms the basis of the emerging fish protein concentrate industry. If American fishermen do not reap the Pacific harvest, Japanese, Russian, or Korean fishermen will—indeed they have already started.

A third sizable fishery resource off California is the jack mackerel.

These are caught in small quantities now—about 30,000 to 40,000 tons a year—but the potential is much greater. Surveys of only a part of the area where mackerel occur lead to an estimate of a 350,000-ton standing crop, and the total is probably much higher.

The above estimates are partly the results of studies of the numbers of eggs and larvae. These studies were stimulated by the disappearance of the sardines, which, even when they were supporting the biggest fishery in the United States, were outnumbered by some other fishes. Anchovies, hake, and jack mackerel supplied about 60 per cent of the eggs and larvae in the plankton hauls. The other 40 per cent were eggs and larvae of deep-sea fishes that are even less known and less exploited than these three, yet which could also support fisheries. The third ranking species (far ahead of jack mackerel, and producing 12.27 per cent of the larvae) was the deep-sea fish *Vincigerria lucetia,* unknown to fishermen, and nothing but a scientific curiosity even to biologists. Sardines ranked only fourth. Two species of lantern fishes, as unknown as *Vincigerria,* ranked fifth and sixth.

Dr. W. M. Chapman summarized the situation off the southern west coast of America this way: "The fishery resources off southern California and northern Mexico are huge and the considerable fisheries in the area are only scratching the surface of the potentials. At a minimum the total fish production of the United States can be doubled within the bounds of maximum sustainable productivity off southern California alone."

Farther north on this coast, the Japanese and Soviets have sent large and efficient fleets into the Bering Sea and the Gulf of Alaska, to the consternation of American and Canadian fishermen but to the satisfaction of the newcomers, since the harvest has been rich. This fishery did not exist until several years after the end of World War II, but by 1965 it was producing enormous quantities of groundfishes, including approximately half the flatfishes caught in the whole world. And while the Japanese and Soviet fishermen were taking the enormous harvest of 2.8 billion pounds, Americans and Canadians were catching only about 200 million pounds of the same species: ocean perch, pollock, black cod, Pacific cod, yellowfin sole.

Pandalid shrimp (mostly ocean pink shrimp, *Pandalus jordani* and *P. borealis*) exist in very large quantities in Alaskan waters—an estimated 2.3 billion pounds of standing crop. These are small shrimp and their market demand is consequently less than for the larger species from the Gulf of Mexico and the South Atlantic, so that the Alaskan fishery has been slow in developing.

The catch of Alaskan king crabs has rocketed since World War II.

The American catch in 1966 was 159 million pounds, and Japanese and Soviet fishermen catch millions more. A second crab, the tanner (*Chionoectes*) may be even more abundant than the king crab—and its fishery is barely starting.

Information is much poorer about the potential of pelagic fishes and invertebrates in the northern area. There is no doubt, however, that such species as smelt, jack mackerel, rockfishes, pomfrets, sauries, and squids are available for greatly increased production.

The area to the south, the ocean off the west coast of South America, offers considerable room for expansion of the fisheries. One of the great upwelling areas of the world ocean occurs here, enriching the surface waters with minerals swept up from the deep sea. These waters are cold, and since they are carried north in the Humboldt Current it was once thought that they originated in the Antarctic. Actually, they well up from the depths offshore to replace surface waters swept seaward by the prevailing southerly and southwesterly winds blowing off Peru and Chile. These waters, rich in nitrates and phosphates, make possible the luxuriant growth of the microscopic algae that feed the planktonic crustacea and thus support the whole food web of the sea. The quantities of minerals are enormous, and therefore so are the quantities of fishes. In particular, anchovies occur in tremendous numbers, to be counted in the billions. The anchovies support the enormous fish meal industry, which brings Peru more foreign-exchange income than any other single source.

The rise of the anchovy industry has been so dazzlingly profitable to the fishermen of Peru and Chile that they have nearly ignored the other fishery resources of their rich waters. But it will not be long before attention will be turned to such species as the tuna, bonita, and mackerel, marlin and swordfish, cod and hake, redfish, pilchard, jack, shrimp, lobster, and squid. The potential of these is unknown, but it may be very large.

The western South Atlantic Ocean includes waters from Cabo Frio in southern Brazil southward to the tip of the continent. Despite increased activity in recent years, fishing is still light in most parts of this ocean, including vast stretches of Brazil and considerable parts of Argentina and other countries.

The important species are tuna, *Sardinella,* menhaden, anchovies, and various bottom-living fishes. Very large populations of the sardine-like fishes occur in the waters of the South Atlantic, but so far they are lightly exploited. For example, the stocks of menhaden in southern Brazil appear to be large, but they are not fished at all.

In Brazil, trawlers in the southern part of the country have in-

[153]

creased their landings considerably in recent years. The chief species are hake, croakers, sea trout, and catfish. For hake especially there appears to be a large potential for expansion. The southern Brazil-Uruguay region may be one of the best croaker grounds in the world. Argentina has trawl fisheries, again principally for hake, but the best grounds appear to be underexploited.

It would appear from a theoretical point of view that the extensive Patagonian Shelf off southern Argentina should be able to support very much greater catches of fish, but experience has dampened this hope. These grounds have been compared to the North Sea because of their geographic location and physical features. The Shelf is actually larger than the North Sea and is the biggest trawlable area in the Southern Hemisphere. But the fish fauna is not rich in species—there being fewer than a third of the number that occur in the North Sea and half the number in the Gulf of Mexico—nor in abundance of any one species. Hake would support a trawl fishery, but its abundance seems to decrease sharply south of 45°S. latitude. There are moderate numbers of a crab, *Centolla*. Altogether, however, results of exploratory fishing for bottom species have been disappointing, and apparently the area does not support as large populations of fish as theoretical considerations would suppose. In addition, the remoteness from ports, and the severe weather commonly encountered in the area make exploitation of fish difficult.

It is plain that the waters of the countries from southern Brazil to Argentina are underexploited, but compared to coastal waters of the eastern edges of continents, this area will probably yield only moderately large sustained catches. As economic, legal, and social factors improve, better use of the fishery products of the area will be made and the ultimate potential may be considerably larger than our presently inadequate knowledge indicates.

The area from Cabo Frio, Brazil, north along the South American coast and extending through the Caribbean includes both regions of low productivity and others where catches and potentials are moderate to high. In general this ocean region lacks the massive overturns that bring nutrient-rich waters to the surface, and consequently it is generally low in fish production.

Shrimp are the resource of highest value in the central western Atlantic, and they are fished from the southern United States around the rim of the Caribbean, off the Guianas and Brazil. Only insignificant subsistence fisheries existed for shrimp in Brazil until recently, when a new industry developed in the southern part of the country. Most of the likely shrimp areas have been examined at least superficially, with the possible exception of some of the more remote sections of the coast of Brazil.

There are large unexploited populations of small shrimp called seabobs (*Xiphopenaeus kroyeri*), and greatly increased catches of these can be made. But the market for seabobs is much weaker than that for the bigger individuals of the several species of *Penaeus,* and this resource will remain underexploited as long as the demand remains at its present low level.

Although tuna represent one of the largest fishery resources of the western South Atlantic, their commercial exploitation is of surprisingly recent origin. It was not until 1957, when Japanese long-liners first appeared in the tropical Atlantic, that this fishery was conducted with any degree of intensity. Before that there was only a small fishery in Cuba and insignificant, unorganized fisheries in various places along the coasts of both the Americas. The Japanese are still the most active tuna fishermen in the area, but Koreans, Formosans, and Americans are beginning to operate more vigorously. Tuna catches have leveled off in this region in recent years. In 1957 Japanese vessels caught approximately 15,000 metric tons. This increased steadily until 1964, when it peaked at something over 110,000 metric tons. Exploitation of the most desirable species, the yellowfins and albacore, is intensive, especially by Japanese long-line vessels, and larger catches of these species may not be possible.

Sardines support a commercial fishery in eastern Venezuela. There is room for considerable expansion of this industry since the sardines are caught by beach seine only and the fishery appears to exploit only the edge of the resource. Efficient gear like the purse seine would unquestionably take much larger catches.

Off South America bottom species can support heavier fishing. In the late 1950's it was revealed that good trawl catches could be made off the coasts of the Guianas, on the northeast coast of South America. Since then small numbers of vessels have engaged in fishing there, and more could be accommodated. Fish are available the year round, out to depths of 120 to 180 feet off various parts of the coast. In the 1960's trawlers were making good catches of sea trout, catfish, and croakers.

Farther north, off the southeastern coast of North America, menhaden support the largest fishery in the United States (at its peak, well over 2 billion pounds), but they seem to be only the third most abundant fish in the region—and they may be only the fifth. Anchovy and thread-herring stocks are certainly bigger, but they are lightly fished. They may be able to support landings of millions of pounds annually. These and other pelagic species (including squids) undoubt-

FIGURE 10.4. *Primitive fish processing in Central America. On a temporary platform built over shallow water off the coast of British Honduras, fishermen salt their catch of black grouper for the Lenten market of Guatemala and their own country.*

C. P. Idyll

edly represent the greatest unexploited fishery resources of the region.

Across the Atlantic, off the west coast of Africa, there exists a rich area of ocean that has been grossly underexploited until recently. Africa lies largely in the tropics and the subtropics, where cooling of surface waters never takes place. But the west coast, like the west coasts of other continents, is enriched by the action of the prevailing offshore winds, which skim off surface waters and replace them with rich up-wellings. The areas of enrichment support large populations of several commercially valuable fishes.

The countries of Africa have high human populations and very inadequate supplies of protein. Animal diseases, chiefly trypanosomiasis, carried by the notorious tsetse fly, make it difficult to raise cattle. Fish is a major supplier of animal protein, but in the past much of it has been imported. Nigeria, for example, is one of the greatest consumers of Norwegian salted fish.

Up to about a decade ago the canoe fishermen of twenty countries from Senegal to Nigeria scarcely ventured beyond the surf line. They were active enough, however, to bring most near-shore fish stocks to full exploitation, and now a vigorous exploitation of the offshore waters has begun. In addition to African vessels, ships from Japan, the USSR, France, Portugal, Italy, Spain, Poland, Greece, Israel, Formosa, and Korea are there in large numbers.

[156]

In the mid-1960's an estimated 250 trawlers were operating the year round on the banks off Mauritania, Senegal, and the Spanish Sahara alone. Other areas are less heavily fished, but Russian factory trawlers and ships from other nations are fishing parts of the continental shelf. The richest trawling grounds are areas of northern and southern upwellings. There are less productive regions off Nigeria to Cape Lopez, and off southern Liberia and the western Ivory Coast.

On the northern part of the African west coast, fishing has already imposed a heavy exploitation on the most valuable bottom-living species. Despite this, considerable expansion is probably possible, especially for some species presently less popular and for some heavily fished species, provided management is applied to avoid the waste caused by overfishing. This management will have to be exceptionally skillful to balance the requirements of different species and different national fisheries.

Pelagic species also show much greater promise of supporting expanding fisheries. Pilchard, anchovies, sardines, scad, jack mackerel, horse mackerel, and squids occur in considerable quantities. Two to five times present catches may be possible. Tuna have been caught with such vigor in the few years since this fishery started in the 1950's that they may already have reached the limit of their productivity.

Altogether, the west coast of Africa north of the Congo may be able to support 3.5 to 5 million tons of production a year, compared to 1.3 million in 1968, while the southern area has potential for considerably increased catches of pelagic species.

If western Africa offers one of the most hopeful areas of the world ocean for expansion of fish production, the other side of the continent promises much less. Although East Africa has been occupied for centuries by Arabian, Indian, and Chinese adventurers, its fisheries are still at a primitive level. The traditional vessels are the ngalawa—a crude dugout canoe with an outrigger—and two somewhat larger types of vessels, the mashua and the dhow. Few advanced vessels are in use here even today.

The middle east coast of Africa has three disadvantages in respect to oceanic production: it lies in the tropics, so that there is no upwelling of deep water caused by the cooling of the surface; it lacks the prevailing offshore winds that induce upwellings on the west coast of continents; and it has a narrow continental shelf. Besides being small, the shelf off East Africa is rough with coral, especially in the northern section. The coral tears up nets, with the result that trawling, normally one of the cheapest methods of fishing, is difficult and expensive in this area. More trawl fishing is possible in the southern part of the area, and

[157]

the Gulf of Aden also offers promise. Shrimp and prawns are caught in nearly all the river deltas; these are underexploited but the extent of this resource is unknown. Sardinella are caught off Tanzania; sharks and other fishes, over the whole coast. Even if the ultimate potential of this area is hazy, and if it is likely to be smaller than for many other regions of the ocean, an increase in landings is possible.

Development of fisheries in other parts of the Indian Ocean has been equally as slow as in the case of the East African fisheries, despite the existence of civilization from ancient times in the countries around this ocean. Compared to the Atlantic and the Pacific, the Indian Ocean produces only about one fifth of the catch per unit area. This is partly due to a low level of technological development, but it may also be a consequence of relatively low productivity of some of these waters. Only in very recent years, following the researches conducted in the course of the International Indian Ocean Expedition of 1959–1965, have any extensive oceanographic data been available.

The continental shelf is narrow around most of the Indian Ocean, occupying only about a quarter to a fifth of the areas of shelf in the Pacific and Atlantic oceans. Thus the shallow area of high fish produc-

FIGURE 10.5. *Beach-seine fishing in Mullativu, Ceylon. All over the Indian Ocean dugout canoes, like those seen in the background, operate primitive gear. Modern methods of catching and distributing fish can probably increase production substantially.*

Food and Agriculture Organization

tion and easy fishing is much reduced proportionately, making supplies of fish low and their harvest difficult. Add to these problems a deficiency of oxygen, which sometimes occurs in bottom waters, and frequent red tides that kill fish in large quantities, and the area presents severe restrictions to fish populations.

Commercial catches from the Indian Ocean are dominated by pelagic species. The bottom dwellers—cod, haddock, whiting, saithe, sole, halibut, flounders—that form the backbone of fisheries of the temperate Atlantic and Pacific oceans are conspicuously scarce. In the western Indian Ocean the oil sardine, the Indian mackerel, the Bombay duck, and other pelagic fishes support most of the catch.

Yet the Indian Ocean, especially the Arabian Sea, can supply far more fish than it does now. On the basis of primary productivity it has been estimated that this ocean can produce 10 million metric tons of fish —compared to less than 1 million produced in the late 1960's. The minimum potential increase seems to be about four times the present catch, while for the west coast of India one biologist has calculated a twenty-five-fold potential to be possible.

Other areas appear to offer less promise than the Arabian Sea but still to be underexploited. The Bay of Bengal can probably produce a minimum of two and a half times the present catch of bottom-living fishes, while the east coast of Thailand is nearly unfished. Indian Ocean waters off Indonesia and the west coast of Australia need only more active fishing for significant increases in catch, especially of pelagic fishes like sardines, anchovies, mackerel, and skipjack tuna. In the Red Sea and the Persian Gulf catches could be considerably higher.

There is also a way in which exploitation could be increased worldwide. The fishes that inhabit the deep sea are usually ignored in discussions of ways to increase food yields from the ocean, probably because they are totally unfamiliar to the general public and hence in no demand. Certainly they are hard to catch, making their potential difficult to realize. But some species come toward the surface at night, and others rise to the very top. Here they have been seen in large numbers at times, encouraging the belief that they represent a very large potential of human food. For example, Michael Graham, the dean of British fishery biologists, says there are enormous populations of black scabbard fishes in the Atlantic, which can be used if methods of harvest can be devised. Among the commonest kinds of deep-sea animals are the lantern fishes. The British weather ship *Weather Observer,* returning to Glasgow from a period of duty at sea, steamed through lantern fishes for five hours one night. Lantern fishes are the main item of diet of the great herds of sea lions inhabiting the Pribilof Islands of Alaska.

FIGURE 10.6. *Skipjack tuna,* Katsuwonus pelamis, *one of the abundant open-ocean fishes. Skipjacks are caught in large quantities in the warm oceans of the world by American, Japanese, and other fishermen.*

Bureau of Commercial Fisheries, Biological Laboratory, Honolulu

Another little-known fish, the deep-sea smelt, *Bathylagus,* is the principal food of a famous Pribilof Island inhabitant, the fur seal. Millions of fur seals haul up on the islands during the mating season, protected and exploited by the United States, Canada, the USSR, and Japan. The quantities of deep-sea smelts eaten by this one predator are astonishing, amounting to more than the combined commercial catch of Canadian and American fishermen of all species in the area during the 1940's—and most fishermen do not even know the deep-sea smelts exist.

Yet neither the scabbard fishes, the lantern fishes, nor the smelts are the most abundant of such species. The bristlemouths, *Cyclothone,* are the commonest deep-sea fishes, and they may even be the most abundant fish in the whole ocean. If so, they must occur in enormous numbers, since herring, sardines, menhaden, and other clupeoids swarm in incredible numbers in some parts of the sea. Hence bristlemouths, which most people have never heard of, must exist in the billions. They are small, and this has caused even those who knew of their existence to disregard them as commercial potential. With the development of fish protein concentrate the possibility of using the bristlemouths and many other deep-sea species seems more promising. But men must first learn to catch them, and the problem seems formidable at the moment.

In the Antarctic enormous blooms of phytoplankton in the spring support equally impressive populations of zooplankton. Curiously, about half the weight of zooplankton consists of krill, *Euphausia superba.* Tens of millions of tons (and perhaps far more) of these are available for harvest. This potential source of animal protein is discussed in Chapter 4.

The chance of large catches of fish in the Antarctic does not seem promising. Some codlike species appear in the summer on the shallows around the South Shetland and South Orkney islands, and deep-water myctophids are abundant in some regions. But fishing would be restricted to the short summer (December to April) and would have to be done under difficult conditions. Squids are numerous and could probably support a sizable fishery.

The great uncertainty expressed throughout this chapter about the fishery potentials of the various parts of the ocean results from ignorance of the sizes of stocks, lack of knowledge about future demands for seafood—especially those types now unfamiliar—and inability to gauge the future rate of technological advances in fish harvesting. Yet, notwithstanding the mist that all these factors cast in front of the picture, it is possible to see clearly that millions of tons of additional seafood can be taken from the sea each year.

11 *Fishing, Now and in the Future*

Despite the contribution that can be made by aquaculture and other techniques, most of the extra bounty from the sea will come from fishing, as it has in the past. This is the "primitive" hunting of wild stocks that has been so roundly scorned but that may be highly sophisticated after all. The principal task facing man is to improve his skills in the hunt even more than he has in recent years.

A common but misleading statement is that we are using the same gear to catch fish that the ancients used a thousand, even two thousand, years ago. But there is only a slight resemblance between the hand-thrown spear of primitive man and the explosive harpoon gun of the modern whaler. A single hook dangled on the end of a yard or so of line, as depicted on Egyptian tombs, is a far cry from the fifty-mile baited lines of the Japanese tuna fleets. The swatch of netting used by ancient fishermen bears no more resemblance to the complicated, three-quarter-mile purse seines than a stone hoe does to the enormous cultivators of an Iowa farmer.

And there are new fishing aids that were never dreamed of a thousand or even a hundred years ago, including echo sounders that permit the hunter to find and track his prey from thousands of feet away, and electrical devices that actually force fish to swim into his nets.

There have been more improvements in fishing methods and gear since World War II than in all the previous history of mankind. In fish-

[162]

ing, as in other industries, the process of change itself has been systematized and institutionalized. Improvements once made mainly through slow and wasteful trial and error are now made by biologist experts in fish behavior, who combine their efforts with those of skilled fishermen and mechanical and electrical engineers to bring about much more rapid and more effective technical innovations. In addition, most of the major sea-fishing nations have well-equipped and well-staffed research laboratories for designing and testing new devices. Experiments with new ideas and gear are carried out on ships attached to these institutions. The result is that fishing boats are now better designed, bigger, and more rugged; their deck equipment is more highly mechanized, and their navigational devices are sharper. The gear on these vessels is made of better materials; it is stronger, larger, better designed, and altogether more efficient. The fishermen themselves are more skillful. And the rate of technical change is likely to increase in the years ahead, reducing still further the resemblance between modern fishing and that of a thousand years—or even of a generation—ago.

Fishing consists of two phases of operation: detection of the prey (sometimes including attraction to the gear) and the actual capture. Of these, detection is often the harder and more time-consuming. Thus, increasing the efficiency of the detection process is the key. Improvements will substantially reduce the cost of fishing, thereby making it economically possible to exploit the food resources of the sea more fully.

In the past, fishermen were obliged to work blind, groping for their prey beneath the surface of a nearly opaque sea. In most waters fish are hidden from view if they are but a few yards beneath the surface, especially when they are some distance ahead of the boat. More often than not the fisherman who is obliged to depend on his eyesight will pass near a school without spotting it. Yet until very recent times the fisherman's sharp eye was his chief weapon of search. He found his quarry by their appearance at the surface, by the ripples or the splashes as they broke the water, or by the dark color of surface schools. In the last few decades this simple procedure has been improved by the use of powerful binoculars.

From time immemorial the fisherman has also used the hunting skills of birds. A school near the surface may be indicated by sea birds diving into it. Sometimes even the kind of fish can be determined by the species of bird "working" the school. Anchovies are usually pursued by pelicans and other diving birds, tuna and bonita by a small white gull.

On a dark night a school may be revealed by the "phosphorescence" produced when fish move among microscopic luminescent organisms. Before echo sounders were perfected to detect fish in the daytime this was virtually the sole method used by sardine purse-seine fishermen to locate their prey.

The higher the fish spotter climbs above the sea the more effective are his observations, so fishermen seeking tuna, menhaden, and other prey by eye build high crow's nests on the masts of their vessels. In some cases they even take to the air. Skilled spotters in small airplanes radio the position of schools to the vessels below, and an enormous amount of time is saved in locating fish. The United States menhaden fleets have used this method for years, and some of the bigger American tuna purse-seine vessels can carry small float planes or helicopters on their upper decks, although a high accident rate has been a deterrent to their use. Schools are spotted most often by their color.

Planes are also used increasingly to guide the actual fishing operations, radioing to the skipper exactly when to put his net overboard and how to compensate for such variables as changes in the shape or movement of the school. Sometimes the vessel captain never sees the fish until they come aboard his boat, his whole procedure having been directed by the airplane pilot. In the Chilean anchovy fishery a single pilot can sometimes direct five boats working simultaneously on different schools.

Surface signs of fish are effective only for purse-seine or gill-net fishermen. For the trawler working on the seabed, other methods of search are necessary. In many fisheries the trawlerman will put over his gear on grounds he has fished successfully before and make a short drag

FIGURE 11.1. *One of the powerful modern tools of the fisherman is the echo sounder. It reveals the depth of water (shown here as the dark line on the moving paper) and the kind of bottom. It also depicts the presence of fish below the boat, acting as the fisherman's eyes in penetrating the murky water.*

D. H. Cushing, *The Arctic Cod*

to see whether fish are present. In the shrimp fishery of Florida and elsewhere, the fishermen drag miniature trawls called "try nets" and decide on the basis of such trials whether it is worthwhile to put the main gear overboard.

A major breakthrough in the search phase of fishing was made after World War II with the use of echo-sounding devices. These render the opaque sea transparent, revealing the presence of fish and guiding the operation of nets. The echo sounder was originally developed to assist navigation by providing a rapid and accurate measurement of water depth. The instrument works by sending an ultrasonic energy impulse vertically through the water and catching its reflection from the bottom. By measuring the time the impulse takes to bounce back to the ship, the machine calculates the distance to the bottom and reports the depth to the captain either as a light on a cathode tube or as a mark of a moving pen on a chart.

Among the first difficulties encountered in interpreting the signals given by depth recorders were the "false bottoms" and "shadows" that appeared. Some of these were quickly recognized as being caused by schools of fish, and the echo sounder's potential as a search tool was soon realized by fishermen. In a remarkably short time the echo sounder became a standard and indispensable tool in many fisheries, especially those pursuing such midwater-swimming fishes as herring, sardines, and anchovies. In most such fleets every boat has one or more echo sounders. These pick up shadows of the schools, telling the fishermen not only that the fish are present, but the size and depth of the schools and their direction and speed of movement. Different kinds of fish produce different kinds of echographs, depending on the size of the fish, how tightly they are schooled, and other characteristics. By this means fishermen can avoid setting their nets on species of no value and can greatly increase the efficiency of their operation by cutting down on search time.

The search for fish can be made still more efficient if the beam of the echo sounder is turned horizontally, to pick up the schools ahead of the boat, or to the side. Such instruments are called echo rangers or sonar. They are harder to use than echo sounders since their energy beams may be intercepted by shallow bottoms or wrecks, or warped out of shape by density differences and bubbles in the water. Echo rangers are being improved constantly, and they are now effective enough under some conditions to be employed alongside depth recorders to assist the fisherman in his search. The Icelandic herring fishery, for example, depends heavily on their use.

Conventional echo sounders are less useful in locating bottom-dwelling fish than mid-water species, since it is hard to distinguish between the echos from the bottom and those from the fish living on or near it. The trawler fisherman uses his machine to give him information about the depth and the character of the bottom (mud and sand give different echos than rocks), but he requires a specially adapted echo sounder to "see" the fish he is trying to catch. These new echo sounders are designed ingeniously so that the high-energy impulses reflected from the sea bottom do not register on the recording paper in the wheelhouse, while the weaker echos from fish on or close to the bottom show up as dark marks. This "white line recording" gives the trawlerman nearly the same amount of information that the standard echo sounder provides the purse-seine fisherman.

Some highly advanced fleets, such as those in the British fisheries for cod, haddock, and other groundfishes, make great use of echo devices. Most vessels have at least three: a standard type; a second that is often capable of magnifying a particular small segment of the water column, so that far more detail can be obtained of the exact region where the fish are located; and an echo ranger, capable of swinging 20 degrees to either side of the bow, to guide the ship to the highest concentration of fish.

Echo sounders are also being carried aloft on towed kites to help penetrate the surface layers. Tests are being contemplated of the use of laser beams to make it easier to "see" below the surface.

Television has been used to spy into hard-to-reach corners of the world, and it has been tried underwater. It has been used to advantage in fishery research, especially to reveal the action of nets and to watch the behavior of fish. So far it has not helped much in the direct location of schools, since there is so little light underwater, but it may offer more promise as technology improves.

Many marine animals make characteristic noises, and with experience fishermen can learn to detect the presence of their quarry in this way. Some marine animals, notably the mammals, actually communicate with sounds. Whales make noises that vary in pitch and intensity under different kinds of situations, and they may be "talking" to each other. Dolphins emit a variety of squeals and clicks, and it has been suggested that these sounds have meanings precise enough to constitute a language that could be learned by man. Whether this is possible or not, there are many fishes and invertebrates in addition to the mammals that make recognizable sounds.

The drums are the best-known sound producers among the fishes. These include the weakfishes or sea trout, the red and black drums, the croakers, and others. They make sounds by grinding their teeth and amplify the noise by setting their gas-filled swim bladders into resonant vibrations as they slowly contract drumming muscles attached to the backbone or skull.

Fish sounds are of several kinds, including those made deliberately (mating calls or expressions of pain or threat) and those emitted accidentally (while feeding, swimming, or releasing gas from the "air bladder" to adjust pressure).

Many of the noises fishes make are associated with spawning. Several species make courting calls. The female may bring a male fish to her side with a suitable enticing grunt or grinding of her teeth. The spawning song of gobies in the Sea of Azov consists of a weak quacking followed by a chirping chorus. The spawning concerts of drumfishes and some South American catfishes are sometimes impressively loud. These noises commonly increase at sunset, perhaps because communication by sight has to be replaced by sound as the light fails.

In the Barents Sea, Soviet scientists have recorded low muttering sounds made by haddock and cod, apparently threats emitted when strange fish appear.

Because water is denser than air it transmits sound better. Snapping shrimp "crack their knuckles" by clicking the two joints of their large claw, and this racket can be heard as much as two and a half miles away. Moderately intense underwater noises can easily be heard fifteen miles away, and some sounds have been detected from far greater distances.

Underwater sounds, if they are moderately loud and fairly near, can readily be heard with the unaided ear; weaker sounds can be picked up with microphones, amplified, and used in tracking down the source.

Acoustical tracking of fish is in the process of becoming a sophisticated art. Buoys have been designed that would be placed strategically to pick up the sounds of passing schools and to relay the information to ships. It may also prove feasible to put the microphones aboard high-speed, unmanned submarines to range among the schools and to radio data to the fishing fleet. A "library" of known sound patterns stored in the memory of the subs' computers would be compared to the incoming sounds, and the species and size of the school would be relayed to the ship, along with the direction and speed of swimming.

Detection of fish can also be improved by correlating their occurrence with hydrographic conditions. Fish have decided preferences for different water conditions, and these preferences vary widely according to species. Key variables include water clarity, salinity, and—most important of all—temperature. Most marine animals are restricted in their range by the water temperature; in some cases the preference is

[167]

sharply defined. When such limits are known it is sometimes possible to locate concentrations of fishes more efficiently by measuring the temperature. Schools of herring, saithe, and ocean perch have been located by water-temperature determination. In the Atlantic, some populations of cod swarm thickest in a narrow temperature range of 1.75° to 3°C., and haddock show a preference for water from 5° to 13.5°C. On the west coast of the United States the fishery for albacore tuna depends to an important extent on the marked temperature preference of these fish, and the thermometer is an important tool of the fishermen. The Japanese have made the most use of temperature measurements to locate fish, particularly tuna. Research ships probe likely areas of the ocean and radio to the fleets when favorable temperature zones are located. Many fishing boats carry their own thermometers.

The efficiency of fishing would be improved if more accurate and more timely temperature measurements were available over wide areas. Radio-equipped temperature buoys spaced widely over the ocean could give fleets a view of the overall temperature pattern and help speed vessels to likely areas. Exceedingly rapid and accurate measurements of surface water temperature can be made by planes carrying infrared sensors. Maps made this way and delivered quickly to the fisherman could improve his efficiency. It has been suggested also that schools of some fishes, notably tuna, might be detected by aerial infrared sensing of the temperature difference of the fish compared to the surrounding water.

The measurement of temperature is mechanical and can easily be done with present technology. The *use* of such data is more difficult. The relationship between the presence of fish and various hydrographic conditions will only become clearer after much more research has been done—a hard and slogging job for high-seas oceanographers for many years to come.

While the biggest savings in the cost of fishing undoubtedly will be made by increasing the efficiency of search methods, substantial improvements can also be made in the attraction and capture phases of fishing operations.

Very little is yet known about the stimuli that are attractive to fish, but data are being rapidly accumulated, and some of the most exciting work in oceanography is being done in this area. Fish are attracted or repelled principally by light, sound, and chemicals. In addition, electricity affects fish in curious ways. The proper use of these stimuli promises to give fishermen greater control over the movements of their prey.

Since ancient times men have known that they could lure fish within range of their spears by holding torches over the water. This technique is still used in many parts of the world. In modern times light is used to concentrate fish into a school tight enough for a seine to surround them. In the Mediterranean, oil or gas lamps are still used in catching sardines, and the same method is employed by fishermen of Zanzibar, Martinique, and many other areas scattered over the world ocean.

The development of the electric lamp has enabled fishermen to make many refinements in the age-old technique of attracting fish with light. Since World War II Japan and the Soviet Union have pioneered in this area. In the Caspian Sea herringlike fish, kilka (*Clupeonella*), are attracted by an underwater light to the intake of a powerful airlift pump that sweeps them aboard the ship. More than 100 Soviet vessels were engaged in this fishery in the late 1960's.

In 1941 a Japanese fishery scientist, Dr. H. Fukahara, developed a method of light-fishing for saury, a small fish with a good market in Japan. The light is suspended above the water, since this produces better results than the submerged light used for kilka. Many thousands of tons of saury have been caught by this method.

In 1965 the Soviets caught 200,000 tons of anchovies in the Pacific using lights. Russian fishermen catch Atlantic sardines and Black Sea mackerel, and the Japanese catch sardines, mackerel, horse mackerel, and squids with this technique. Canadian and Italian fishermen use it to attract sardines to their gear.

Lights have been used on gill nets to lure the fish into the entangling webs, on trawls to bring them into the mouth of the net, and over a submerged lift net, which is quickly raised when a school has gathered. A complicated "lighted road" has been set in some Japanese areas, with electric lights snapped on at stations successively closer to a trap, attracting fish to their doom a step at a time.

Attraction by light can be improved by research into the behavioral reaction of fish to the stimulus. It has been discovered that this varies considerably among different species. It has already been pointed out that for saury a light above the water is most efficient, while for kilka the illumination should be submerged. Color may be important: red light seems to be best for saury and white for some herringlike fishes. Certain sardines, however, appear to have no color preference. Some species react more vigorously to blinking light than to a steady illumination. Some species swim right into the brightest part of a lighted area, while others, including the herringlike *Sardinella*, lurk in the twilight zone, moving closer to the nets if the light is dimmed. Young of this species stay closer to light than the adults.

Many fishes track their prey partly by the use of sounds, and

[169]

fishermen are beginning to use them as a lure. The sounds of pain made by an injured fish (which presumably suggest to the predator that an easy meal is available) serve as effective lures. So do the characteristic noises of prey species. When the nature of such sounds has been determined with underwater listening devices, recordings can be played back into the water. Some remarkable responses have been obtained in this way. For example, at the Institute of Marine and Atmospheric Sciences in Miami, Dr. Arthur Myrberg and his associates have succeeded in bringing several species of sharks up to a speaker emitting particular irregularly pulsed sounds. The predators can be pulled in from at least as far as eighty feet, presumably by the hope of a meal.

Predators are also attracted by the sounds of fish feeding. In the Black Sea the Soviets transmit feeding sounds to attract labrids. Within five minutes fish begin to appear around the sound source; individuals can be brought from a distance of 150 to 200 feet within fifteen to twenty minutes.

Russian biologists have herded cod and herring from mid-water positions down to within six to ten feet of the bottom by playing a low-frequency sound in the water. The fish responded immediately to the sound by descending, and rose again when the recording was turned off. When the noise resumed the fish swam down again, but they soon became used to the stimulus and failed to react. More marked and lasting effects were obtained when the sounds of fish predators and of toothed whales were played into the water. Herring schools were driven down deeper in a dramatic fashion, and they stayed at the lower depth as long as the sounds continued. This represents a total change in the behavior of the fish and opens up exciting possibilities of manipulating their position so that gear can get at them more easily. It was estimated that catches increased three to five times when sounds were used in association with the trawls.

A difficulty encountered in the use of sounds to attract fish to gear is that the attention span of the fish seems to be short: they cease to react after a relatively short period, and any system would presumably then become ineffective. Clearly, much more research is required in this area, not only to overcome this difficulty (perhaps by varying the volume, pitch, or other characteristics to arouse the interest of the quarry again), but to determine the nature of the widely varying responses of commercially valuable fishes to sound.

As is the case in many other aspects of fishery research, Soviet scientists are at the forefront in fish-behavior studies. Their research ship *Boridev* is a floating acoustical laboratory, with twenty-four different kinds of echo-sounding devices on board. In 1967 she had more electronic equipment than the combined ships of the United States Bureau of Commercial Fisheries.

The Russians are investigating such aspects of fish behavior as the "opto-motor reaction." This is the behavior of a fish in following a moving object or reference point, and is a skill that enables it to orient itself when visual reference points are available. If these reference points are the parts of a trawl net, for example, some scientists believe that it may be possible to alter the patterns of the webbing in such a way that the opto-motor reaction is created in some parts of the net and not in others; if the control is clever enough the fish may be persuaded not to try to swim out of the net! One Soviet behaviorist, Professor D. V. Radakov, believes that the escape of fish from trawl gear can be reduced by creating a "secondary stimulus"—confusing the fish so that its natural escape reaction on the sight of the net is submerged by some other stimulus—for example the sounds of predators around the net.

Soviet behaviorists have used the submarine *Severyanka* for several years to study schools of herring and other species. It is now clear that this submarine is too big, expensive, and difficult to maintain for this purpose, and a smaller submersible, the *North I,* is being built specifically for fish-behavior work. She will be able to descend to 2,000 meters and run at 5 knots submerged. She will study the reactions of fish to gear and will conduct experiments in fish detection and scouting. The British are using two-man submarines to study the actions of trawls; American scientists also advocate the construction of research submersibles for the direct observation of fishes' reaction to gear.

Some fishes have acute organs of taste and odor reception, being attracted to or repelled by dissolved substances, often at astonishingly low dilutions. Pacific salmon can perceive dilutions of one part per billion; eels can detect alcohol in water in proportions equal to a teaspoonful in Lake Superior; a sea burbot (*Gaidropsarus*) became greatly excited when two liters (a little over two quarts) of water were poured into its aquarium, apparently because it detected the odor of a sand-smelt that had been allowed to swim in fifteen liters of this water. Salmon are believed to find their way back to ancestral spawning grounds by following to their source the characteristic organic odors of that part of the watershed, even though these odors may be enormously diluted in a big river system. Perhaps man can make use of such highly developed abilities to attract and concentrate fishes for their easier capture.

While efforts to improve methods of locating fish and attracting them to gear will continue with renewed vigor in the years to come, the gear itself must be improved if world catches are to rise significantly.

[171]

Fishing gear constantly becomes better, sometimes by small improvements in design or materials, occasionally by substantial leaps as some good new idea is developed.

An important advantage that modern fishermen have over those of even the recent past is the possession of rot-resistant, light, strong, synthetic fibers for their nets and lines. Even with constant care, including tedious washing and dipping in preservatives, nets made from cotton and linen have short lives, rotting from bacterial action and wearing out from abrasion. The introduction of the polyamids (nylon, perlon) and other man-made fibers has greatly increased the catching capacity of fishing gear and has reduced the cost of capture. Besides resistance to rotting and abrasion, synthetics exhibit higher tensile strength and elasticity.

The new fibers have been particularly useful in making gill nets that operate by entangling fish trying to swim through the gear. The efficiency of gill nets depends on their strength and invisibility. Because monofilament synthetics are stronger than traditional materials they can be made much finer, with the result that their efficiency is as much as ten times greater for species like salmon, trout, and whitefish. Trawl nets made of synthetic materials can now be as large as 280 feet long and 250 feet across the mouth. High-seas Japanese drift gill nets of synthetic materials range from six and a half to ten and a half miles in length. Icelandic herring seines are often 1,800 feet long and 600 feet deep.

Two substantial advances in fishing methods were the introduction of trawling about 1850 and the invention of purse seining early in this century. A trawl is a conical net dragged over the bottom of the sea, scooping up fish as it passes. It is a highly efficient gear, capable of catching more fish in less time and in rougher weather than most other kinds of apparatus. The purse seine is used to pursue surface-swimming fish, encircling them with a great wall of netting. When the ends are brought together a "draw string" cable at the lower end of the net closes it like an old-fashioned purse, trapping the fish in a big bowl.

Worldwide, these two types of gear catch more fish than any other devices. Both have been considerably improved in efficiency over the years. The earliest trawls were held open at the mouth by a beam supported on runners. In 1893 otter boards—kitelike devices that keep the mouth of the trawl net open as the gear is dragged forward in the water—began to supersede the clumsy rigid beam. This improvement allowed the height of the net to be increased. In recent years the operation of trawls has been much improved by fishing them from the stern instead of from the side of the vessel. The resulting greater safety, speed, and general efficiency have produced much larger catches.

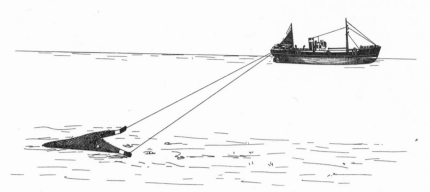

FIGURE 11.2. *Worldwide, trawling is the most important kind of fishing. Its advantages are that it catches more fish at lower cost and can be carried on in heavier weather than other methods. Here an otter trawl is dragged behind a steam vessel in the European fisheries.*

D. H. Cushing, *The Arctic Cod*

Some modern trawlers are immense, the biggest being Soviet vessels, which range up to 423 feet in length and have running speeds to 16 knots and trawling speeds to 4 or 5 knots. Such large vessels are capable of fishing in gales as strong as 60 miles an hour, so that they are obliged to spend far less time in port because of bad weather than any other kind of fishing boat. Modern trawlers have a bewildering array of electronic equipment: navigation aids such as radar, Decca, and loran; radio direction finders; ship-to-ship and ship-to-shore radios; automatic pilots; and fish-detection equipment, including two or three kinds of echo sounders and echo rangers. British trawler owners in Aberdeen can talk to their captains fishing on arctic, Greenland, or Newfoundland banks; skippers can converse with other ships 500 miles or more distant. Some of these big trawlers are also factory ships, processing their own catch and that of smaller vessels by freezing, canning, and reducing it to meal.

In some cases the trend to bigger trawlers may have gone too far. Nations like West Germany and the United Kingdom are having difficulty making the biggest trawlers pay their way. British ships must catch a minimum of twelve tons of fish a day to break even. Part of the problem is persuading men to work on these vessels, because to make a profit the owner must keep them at sea longer and for more days of the year than most fishermen like. Adjustments are being made in size

FIGURE 11.3. *Deck machinery has improved greatly in modern times, and in addition many fishing ships carry sophisticated processing plants. A high-speed filleting machine operates in the hold of a German trawler, preparing cod for freezing.*

Hans Saebens

to combat these and other problems, and the optimum sizes of trawlers for particular cases will gradually emerge.

Meantime, a new kind of trawling gear is being developed for mid-water fishing. This promises to open up a vast area of the ocean that has been nearly inaccessible hitherto. Trawls that drag the bottom catch demersal fish; purse seines and other gears harvest those that school near the surface; but there have been few devices capable of efficient capture of species in mid-water. Right after World War II, experiments started in Scandinavia on mid-water trawls. Their development has been slower than expected. It was found that merely lifting a bottom trawl up into mid-water would not work; the shape was wrong and an entirely new design was necessary. Mid-water fishes are, in general, faster swimmers than those living on the bottom, and they are likely to be dispersed over a great distance vertically. Thus, trawls had to be pulled faster and have a much larger vertical opening than bottom trawls. This required new hydrodynamic configurations, new materials that were lighter and stronger, and faster ships. In addition, to use the gear successfully it was necessary to know with accuracy the position, direction, and swimming speed of the schools sought. New echo sounders and other devices had to be developed to locate not only the schools but the net, and new skills had to be learned—how to put the gear "on the fish" and keep it there. Echo sounders are now attached to the headrope of the trawl as well as to the boat, so that the skipper knows instantly where his net is in relation to the bottom and to the fish.

Mid-water trawls are in common operation only in a few fisheries, but experimental results give hope that it may not be long before this gear will be an important factor in fish production. In Europe, herring are caught with mid-water trawls, and the size of the catches is encouraging. A fleet of 275 vessels catches shrimp with mid-water trawls in the East China Sea. Huge catches of herring have been made by experimental Canadian mid-water trawls in the Gulf of St. Lawrence. The *J. B. Nickerson*, a 156-foot stern trawler, landed 1,227 tons in one week of fishing in early November 1968.

FIGURE 11.4. *A gill net catches fish by entangling them in slack meshes as they try to push their way through. This sketch is of a sunken gill net used in the North Atlantic to catch cod and other bottom species.*

Bureau of Commercial Fisheries

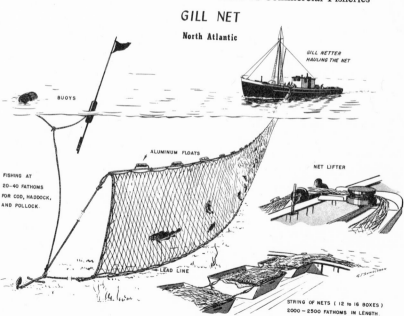

GILL NET

North Atlantic

FIGURE 11.5. *Trawling methods and gear have been greatly improved in recent years. Here the German stern trawler* Bremerhaven *drags a full net up its ramp, while the* Berlin *stands by in the background.*

Gerhard Binanzer

In Puget Sound and off the coast of Washington a commercial mid-water trawl hake fishery produced good catches for three years: 6 million pounds in 1966, 9 million in 1967, and 20 million in 1968. Some vessels averaged 12,000 pounds of fish per hour and the top vessel averaged 14,000. Single catches of approximately 50,000 pounds were common and several over 100,000 pounds were made. These yields provided the fishermen with average daily earnings equal to, or better than, those they had experienced with other kinds of gear in previous years. Yet the fishery stopped, and the reason for this sheds a good deal of light on the problems faced by vessel owners in attracting crewmen. Crews could not be recruited merely by promises of good earnings, reasonably sustained; they had to have the hope of a bonanza catch—which the mid-water trawl fishery for the low-priced hake apparently could not provide!

Purse seines have changed less than trawls, partly because they have had a shorter history. But their efficiency has increased greatly in recent years. One major United States fishery—that for tuna—was rejuvenated by adopting an improved purse seine. This fishery, operating out of California, used to catch its fish by attracting them to the side of the vessel with live bait (anchovies, sardines, or similar small species) and then hooking them one at a time with pole-and-line gear. This was relatively inefficient, and the industry slumped in the face of dwindling profits. Then it became possible to build and operate enormous purse seines, big enough to surround and catch the swift-swimming yellowfin and skipjack tunas. This was done by making the nets of light, strong nylon or other synthetic fibers that allowed the gear to be far larger than the bulky and weaker manila, sisal, linen, or cotton nets. Then, a new device called a power block was invented by a Seattle fisherman, permitting big nets to be hauled, and using the muscle of the engine instead of the fisherman. Tuna seines 4,000 feet long and 200 feet deep are now in use, and the United States is again a power in the tuna industry.

This kind of development in gear is necessary and useful, but if really substantial increases are to take place in world fish production, some spectacular *new* kinds of capture appear necessary. Perhaps some of these will involve the use of electricity. In fresh water, electrical fishing gear has been used for a good many years. This depends on a series of curious effects that electricity has on the behavior of fish and other creatures. When an alternating-current electrical field is set up in water, fish are frightened away. But in a weak direct current the animals line up in the field like iron filings over a magnet, with their heads toward the positive pole. As the power is increased the fish are forced to

FIGURE 11.6. *Tuna fishermen begin to stack a purse seine after completing a haul. The power block at the head of the boom pulls the net (which may be 3,000 feet long and 300 feet deep) from the water, greatly increasing the efficiency of operation.*

Garth I. Murphy

swim toward the positive pole from as far away as fifteen or twenty feet, and eventually they are immobilized or killed.

When this odd behavior was discovered high hopes were raised that electrical fishing gear could be developed to pull fish from distant hiding places, and make their capture easy by reducing their struggles or by killing them in the gear. This hope has been realized to some extent in fresh or slightly brackish water. In the Sea of Okhotsk the Soviets operate a major fishery on the saury, *Cololabis saira,* the fish being concentrated around a pump by lights combined with electricity. In the freshwater Borok Reservoir in the Soviet Union, electrical poles are being tested on the mouths of trawls. The objective is to attract fish to the gear and then render them selseless so they cannot avoid the net.

Earnest attempts have been made to develop electrical fishing gear in the sea, but so far progress in developing revoluntionary gear has been disappointing. This is partly a consequence of the considerably greater amounts of power required to produce a reaction in fish in salt water compared to those required in fresh water. The conductivity of the water increases with the amount of dissolved salts, and (contrary to the expectation of most people) more and more power is required to affect the fish; the increase may have to be as much as 1,000 times. This makes electrical fishing in the sea far too expensive unless adaptations can be made in the design of the apparatus.

Such adaptations are slowly being made. An important one is to use interrupted current, keeping the current on only a small fraction of the time, with proportionate savings in power but with no diminution of its effect on the nervous systems of the fish. With this and other refinements electrical apparatus has been developed to concentrate menhaden in purse-seine nets off the east coast of the United States. These fish crowd to the bottom of the net after they are caught, making heavy work for the fishermen to pull them aboard along with the big net. This work is lightened enormously if a pump is put among the fish in the net and the end of the pump is made the positive pole of an electrical system. A current is set up with the negative pole on the hull of the vessel, forcing the fish to swim to the pump head, where they are swept aboard the boat.

But useful as this device is, it is a means of loading fish, not *catching* them; so far no fully satisfactory "electrical net" has been developed. One serious problem is the short range over which current is effective—about twenty feet for most fish. But research is proceeding with the object of perfecting such types of gear as a "netless seine," consisting of a cable within whose electrical field fish may be trapped and concentrated.

[179]

BRIDGE AND
FUNNEL ON
STARBOARD SIDE.

FISH
HOLD.

SUPERFLUOUS WATER
FROM FISH HOLD.

FISH AVOIDING
CURRENT AREA

SURFACE.

UP-PIPE

STERN ELECTRODE

CENTRAL ELECTRODE
AND INTAKE.

FISH BEING
SUCKED INTO
FUNNEL

ALTERNATING CURRENT

DIRECTION OF SHOAL
OF FISH

BOW ELECTRODE.
BOW AND STERN
ELECTRODES ARE
OF OPPOSITE
POLARITY TO
CENTRAL ELECTRODE

G. H. DAVIS
1952

It has been found that electrical currents can also affect shrimp, forcing them to leap out of the bottom mud and sand under the influence of certain kinds of low-voltage impulses. Some species are nocturnal, and fishing is poor during the day when they are buried in the mud. High hopes are held that the attachment of electrical devices to shrimp trawls might make fishing possible around the clock and at a high rate of efficiency. Such devices have been manufactured by a firm in north Florida. These, and other aids now unguessed, may well promote great improvements in man's ability to catch fish efficiently.

The efficiency of catching operations depends to a large extent on whether the fish are closely concentrated. One method of increasing the concentration is to prevent their movement away from an area by imposing some kind of barrier to migration. This might involve taking advantage of the reactions of fish to amazingly small concentrations of some substances. By discovering which ones repel certain species, it might be possible to erect chemical barriers that prevented the fish from moving away until catching gear could be deployed. Experiments have been performed using this principle, and other tests have employed dye, acoustical, and electrical barriers. Bubble curtains have already shown themselves to be effective. In Maine, for example, herring fishermen keep schools penned up, and guide them to areas where capture is easier, by creating a bubble curtain with compressed air forced through a perforated hose laid on the bottom in shallow water.

Some other directions for the future are already clear, or can be guessed. The use of self-propelled, unmanned trawls under remote radio control from a mother ship some miles away is a common suggestion. In 1967 Dr. N. Andreev described on Moscow radio plans that his country has for amazing crewless vessels to fish at depths to 2,500 feet. Said the Soviet scientist, "Fishermen will soon join the chanties, widows' walks, and ghosts-ships of folklore." "Soon" seems to overstate the case, but this kind of development may come in time.

FIGURE 11.7. *If electricity can be harnessed, and the curious reactions of fish to electrical fields made to work for the fisherman, ocean fishing could enter an exciting new era. At present the technical difficulties are formidable, and most electrical fishing is limited to fresh or brackish waters. Here a Soviet ship sets up an electrical field in brackish water, using a pump-head as the positive pole. Fish are forced to swim to the anode and are sucked aboard into the hold of the vessel.*

Illustrated London News

FIGURE 11.8. *A spectacular catch of herring by the Canadian mid-water trawler* Lady Ann *off Newfoundland in the winter of 1968. One tow produced eighty tons of fish in approximately four minutes. This kind of gear is opening up a new part of the ocean to exploitation.*

Deparment of Fisheries and Forestry of Canada

It has been suggested that submarines may take over from surface vessels the task of catching fish. This seems unlikely in most cases, since it appears that their chief value would be to allow fishing in worse weather than at present, and the costs and other problems associated with operating submarine fishing vessels might overbalance the advantages to be gained. But whether submarines or crewless fishing vessels ever come into common use, vessels and gear will certainly improve in the future. And so will fishing strategy.

Fishing is a skilled trade, an art. In any fishing fleet the boats sort themselves out in terms of the amount of fish caught in a season, with certain vessels always coming near the top of the list. Usually these "high-liners" are more than ordinarily successful because of the skill of the captain. The artfulness comes in his ability to integrate a complex set of circumstances: by weighing the various effects of weather, sea state, depth, bottom conditions, water currents, and other variables, he decides where fish are likely to be concentrated within reach of his gear. The skipper does this by relying on his recollection of where fish were caught on previous trips in relation to a given set of conditions. He may refer to records he has kept of his fishing operations of the past, or he may operate solely from memory.

If the captain has at his command up-to-date and accurate information in addition to his own experience, his effectiveness will increase. In many of the largest of the world fisheries, systematic programs have been developed to provide such information, in amounts far beyond that which any individual fisherman could gain on his own. A highly successful example of this is provided by the Icelandic "herring search system," where government and industry cooperate in providing skippers with information about the location of schools and their likely movements.

The Icelandic herring fishery is conducted with purse seines. In this kind of fishing 80 to 90 per cent or more of a vessel's time is spent running to and from the grounds and searching for the fish. In this particular fishery the search must be made over a vast area of ocean, since the Icelandic-Norwegian herring undertake long feeding and spawning migrations: in winter the fish are off the Norwegian coast for spawning; in the spring and summer they migrate west across the Norwegian Sea to the east coast of Iceland. Fishermen in years past located their quarry by sighting schools on the surface. But about twenty years ago the behavior of the fish changed and the herring schools did not appear at the surface as they had previously. As a result, the Icelandic government instituted a systematic search system, whose success has been spectacular.

The Icelandic system involves the use of three vessels, a research boat and two scout boats, equipped with echo-ranging equipment. These seek out the schools and report their presence to the fishing vessels. Before the herring season starts, the research vessel makes surveys of the grounds to determine the location of the schools and to make observations of temperature, currents, and other hydrographic conditions. On the basis of these data, forecasts are prepared and relayed to the fishing fleet of the probable movements of the herring in the next weeks and months. Then the two scouting vessels join the research ship, and the schools of herring are precisely located. Fishing boats begin to arrive, and they are directed to the schools; they begin fishing immediately, without the long and profitless delays that are so characteristic of ordinary fishing operations. All the fishing vessels are required to report their catches and the location, size, and movements of herring schools. This information, plus the reports of the research and scouting ships, is integrated by the research vessels, which issue two broadcasts a day to the fleet. When storms break up and scatter the schools the whole fleet undertakes a collective search, reporting its findings to the research ship.

The success of this system has been so great that fishing can be carried on continuously eight months of the year instead of the two or three months in years past. Catches have zoomed. The men who developed the system, Dr. F. Devold and Dr. Jakob Jakobsson, are national heroes. The ultimate proof of confidence by the fishermen was their willingness in 1966 to spend more than $1,000,000 of their own money to buy and equip another herring-survey vessel.

Other successful fisheries also use integrated programs to guide the operation of the fishing fleets. The Soviets, as was pointed out in Chapter 8, have established a coordinated procedure whereby the kinds and quantities of fish caught by each boat and the exact location of capture are reported to a central command vessel, which then deploys the boats to produce the maximum catch possible. The Japanese make effective use of similar techniques. Japanese prefectural fisheries schools and federal government fishery laboratories often maintain exploratory and scouting vessels whose job it is to direct commercial boats to fish schools as quickly and efficiently as possible. The Japanese tuna fleets cooperate fully, reporting to each other where they are fishing and what success they are having.

Clearly, such coordinated operations portend the shape of the future for world fishing. With increases in man's knowledge and skill in interpreting the meaning of oceanographic data (weather, temperature, currents) in terms of the schooling and movements of fish, integrated fishing operations will become more complex and sophisticated. Perhaps hundreds of vessels over thousands of square miles of ocean will have their fishing directed by a nerve center equipped with computers to receive, digest, and integrate thousands of pieces of information about the location, kind and abundance of fish (as reported by fishing vessels and government survey boats) and about the temperature, salinity, height of waves, and depth and sharpness of the thermocline (as reported by research vessels and fixed buoys). The World Meteorological Office will soon put into operation a World Weather Watch, designed to coordinate weather observations, and the data from this will be available for fishing fleets.

In the report of the Second World Fishing Gear Congress of 1963, Dr. Dayton L. Alverson of the U. S. Bureau of Commercial Fisheries in Seattle and Dr. Norman J. Wilimovsky of the Institute of Fisheries of the University of British Columbia describe how such a fishery nerve center might work:

Let us visualize how fishing might be conducted in the future . . . an office, "Hydro-central," operating a network of unmanned buoys and automatic patrol submersibles. From data collected over several years, patterns of distribution of biological resources have, we may suppose, been plotted. The buoys are interrogated at regular intervals by radio via satellites and they respond with information from their own instruments and also from instruments at various depths in the sea relayed to the buoys by pulse-coded acoustic waves. As the fresh data come into "Hydro-central" computers work to reduce them to contoured plots of biological, oceanographic, and meteorological conditions. Facsimiles of the data summaries are transmitted to the research laboratories and fishing centers of the world.

When a school of fish is detected, the nearest buoy is automatically instructed to assess its nature with high-resolution sonar and analyses of the odors. The results are transmitted back to the "Hydro-central" for computer and human interpretation. The movements of the identified fish are tracked. In some instances it may be necessary to verify the identification by an on-the-spot check using aircraft, perhaps equipped with lasers, or hydrofoil research craft deploying high-speed submersible television vehicles. Depending on the species, the main fishing fleets may be deployed onto the path of the fish; alternately, suitable means of guidance may be used to bring the fish to the catchers. In the latter case, aircraft could disperse olfactory pellets, or remote-controlled underwater vehicles could produce the necessary electric, sonic, or bubble barrier to perform the same function. Depending on the depth of the fish, they are finally caught directly by catcher boats assigned to permanently anchored factory ships, or by net-towing submersibles operated from ship to shore stations.

These procedures still constitute a "hunting" operation—the kind that many people consider too primitive to fill mankind's needs. But the operation is becoming highly sophisticated, and the hunter is using far sharper weapons than in the past.

12   *Freedom to Fish*

The rising tide of fishing effort over the world oceans assures that more and more of the potential of the sea's food will be won for the benefit of mankind. But this rapidly increasing fishing pressure has other effects too—reduction in the efficiency of capture, duplication of effort, depletion of stocks, and rancorous disputes when two countries aim their gear at the same quarry.

The world faces a monumental task in trying to untie this complex knot, but if it cannot succeed in this and in other problems requiring international goodwill and cooperation, mankind will lose heavily in the amount of food it harvests from the sea.

One major aspect of the law of the sea is that oceanic fish stocks are common property: they belong to all, therefore to none. As a result, they are grabbed as fast as possible, since otherwise someone else will take them. With no ownership, there is no husbandry, no benefit to be gained from controlled and rational exploitation, unless agreements can be worked out among competing nations.

The concept of freedom of the seas became firmly established in the sixteenth and seventeenth centuries following rejection by the international community of Spanish and Portuguese claims over vast expanses of the Atlantic. The concept has always involved both freedom of navigation and freedom to fish. However, the use of the ocean for transport was historically more valuable, and prior to the twentieth century most of the fishing was done in coastal and offshore waters, with only a few areas of international discord. Hence, in the minds of most people freedom of navigation has been the principal concern. In recent years, as the pursuit of fish has become so much more important and as conflicts over who shall take them on the high seas have become frequent and bitter, the second principle—freedom to fish—has become a public issue.

The two principles are significantly different in one important aspect: freedom of navigation removes nothing from the sea; freedom to fish results in the physical removal of something of value, preventing others from realizing the same gain.

For centuries freedom to fish caused only locally irritating problems, where too many boats crowded onto especially rich fishing grounds inside national waters. Unrestricted access to all extraterritorial waters and all high-seas stocks was generally acceptable as long as everyone believed the stocks to be inexhaustible. But oceanic fish stocks are *not* inexhaustible: there are only certain limited quantities that can be taken before the population is harmfully reduced and subsequent harvest diminished. Already some of the more valuable and heavily fished populations are overexploited, and as world fishing increases, more and more stocks will become biologically depleted and their fisheries economically unprofitable.

Thus, the concept of freedom of the seas has led to unlimited entry into the fisheries, sometimes to the detriment of the total harvest and the profits of fishermen. Some limitation is clearly necessary lest the whole freedom be destroyed; some workable system of law must be developed if more serious clashes and damage to fish stocks are to be avoided.

The problem exists on national and international levels. Some countries have found national solutions that are partly satisfactory. Japan, for example, has tightly organized federal control of fisheries, issuing licenses only in numbers believed proper to maintain reasonable profits to the operators. Most other nations—including the United States—are far from having a workable system on the national level.

On the international level the problem looms even larger. Seizures by Peru of American tuna boats and Greek whaling vessels have produced headlines on the front page; arrests by the United States of Soviet and Japanese vessels off Alaska have caused abrasive reactions in those countries; the seizure of a Soviet ship by Ghana and the month-long imprisonment of its crew disturbed diplomats and high-seas fishermen everywhere.

For centuries it has been universally accepted that within a certain distance from its shores a nation enjoys exclusive privileges, subject to the right of "innocent passage" of foreign vessels. This exclusive zone is part of the territory of the country. Britain, the United States, and many other nations have long claimed three miles as their territorial sea, but

[187]

this has never been the case universally. And in recent years there has been a strong tendency to claim greater widths. In 1968 three countries claimed four miles, one five; sixteen countries claimed six, one nine miles, and many others greater widths, including eight states (Argentina, Chile, Costa Rica, Ecuador, El Salvador, Nicaragua, Peru, and Panama) that claimed 200 miles, either as territorial seas or as exclusive fishing zones. A number of these states collect license fees from foreign ships operating in the exclusive zones. Peru and Ecuador have backed their claims by seizing fishing vessels of other nations far offshore, confiscating their catches, and imposing heavy fines on their owners. Other nations reject the claims, but short of sending gunboats to accompany their fishing vessels they can only protest the seizures and pay the fines levied on their fishermen.

In some countries an internal conflict arises from the opposing desires to have universally narrow territorial seas, so that their navigation is unimpeded, but to have wide zones off their own shores, so that

FIGURE 12.1. *The king crab,* Paralithodes camtschatica, *a creature of the continental shelf. By international agreement at a 1958 conference in Geneva, animals that live on the bottom of the sea are regarded as the property of the adjacent coastal state. The United States has declared that king crabs, abalones, sponges, and other valuable animals are the possession of this country, even though they sometimes occur outside the twelve-mile exclusive fishing zone.*

C. P. Idyll

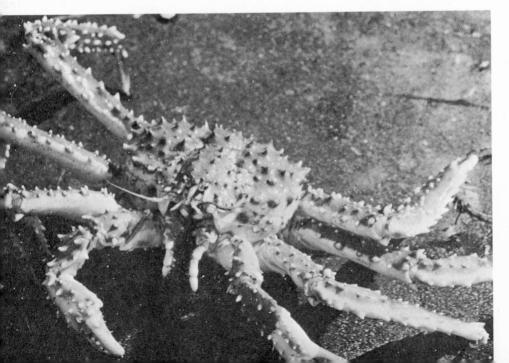

they can keep for themselves the fish and mineral resources of these regions. As a result, a new concept has developed recently—that of exclusive fishing zones beyond the territorial seas. Following the failure in 1958 and 1960 of international conferences on the law of the sea to agree on the width of territorial waters, many countries have claimed exclusive right to fish within twelve miles of their shores. By 1968 more than thirty nations (including the United States) had claimed such exclusive fishing zones. (These claims are often tempered, however, by exceptions.) To the extent that this concept is accepted, the ocean seaward from twelve miles offshore is still considered "high seas," open to exploitation by all comers.

There is, however, one further new limitation on the freedom to fish. At the international conference in Geneva in 1958 the continental shelf, its mineral resources, and its fishery resources living on the bottom were declared the exclusive property of the coastal nation. Under this law the United States has claimed that king crabs, abalones, sponges, and some other valuable animals on the sea floor are the possession of this country, even though they may sometimes occur beyond the twelve-mile exclusive fishing zone. This has been formally accepted by the USSR. Both that country and Japan have agreed to quotas on the catch of king crabs beyond the twelve-mile zone in the Bering Sea and the Gulf of Alaska.

The continental shelf is defined by convention as that part of the sea bottom out to a depth of 200 meters (about 656 feet) *or* a further limit at which exploitation can take place. This "open-ended" definition can change the legal limit of the shelf as technology advances the ability to exploit its resources, and therefore it is not workable; it will have to be altered so that the legal limits are fixed and easy to determine.

The difficulties faced by nations in trying to protect marine resources from increasing pressures and in deciding how to divide equitably the limited amounts of fish available are among the most pressing aspects of the general problem of creating a law of the sea. A number of solutions, of varying merit, are available. For example, strong nations with high capacities for exploiting the sea (like the United States, Japan, and the USSR) might proceed much as they are at present, fishing hard wherever it is profitable, and hoping to fend off competition by aggressiveness and superior efficiency. This alternative favors the rich and developed nations, and is not likely to serve as a viable long-term solution.

Another approach, and one already widely used, is for two or more nations to make agreements concerning specific fisheries or certain areas of the ocean. Such agreements have proven to be the only effective means

[189]

FIGURE 12.2. *A Soviet factory ship, the* Spassk, *of the Far Eastern fleet. This impressive vessel, built in 1966, is 571 feet long and carries a crew of 280 men and women. Supplied by a fleet of catcher boats, she freezes, cans, and reduces fish to meal and oil. The Soviets have at least two other factory ships like this one and many more of other designs. These, and hundreds of other vessels, are being used effectively to fish international waters, and the pressures created will increase as the years pass.*

B. Korobeinikov

FIGURE 12.3. *South Korea is one of the most recent participants in global fishing, competing hard with Japan and other veteran fishing nations. Here a fleet of the Korean Samyang Fisheries is anchored in Dutch Harbor, waiting to fish in Alaskan waters.*

Bureau of Commercial Fisheries, Alaska

of dealing with international fishery problems to date. The United States, for example, is a party to eleven treaties for the protection, management, and (sometimes) the division of the catch. The first of these was entered into in 1911, when a treaty was signed with Great Britain (including Canada), Japan, and Russia for the protection of the fur seals of Alaskan waters. This has been one of the most successful treaties, resulting in the restoration of a badly damaged resource (from an estimated 200,000 animals in 1911 to herds now numbering 1.5 million) and a stabilized yearly harvest of furs. Treaties with Canada have been notably successful in managing the halibut of the North Pacific and the salmon of the Fraser River near the Canadian-American border.

Other fishery agreements that include the United States are more complicated and in most cases less successful to date than the fur seal, salmon, and halibut treaties. One dealing with the northwest Atlantic (the Grand Banks and other historic shallows) is shared by fourteen nations and covers cod, haddock, ocean perch, and many other fishes. The multiplicity of countries and species involved has made this effort at international conservation difficult to study and to administer and therefore not fully effective. And some agreements are nearly failures. The International Whaling Commission has no effective international inspection system and it is without power to enforce its suggested regulations. It has been unable to prevent the near-destruction of some species of whales by countries that catch antarctic whales in the open sea.

However, the United States is happy with most of these agreements. Indeed, they have resulted in more effective conservation regulations and management of fish stocks than most efforts at internal management of domestic fisheries. But the treaties have not solved all the problems. In the halibut fishery of the North Pacific, for example, the success of the International Halibut Fisheries Commission of Canada and the United States in restoring the populations of halibut has been partially mitigated by the entrance of such large numbers of boats from the two nations into the fishery that profits to individuals have been far less than if fewer were engaged. And in recent years Japan, the USSR, Korea, and others have shown strong interest in halibut and other of the region controlled by the Halibut Commission, threaten other burden of fishing pressure and posing vexing problems of con. and equitable division of the harvest.

Other countries besides the United States have used the technique of bilateral or multilateral fishery agreements. But as more and more nations enter the competition these kinds of agreements will become less effective, since they require the consent of all who have prospects of exploiting the fish. Ambassador Donald L. McKernan, the American

[191]

FIGURE 12.4. *Japan and the USSR have replaced the traditional whaling nations—the United States, Great Britain, Norway—as the leading catchers of whales. Here a whale is being butchered on a Japanese vessel in the Antarctic. International control of whaling has been a dismal failure; some species are seriously depleted and others are in danger of actual extinction.*

Consulate General of Japan,
New York

official most responsible for this nation's activities in the international fishery field, has said that "the present system of international arrangements . . . is only transitory in nature and only foreshadows dimly future international arrangements."

Another possible method of attacking the problem is through general international control of high-seas fishery resources. Such control would require a central organization—the United Nations, one of its presently existing specialized agencies (presumably the Food and Agriculture Organization), or a newly created body inside or outside the UN. This body would have the responsibility for controlling fishing effort, for establishing national quotas, for limiting entry into fisheries already fully exploited, and for enforcing its decisions in all of these matters. This implies an international governmental apparatus, a level of agreement among nations, and an effective machinery of enforcement that are far beyond anything the world has yet achieved.

A fourth alternative, even more Utopian, would involve not merely control of high-seas fishing by an international agency, but actual ownership of these resources by such an agency.

In May 1966 the Commission to Study the Organization of Peace, a research affiliate of the United Nations Association of the U.S.A., recommended the establishment of a United Nations Marine Resources Agency to control and administer international marine resources, hold ownership rights, and grant, lease, or use these rights in accordance with the principles of economic efficiency. Utilization of the proceeds would be decided upon by the United Nations General Assembly.

In July 1967 the World Peace Through Law Conference held in Geneva recommended that the General Assembly of the United Nations proclaim that the nonfishery resources of the high seas outside the territorial waters of any state and the bed of the sea beyond the continental shelf "appertain to the United Nations and are subject to its jurisdiction and control."

On August 17, 1967, a proposal was put forward in respect to the seabed and its mineral resources by Arvid Pardo, the Ambassador to the United Nations from Malta. The "Maltese Proposition," which has attracted much interest in the United Nations, would put mineral resources under international ownership but would exclude plant and animal resources in the water above the seabed from such ownership. In practice, however, it would be impossible to control one and not the other, since they are inseparably connected ecologically. Thus, since Ambassador Pardo made his suggestion, others have taken the obvious next step and proposed that living resources of the sea also be claimed by the community of nations as the property of mankind as a whole, and that they be managed and divided among nations in respect to need instead of ability to exploit them.

The arguments in favor of international ownership of marine resources and their management for the sake of needy nations are compelling. Dr. Carl Q. Christol, Professor of International Law and Political Science at the University of Southern California, is one of those advancing such arguments. He states that "the rising tide of human expectations" is demanding a worldwide sharing of the world's riches and that in effect the ocean belongs to all of mankind. "It is my view that the United Nations . . . should assert a claim for the permanent and exclusive right to the marine resources of the high seas." Control would be delegated to "a competent commission."

The plea for the internationalization of the high seas and their resources also has been put forward persuasively by Elizabeth Mann Borgese, daughter of the famed German author Thomas Mann. In an article in *The Center Magazine* of May 1968, she proposes a "Republic of the Deep Seas." In the past, says Mrs. Borgese, oceans have tended to separate peoples and nations as much as to unite them.

Today technology has changed all this. Distance has shrunk. Dark depths have become shallow and transparent. The ocean floors, their gorges and mountain ranges and peaks, have been charted and mapped, and found to hold copper and zinc, manganese and nickel, in untold quantities—everyman's wealth in no man's land, waiting for science-fiction vessels to bring it to the surface. . . .

[193]

Not only the mineral wealth of this vast expanse that covers seven-tenths of the surface is there for the asking; ocean flora and fauna may yet furnish a major share of the food for the growing world population—plankton cultivated in portions of the ocean whose temperature may be raised by atomic energy, "trash fish" until recently despised and unused but now husbanded and herded by dolphin sheep dogs into fish protein concentrate. . . .

Efforts directed to the oceans that could begin almost at once to add billions of dollars to the world's riches may instead produce depletion and pollution, a wasteland of wonderland, a globe-encompassing Dead Sea. . . . Exploration and exploitation of the deep seas beyond national jurisdiction could procede in an orderly, planned and cooperative manner under the direction and control of an international agency—which, as UN Ambassador Arthur Goldberg observed with regard to the Space Treaty, might provide "a framework, if only skeletal in form, for the future pattern of man's activities." Or, it could proceed competitively, anarchically, chaotically, disastrously, in a new era of imperialism that would carve up a new submarine continent among the few wealthy and technologically developed nations to the detriment of all the others, and, in the end, to themselves as well.

The choice must be made without delay.

The force of such arguments, so eloquently presented, is difficult to resist. But whether, in its present state of social development, the world is capable of implementing a "Republic of the Deep Seas" is highly questionable. If efficiency of capture and conservation of resources are to be achieved under such an arrangement, control must be exercised by an impartial international agency. Where full control over the fishermen is possible, fishery biologists have approached this ideal for a few stocks. But not for most, and technical problems of international control of fisheries would be difficult.

But consider the far more difficult social, economic, political, and legal questions that the international controlling body would have to answer:

How much fishing can be allowed to achieve the maximum *economic* yield, that is, to permit the maximum efficiency of operation? In making this decision, how will different methods of determining costs and profits, resulting from different social and economic systems, be taken into account?

Which countries will be allowed to fish in a particular area, keeping in mind the rights of the adjacent coastal states, the rights of rich versus poor nations, the rights of nations that have fished there historically versus newcomers who are eager to begin sharing

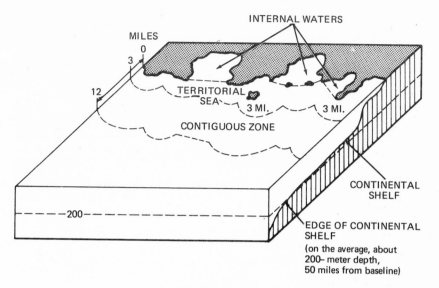

DEPTHS IN METERS

FIGURE. 12.5. *Relationship of internal waters, the territorial sea, the contiguous zone and the continental shelf, in terms of United States policy. This policy, with some variations, is a common one among maritime nations. But other nations claim different widths of territorial sea. The definition of the continental shelf (out to 200 meters depth or the limit of exploitation) is not satisfactory as a permanent system.*

U. S. Commission on Marine Science, Engineering, and Resources

the bounty, and the rights of nations that have invested heavily in money, fleets, research, and control of their own fishermen versus those that have spent nothing?

What machinery can be erected to ensure that enforcement of regulations would be prompt and effective?

Answers to these questions are not apparent. The hard fact is that the nations of the world have not yet come to the point of permitting an international body to make the kinds of economic, social, or political decisions that would be necessary for a "Republic of the Deep Seas" to work.

The various proposals for internationalization of the resources of the deep seas are weak economically too. Internationalization is very appealing to poor nations as a means of sharing what the wealthy nations are now taking from the ocean. Moreover, the attractive idea has been suggested that the wealth of the sea can finance the operations of the United Nations, and thus hasten the development of world government. But it is naive to expect that regulated access is all that is required "to add billions of dollars to the world's riches." Where profits are to be made by the exploitation of these resources, they are being vigorously pursued now by private companies or by national governments. So far, except for oil, ocean-bottom minerals have not usually supported profitable industries—and those that have are in territorial waters or on the continental shelf, both the acknowledged property of individual nations. Later, as technology reduces the cost of extraction, exploitation will be pursued for true high-seas mineral resources. But this has barely begun, and it will be many years before enough money will be derived from the international exploitation of these resources to pay for the necessary new administrative machinery, let alone the financing of the present United Nations organizations.

It is unrealistic, moreover, to believe that the harvest of fish would be increased by the substitution of internationalized fishing for the present profit-driven fishing of national fleets. Japan, the United States, Norway, and other countries cannot be expected to give up something they have developed at great cost over the centuries, and if they did the world would suffer heavily in loss of protein supplies, since international social and administrative machinery is not yet as efficient as private or national operations.

Hence there seems to be no prospect in the near future of a worldwide agency assuming the control and development of high-seas resources. The likely trend will be increased bilateral and multilateral agreements among nations. This may lead in time to a limited world government control; as soon as international amity, sophistication, and the skills of international organizations will permit, some world body should be given the authority to develop and enforce high-seas conservation practices. This might be the existing Department of Fisheries of the FAO, or an entirely new body, but in either case it will have to be endowed with a special wisdom and patience, and staffed with supermen. If such a development takes place it may be the opening wedge toward true international government and represent a new plateau in human achievement. If it does not, mankind will never realize the full potential of the ocean.

13   *The Realities*

It is widely believed by the world's leaders and wise men as well as by the general public that the ocean alone can overcome present and future malnutrition and famine. One of the world's most highly respected scholars, Professor Arnold Toynbee, author of the monumental *Study of History*, has expressed the view that the sea will eventually contribute more food than the land. Following the orbiting of the moon by astronauts in late 1968, Professor Toynbee urged that the United States (and the rest of the world) turn the enormous efforts being expended on "the dead end" of space exploration toward the solution of problems of extracting food from the sea. "Here," he said, "is a vast accessible field for mankind's enterprise, and also a sure guarantee for our race's survival even if our descendants are going to be ten times as numerous as we are today. Even in these numbers our descendants will not starve, since the quantities of edible fish will have multiplied, in domestication, far more sensationally."

Fictional and pseudoscientific accounts of ocean exploitation support the same view. In his skillful novel, *The Deep Range*, Arthur Clarke describes his hero, a latter-day marine scientist, as "holding at bay the specter of famine which had confronted all earlier ages, but which would never threaten the world again while the great plankton farms harvested their millions of tons of protein, and the whale herds obeyed their new masters . . . until the oceans froze [man] would never be hungry again."

Unfortunately, such hopes are unlikely to be fulfilled. Professor Toynbee makes the assumption that man will abandon the process of "skimming food from the sea by the paleolithic method of hunting" in

[197]

favor of "farming the sea by cultivating edible seaweed and by breeding and shepherding fish, as we breed and shepherd sheep." This is undoubtedly the most widely held (or at least, hoped-for) idea about man's future in the sea, but as demonstrated in Chapter 6, it is false.

In Mr. Clarke's case the false assumptions are that plankton offers an economic or nutritionally acceptable source of protein for man, and that the principal food fishes of the ocean can be successfully herded or increased by land-adapted farming techniques—misconceptions that are treated in Chapters 4 through 6.

If we cannot hope for substantial increases in food from the harvest of plankton, and we cannot expect much from sea farming or the transplantation of useful animals to new parts of the ocean, we are left with the hunting of wild fish, as has been the case since the dawn of mankind.

But the situation is not as bad as unadorned statements about "primitive fishing methods" would imply. Indeed, fishing techniques are significantly improved over those of even a generation or so back, and they promise to become far better still.

The exercise of attempting to estimate the potential production of food from the ocean is frustrating because of the lack of knowledge about the basic productivity of most areas and the biology of fish stocks, especially in respect to fluctuations in abundance—information we must have to make rational calculations of these potential yields. But it is nonetheless clear that the total quantity of food material in the sea is far above that needed to meet the needs of the present world population, and even above amounts needed far into the future. So we can start from the important baseline that food material is being manufactured in the sea in very great quantities.

Yet, whatever the magnitude of this potential, it can never be fully realized because of the numerous biological, social, economic, political, and technical barriers.

One of the basic biological barriers is the fact that by removing certain species through fishing, man is often competing with ocean creatures that require these same species for food. Thus, by heavy exploitation of one fish, the harvest of another species on a higher trophic level is reduced. For example, if fishing for the sand lance, *Ammodytes*, increases substantially, enough food may be snatched from the mouths of codfish (which depend heavily on sand lance in their diet) to reduce the catch of cod. There are millions of intricate relationships that may be upset as fishing becomes heavier and more diversified.

Some of the theoretical increase in yield can come about only if much better management is applied and the waste of overfishing is

FIGURE 13.1. *A mixed catch of many species of groundfishes on the deck of a Japanese factory ship operating in Bristol Bay. The problem of managing two species to obtain the maximum catch is far harder than that of managing one, and the difficulties are multiplied as each additional species is added. Some species will suffer overexploitation and others will be underfished.*

Bureau of Commercial Fisheries, Alaska

eliminated. The tools to do this exist for many stocks, and failures are only the consequence of defects in administrative machinery—social and political difficulties. But for other stocks technical problems hamper the framing of effective management. When many different kinds of fishes are exploited in the same area by the same gear, fishing may be too heavy on some species—resulting in lower sustained catches—and too light on others—also resulting in yields below the potential for those stocks. An example exists in the trawl fishery off the west coast of Africa, where a considerable number of fishes of different sizes are caught together. For the overexploited species less fishing with bigger meshes would correct the problem; for the underexploited species exactly the opposite techniques are required. In the growing fishery for sandeels and sand lances in the North Sea, the small meshed trawls used to catch these species are also making sizable incidental catches of juvenile cod and haddock—to the detriment of these stocks.

Among the other technical difficulties delaying full harvest from the sea is the present lack of gear and fishing methods capable of catching certain of the unfished stocks. We cannot, for example, harvest the enormously abundant zooplankton (including the millions of tons of antarctic krill) nor the swarming deep-sea fishes.

In the end, when all the complex calculations have been made of the total annual production of organic material in the sea, when all the guesses have been collected about how much of this or that kind of fish might be harvested from every segment of the ocean, we are forced to adjust all of them in terms of one overriding determinant: how much of the potential food can be landed at a profit? Regardless of how many people need food, fish will not be caught unless the fisherman can sell them for more than it costs him to catch them, including a reasonable return for his labor and his investment in boat and apparatus. Ultimately, the whole equation can be in terms of efficiency of capture, since if this is high enough, so that fish can be caught at a cost low enough, sales can be made at a profit even with weak demand.

A significant amount of the projected increases from the sea would come from the remoter regions of the ocean, or from areas where fishing conditions are so unfavorable due to weather, ocean currents, depths, or types of bottom that exploitation may never be possible. These parts of the estimated potential should therefore be subtracted from the total.

The prospect of doubling or quadrupling the catch of seafood may create the misconception that these extra catches will be constituted by popular species like salmon, sole, shrimp, and lobsters. But most of the stocks of the high-value species are near full exploitation now, or are

FIGURE 13.2. *The octopus, with its odd appearance and curious behavior, causes more revulsion than nearly any other animal, marine or otherwise. As a consequence, in many parts of the world it is not popular, even though it provides excellent food. Mankind will have to learn to eat many such unappealing marine creatures.*

Marineland of Florida

already overfished, and a high proportion of future increases in catch will consist of species of low value and demand—sand lances, squids, and sharks, for example. Many of these will be suitable for direct human consumption only if they are made into fish protein concentrate or some other, now unfamiliar product. Thus it is important to encourage public acceptance of fish in new forms.

The same species that could be transformed into FPC will more likely be manufactured into fish meal, at least for many years. This means that the fish will have to be fed first to chickens or livestock before it can benefit humans. Not only does this reduce the real food potential of an enormous quantity of the possible catch from the ocean, but it makes mankind dependent again on the land farms to serve as channels for food from the sea.

FIGURE 13.3. *Cousin to the octopus, the squid is likewise not a popular food except among the Japanese and some other enlightened peoples. Yet squids, like these from Newfoundland, are among the most numerous and grossly underexploited of the edible animals of the sea.*

Department of Fisheries and Forestry of Canada

The rapid increase in human population is forcing man to make many changes in both the land and sea environments that are reducing his chances of feeding himself. Trends of land use are affecting sea harvests adversely, and threaten worse effects. Land and sea, far from being independent parts of our globe, are intimately interrelated. By far the greatest production of sea animals is supported by the shallow seas over the continental shelves. It has been estimated that as much as 90 per cent of the seafood produced by United States fishermen is of species that must spend part of their lives in the estuaries or nearby shallow waters. But through the destructive process of harbor and land building, and the dumping of enormous quantities of killing pollutants into the estuaries and bays, we are reducing the ability of the sea to produce marine animals. This has already had undoubted effects on the salmon catch, for example, and it may be partly or mostly responsible for the disastrous drop in the landings of menhaden off the Atlantic Coast of the United States. Hence careless handling of our land resources is also destroying our sea resources, and the bright hopes for vast new harvests from the ocean may be vain unless we learn better control of activities along the shore.

It is apparent therefore, that some of the more optimistic estimates of the sea's potential assume not only a perfect world in terms of man's behavior, but the simultaneous occurrence of incompatible events. If we concede imperfection of man and the reality of nature, it is probably realistic to hope that the sea will some day produce 200 to 250 million tons of usable food—four to five times the present yield. To the extent that man becomes more rational in his behavior and that he sharpens his understanding of the complexities of the ocean and his skills in fishing techniques and management, larger harvests will be possible: perhaps 400 million tons without stretching credibility—1 billion as a more remote possibility.

If supplies of food from the land remain at their present level, world fish catches of 250 million tons would constitute about 12 to 15 per cent of the supply of calories. But the amount of food from the land will and must increase, so that the proportion originating from the sea may rise only a little from its present 2 or 3 percent. Furthermore, there will be a great many more people to feed by the time the fishing industry has reached this level of production, since it may take many

FIGURE 13.4. *An estuary near Bayside, New Jersey, fouled by pollution. Edges of the sea are among the most biologically productive areas of the whole earth. If they are destroyed, fish catches from the sea will decrease.*

R. A. Schmidt

FIGURE 13.5. *Regulation of fisheries and the enforcement of these regulations must become more effective for increased catches to become a reality. The meshes of a trawl net are being measured to make sure they are not smaller than the legal size.*

Department of Fisheries
and Forestry of Canada

decades if it is ever achieved. Thus, the average amount of fish available per person may not rise significantly either.

It seems certain, therefore, that food from the sea scarcely constitutes "a sure guarantee for our race's survival," as Arnold Toynbee predicted.

Despite the high hopes of so much of mankind, it appears that the sea alone cannot solve the world's hunger problem. It will take every ounce of straining effort in every way that man can devise to produce the food that is needed—by land farming, by the manufacture of protein from petroleum, by algal culture, by increasing the harvest from the sea.

But this should not be a message of despair, since far greater quantities of food, especially valuable animal protein, can be harvested than is the case now, so that even if hunger cannot be banished by the fruits of the sea alone, one of its most damaging manifestations, protein deficiency, can be blunted.

These prospects make it more than worthwhile—they make it urgently necessary—that mankind put forward the necessary effort to realize the potential of the sea.

Additional Reading

Additional Reading

GENERAL

FIRTH, FRANK E. (ed.). *The Encyclopedia of Marine Resources.* New York: Van Nostrand Reinhold Co., 1969.

IDYLL, C. P. *Abyss: The Deep Sea and the Creatures That Live in It.* New York: Thomas Y. Crowell Co., 1964.

——— (ed.). *Exploring the Ocean World: A History of Oceanography.* New York: Thomas Y. Crowell Co., 1969.

RUSSEL, F. S., and YONGE, C. M. *The Seas.* London: Frederich Harner & Co., 1963.

SMITH, F. G. W., and CHAPIN, HENRY. *The Sun, the Sea, and Tomorrow.* New York: Charles Scribner's Sons, 1954.

CHAPTER 1

BROWN, HARRISON. *The Challenge of Man's Future.* New York: Viking Press, 1964.

OSBORN, FAIRFIELD. *The Limits of the Earth.* Boston: Little, Brown & Co., 1953.

PADDOCK, WILLIAM and PAUL. *Hungry Nations.* Boston: Little, Brown & Co., 1964.

POPULATION REFERENCE BUREAU. Various publications. Washington, D.C.

UNITED STATES SENATE, Committee on Foreign Relations. *World Population and Food Crisis.* Washington, D.C., 1965.

VARIOUS AUTHORS. *Humanity and Subsistence.* Vevey, Switzerland: Symposium Annales Nestlé, 1960.

CHAPTER 2

BORGSTROM, GEORG (ed.). *Fish as Food.* Vols. 1-4. New York: Academic Press, 1961–65.

FOOD AND AGRICULTURE ORGANIZATION OF THE UNITED NATIONS. Various publications.
HEEN, EIRIK, and KREUZER, RUDOLPH (eds.). *Fish in Nutrition.* London: Fishing News (Books) Ltd., 1962.
SCHAEFER, MILNER B. "The Potential Harvest of the Sea." *Trans. American Fisheries Soc.,* Vol. 94, No. 2, 1965.

CHAPTER 3

FRASER, JAMES. *Nature Adrift: The Story of Marine Plankton.* Chester Springs, Pa.: Dufour Editions, 1962.
GRAHAM, MICHAEL (ed.). *Sea Fisheries: Their Investigation in the United Kingdom.* London: Edward Arnold, Ltd., 1956.
HARDY, SIR ALISTER C. *Great Waters.* New York: Harper & Row, 1967.
———. *The Open Sea: Its Natural History.* Part 1. *The World of Plankton.* Boston: Houghton-Mifflin Co., 1956.

CHAPTER 4

BONEY, A. D. *Aspects of the Biology of the Seaweeds of Economic Importance.* Vol. 3, *Advances in Marine Biology.* New York: Academic Press, 1965.
CHAPMAN, V. J. *Seaweeds and Their Uses.* New York: Pitman Publishing Corp., 1952.
DUDDINGTON, C. L. *Flora of the Sea.* New York: Thomas Y. Crowell Co., 1967.
WALFORD, LIONEL A. *Living Resources of the Sea.* New York: The Ronald Press, 1958.

CHAPTER 5

BARDACH, JOHN E., and RYTHER, JOHN H. *The Status and Potential of Aquaculture.* Washington, D.C.: American Institute of Biological Sciences, 1968.
GALTSOFF, PAUL S. "The American Oyster, *Crassostrea virginica* Gmelin." U. S. Fish and Wildlife Service, *Fish. Bull.,* Vol. 64, 1964.
IVERSEN, E. S. *Farming the Edge of the Sea.* London: Fishing News (Books), Ltd., 1968.
SHELBOURNE, J. E. *The Artificial Propagation of Marine Fish.* Vol. 2, *Advances in Marine Biology.* New York: Academic Press, 1964.

CHAPTER 6

AZBELEV, V. V.; SURKOV, S. S.; and YAKOVENKO, A. A. "Information on the Biology of Pink Salmon Acclimatized in the Basins of the White and Barents Seas." *Bull. PINROH* 2 and 3. (Fisheries Research Board of Canada Translation Series No. 437), 1963.

INTERNATIONAL PACIFIC SALMON FISHERIES COMMISSION. Annual Reports, 1948–1968. New Westminster, B.C., Canada.

WIMPENNY, R. S. *The Plaice*. London: Edward Arnold, Ltd., 1953.

CHAPTER 7

BORGSTROM, GEORG. *Japan's World Success in Fishing*. London: Fishing News (Books), Ltd., 1964.

COMMISSION ON MARINE SCIENCE, ENGINEERING, AND RESOURCES. *Our Nation and the Sea*. Washington, D.C.: United States Printing Office, 1969.

COMMISSIONER OF FISH AND FISHERIES OF THE UNITED STATES. Various reports.

GILBERT, DEWITT (ed.). *The Future of the Fishing Industry of the United States*. Seattle: Univ. of Washington Press, 1968.

MATHISEN, OLE A., and BEVAN, DONALD E. *Some International Aspects of Soviet Fisheries*. Unpublished duplicated report. Second Conference on Law, Organization, and Security in the Use of the Ocean. 1967.

CHAPTER 8

STANSBY, MAURICE E. (ed.). *Industrial Fishery Technology*. New York: Reinhold Publishing Co., 1963.

VARIOUS AUTHORS. *Proceedings of the Canadian Herring Fishery Conference*. Canadian Fisheries Reports No. 8. Ottawa: Dept. of Fisheries of Canada, 1966.

VARIOUS AUTHORS. *Proceedings of the Conference on Fish Protein Concentrate*. Canadian Fisheries Reports No. 10. Ottawa: Dept. of Fisheries of Canada, 1967.

CHAPTER 9

ANON. *Economic Benefits from Oceanographic Research*. Publication No. 1228. Washington, D.C.: National Academy of Sciences, 1965.

CUSHING, D. H. *The Arctic Cod*. Oxford, England: Pergamon Press, Ltd., 1966.

KUHNAU, J. (ed.). *Proceedings of the Seventh International Congress of Nutrition, Hamburg, 1966*. Vol. 4, Symposium XV, *Food from the Sea*, pp. 936–1041. Oxford: Pergamon Press, 1967.

CHAPTER 10

ALVERSON, DAYTON L., and WILIMOVSKY, NORMAN J., "Fisheries of the Future." *New Scientist*, No. 342 (1963).

ANON. *Modern Fishing Gear of the World*. Vol. 3. London: Fishing News (Books), Ltd., 1964.

KRISTJONSSON, HILMAR. *Modern Fishing Gear of the World.* London: Fishing News (Books), Ltd., 1962.

PARKES, BASIL A. *The Future of Fish Harvesting.* Canadian Fisheries Reports No. 5. Ottawa: Dept. of Fisheries of Canada, 1965.

SCHARFE, J. "Improvements and Trends of Development in Marine Fishing Methods and Gear." *In the Better Use of the World's Fauna for Food,* ed. by J. D. Ovington. Sympos. of the Institute for Biology, No. 2. New York: Hafner Pub. Co., 1963.

CHAPTER 11

CHRISTY, FRANCIS T., JR., and SCOTT, ANTHONY. *The Common Wealth in Ocean Fisheries.* Baltimore: The Johns Hopkins Press, 1965.

CRUTCHFIELD, JAMES A. (ed.). *The Fisheries: Problems in Resource Management.* Seattle: Univ. of Washington Press, 1965.

GULLION, EDMUND A. *Uses of the Seas.* The American Assembly. Englewood Cliffs, N.J.: Prentice-Hall, Inc., 1968.

CHAPTER 12

CHAPMAN, WILBERT M. *Food Production from the Sea and the Nutritional Requirements of the World.* Unpublished duplicated report. Second Conference on Law, Organization, and Security in the Use of the Ocean. 1967.

CLARKE, ARTHUR C. *The Deep Range.* New York: Harcourt, Brace and Co., 1957.

MACKINTOSH, N. A. *The Stocks of Whales.* Bath, England: Coward & Gerrish, Ltd., 1965.

Index

(Page numbers in italics refer to illustrations)

Guianas, 154, 155
Gulf of Maine, 147
Gulf of Mexico, 100, 140, 152, 154
Gulf of St. Lawrence, 100, 175
Gulf Stream, 16
gull, 163

haddock, 19, 20, 146, 147, *148,* 149,
  166, 191, 200
  hatcheries for, 67
  sounds made by, 167
  water-temperature range preferred
    by, 168
  world catch of, 13 (table)
hake, 19, 128, 137, 138, 142, *144,* 147,
  151, 152, 153, 154, 177
  world catch of, 13 (table)
halibut, 20, 147, *148,* 151, 159, 191
  world catch of, 13 (table)
Hammond Bay, *48*
Hardanger Fjord, 45
Hardy, Alister, 34, 36, 41-42
hatcheries, 67-69
  United States, 65-66, *66, 67,* 68
hatchet fish, *141*
Hawaii, 51, 77, 103
Hebrides, Outer, 62
Hell's Gate River, 105, 106
Herdman, Sir William, 35
herring, 2, 19, *23,* 35, 70, 138, 140,
  147, *148,* 150, 151, 170, 171, 175,
  181
  Icelandic search system for, 183-184
  located by water-temperature deter-
    mination, 168
  mid-water trawl for, *182*
  world catch of, 13 (table)
Hesse, Fanni Eilshemius, 55
Hesse, Walther, 55
Heyerdahl, Thor, 34, 36
Hinkley, Isaac, 129
Hoko Suisan (fishing company), 114
holdfast of seaweed, 47, *53, 57*
Holland, *see* Netherlands
Homarus, 85, 86
Hong Kong, *71,* 77
Horns Reef, in North Sea, 98
Hudson River, 100, 103
Humboldt Current, 153

hunger:
  dual aspect of, 6
  geography of, *6*
  number of people suffering from
    (1966), 7
Hutchinson, Samuel, 104

Iceland, 49, 108, 111 (table), 165
  herring search system developed by,
    183-184
India, 37, 61, 70, 138, 139, 159
  fish caught by (1968), 111 (table)
  fish consumed in, 11
  as fishing nation, 123 (table)
  milkfish ponds in, 77
Indochina, 37
Indonesia, 51, 159
  fish caught by (1968), 111 (table)
  milkfish ponds in, 76, 77
  Service of Sea Fisheries of, 38
  shrimp culture in, 80
Inland Sea (Japan), 51, *60,* 83, 84
Institute of Fisheries of the University
  of British Columbia, 184
Institute of Marine and Atmospheric
  Sciences, 84, 86, 170
Institute of Seaweed Research, 62
internal waters, and U.S. policy, *195*
International Council for the Explora-
  tion of the Sea, 96
International Halibut Fisheries Com-
  mission of Canada and the United
  States, 191
International Indian Ocean Expedition
  (1959–1965), 158
International Salmon Commission, 106,
  107
International Whaling Commission, 191
iodine, 54
  in fish meal, 131
Ireland, 58, 59, 103
Irish moss (*Chondrus crispus*), 47, 49,
  50, 57-58, *58, 59*
iron, 14, 54
  in fish meal, 131
Israel, 156
Italy, 84, 103, 156
  valli da pesca in, 78-79
Ivory Coast, 157

639   14409
I   Idyll, C.P.
     The sea against hunger